INTERNAL SECURITY THREATS IN SOUTH ASIA

INTERNAL SECURITY THREATS IN SOUTH ASIA

MANAN DWIVEDI
DEVADITYA CHAKRAVARTY

KALPAZ

Internal Security Threats in South Asia

ISBN: 978-81-7835-887-1

Published in 2013 in India by
Kalpaz Publications
C-30, Satyawati Nagar,
Delhi-110052
E-mail: kalpaz@hotmail.com
Phone : 9212729499

Lasser Type Setting by: Rudra Computer Graphics, Delhi
Printed at : G. Print Process.Delhi

Contents

Preface

IS or Internal security is avowedly a benign term in the contemporary context as it involves a great deal of concerns within the ambit of the domestic concerns of nation states in a specifically given regional context. The present work is an honest attempt to delve inside the brass tacks of South Asian internal security paradigm, where-in, the concerns of law and order, the upkeep of security and peace in the nation state along with the notion of tackling the scourge of terrorism, drug trafficking, energy security, food security and the attendant concerns of gender empowerment and human rights consciousness in a nation and a region at large needs to be underscored with a bright indexing of all these emergent concerns in the South Asian context. The notion of security too needs to be delved inside with some detail as the traditional power centric approach of 'hard security' needs to be reinvented with a great deal of academic verve and rigour and its supplanting, if not an avid replacement with the notion of 'Soft Power approach' needs to be the order of the day in the context of regional security. The attendant notions of globalisation, transnationalism, convergence and the universality of the human and the comprehensive discourse needs to be pinpointed with renewed vigor and alacrity.

The book aims to weave together a narrative of the South Asian region with the centrifugal tendencies of cross border terrorism along with the notion of parallel economies and the inherent sense of *estragruffen* being felt by the younger and unemployed populations of the South Asian nation states. The colour of rebellion as sketched by Shepard Fairy in the Obama posters during the 2008 election campaign in the United States, equally, reflects the estrangement with the state felt by some segmented scions of the national populations all across the South Asian sub-continent. The state ordained sovereignty issues still cannot be tidied over but still the notion of weaving together a narrative of South Asian bonhomie needs to be reserved as the acme of the bilateral and multilateral coalitions in the South Asian region. The individual nation states of the order of India (the benign hegemon), China, (the new interested state party in the region), United States (the eternal keeper of order in the frontiers in the region) along with the individual states of the order of Pakistan, Sri Lanka, Maldives, Nepal, Bhutan, Bangladesh and the latest entrant inside the rubric of the South Asian Association of Regional Cooperation, form the contemporary narrative and a significant sub text within the fast changing contours of the present day international system. The nations face their own internal challenges of the order of third party interventions, poverty issues, food insecurity, externally supported rebels and the rising tide of insurgency and terrorism in its various variants in some of these nation states in South Asia.

The debates of race questions in South Asia, along with the flickers of self determination in some of the nations, casts, a vivisecting and debilitating shadow upon the norm and practice of internal security in these nation states. The fulcrum of the South Asian nations incidentally revolves around India which is sometimes uncomfortably ensconced within the nomenclature of, "benign hegemony" much to the Indian consternation. Also, the internal foibles of the criminal justice systems in this developing part of the international system, also, leads to a rumination over the chaotic barometer in the South Asian nation states. The order of the day is to spawn a balance between the internal scenario (socio-political, economic, cultural) of these receptacle nation states along with the foreign relations amongst the nations in South Asia. The internal security paradigm primarily, delves inside the norm that, the national mandarins need to learn to secure their specific houses in order before launching forth with the personification of their international visages in the global order. It is this enmeshing with the internal/ national security motifs in South Asia with the much larger regional security rubric which forms the core content of the presented work. The idiom of international relations ascertains the conditionality that the theme of internal security cannot be perceived in isolation and sequestration from the lore and norm of *telling bilaterals* between the myriad nation states in South Asia and also from the regional and international organisational perspective. Also, the tribal and race dimension of the notion of internal security dispensation in South Asia is an eager beaver theme which should not be relegated to the politico-strategic backburner. Two instances of Maoism in India and the SWAT in the western frontiers of Pakistan hold a key to the internal disequilibrium in the region, which is far diverse an approach to lambaste the American intrusion in the region or to cap the honour of being the eternal enemy on Pakistan. The failure of land reforms and the want of something more than a mere trickling down impact upon the tribal populations in India has aggravated the naxal threat where the security denomination faces an alien terrain and an uphill task. In the same manner, the diversion of Frontier Corps to the western SWAT and FATA's turmoiled terrain has made the task far much difficult for Frontier Corps to militate against their own brethren in the terrain. The strategy being to keep the mainstream Pakistani army away from direct and the much needed counter insurgency operation in the tough valleys of a *neo-Afghanistanised* SAWT and FATA in the confines of a compromised Pakistan. Thus, the work posits a narrative for a light hearted evaluation and resolution of the notion, and operation of the conditionality of internal security in the nation and the South Asian region at large. The work is all about this narrative and is an academic weaving of a significant tale and more of it, as, a reader skims through and discovers more of it, through the pages.

Manan Dwivedi
Devaditya Chakravarty

Acknowledgements

An Ode to *Papa Dam Oak*

Hoary days, divine anthems, and protected networks, all are a thing of the past. God takes a toll and I am born anew. Sturdier if he had been, I would have been frail. Gone are the days, gone are the times when my guardian lifted me up across the knee high green hollow enchained poles of India Gate and led me to an auto to disembark upon the gates of Modern School Barakhamba Road to make me participate and paint in the Shankar's art competition as a much tom-tommed annual event. The guardian parts company but not the distillation of his memories which leads me on from one creative coming to the other in the realm of writing. I, then, pictorially depicted war, and now, I do it with a word processor but the shelter and his all 'subsuming awe' drives me on from one jotting to the other. He eggs me on and I drive on in the labyrinth. The work is a labour of love which has many firsts for me as a writer and a researcher with South Asia to coming to prominence in an Asian century with the avowed zeal of an American emphasis. I dedicate the work to my father, *Papa Dam Oak*, who cherished and cleaned my first Book, "South Asia Security" repeatedly on the drawing room's mantelpiece every day and hoped for more to come. He drove all the way from Gandhinagar to Baroda to take my few Books to my Chacha, so that I could write on with my teaching fixtures in *Gnlu* and so that I may not go in the unsparing heat. It is his earnestness and the glassy eyes which dream on for me as a person and as a writer as his visage cowers down to pick up the dusty cloth to clean my First Book on the mantelpiece. Pa's mantlepiece in Jaipur is dirty now as the house is closed but the books will keep on increasing in number and quality as he bears witness to my cavalcade of works in times to come and present.

I am whole heartedly thankful to Professor B M Sharma for having steadied a ship by providing me with academic guidance and familial succor in my initial days in the Indian Institute of Public Administration. Kamal Chenoy Sir stayed in a far off Delhi but in various meetings with him I spruced up and sharpened by argumentative skills, which finds some echo in the work here. Sir is our 'cult hero' in the good ol' MA days with the batch of 1998 in SIS. I extend my warmest thankfulness to the Professor V S Mani for having taught me the nuances of research and patience in reading as he is the tangibility behind my first book during his stay in *Gnlu* as the founding Vice Chancellor of the University. Professor Radhakant Barik, too, is a forerunner in the schemata of things as he enshrined in me the comprehension of the notion that even teachers have to earn their bread. It is Barik Sir's constant goading and casual cajoling which made me stay up in the Institute and write on till the early hours of dispersal in the Institute. Professor B M Jain constantly directed me telephonically about the latest in the South Asian literature and made me aware of the tenet of consistence and conscience in reading and writing honestly. Devaditya Chakravarti my co-author has been a good person as he supplied me with the relevant chapters in the midst of his testing interludes in *Gnlu*. He has rendered my noble and sole cause a great deal of good yeomanly service which I am indebted to with his state of the art research and writing zeal and skills much known to me as I occasioned to teach him for a semester in *Gnlu* in the stream of International Relations and Political Science. I extend my heartfelt thanks to my student Shreyas Dube for sharing a couple of chapters in the book when the conceptualisation of the book was in an entophytic stage and his quick and sagacious inputs complemented the initial research efforts. My Mother and better half Pooja share the burden for waking me up in the mornings to revise my juvenile jottings. My Mother shares all this with me.

The Raven croaks but the child comes. Pal Dwivedi strives to tear apart my study in her infantile ministrations but that makes me wake up when she sleeps and I write on. Pal has to make ends meet with the Bolts, Spidermans, avengers, Pheneases, Pherbs and the Platypus Parry's, as she is on my side. The World will soon be. Pal pesters me only to delete words from my file but I re-write and don the mantle of a significant author. She owes it to her Dadaji. She pays homage and so do I.

Manan Dwivedi
Devaditya Chakravarty

1

The Meaning, Nature and Scope of Security: An International Relations Perspective

Security in the realm of International Relations is home to innumerable debates and discussions, wherein the theme of security dilemma and an attendant dilemmatic conditionality become the order of the day. As an instance, in a statement attributed to Director General of Police, K.P.S. Gill, he went to relate during the heydays of militancy in Punjab that, "I write out a message for the youth of the State of Punjab. If you side with the terrorists then you will eventually end up as a corpse and nobody will be able to take care of your family and if you enroll yourselves as a defense and security personnel then you will be able to get a healthy stipend and if you perish in the war against terror then you will perish as a martyr, a patriot and will be mentioned in the annals of history as a person who selflessly laid down his life for the country." Thus, such a genre of security dilemma is faced by denizens of India (North-East, Punjab, the red Indian corridor permeated and run by the Naxals), the people in Sri Lanka and the choice of the right fences in the Swat in the Islamic Republic of Pakistan along with the Afghani locals who tend to side with the Talibanists on the foundation of their being the Pashtuns which is the single most largest population in the body politique of Afghanistan in the South Asian firmament which we are concerned about. It is the new notion of keeping intact the internal order of the nation in order to transmit to it the standard achievement of external dividends of peace and stolidity in the regional and the international context.

Joseph Nye Jr-[1] has recommended a new and untraditional aspect of security which is very much different from the traditional aspect of security which we have all learnt to identify as the conventional and commonly utilised format of security amongst the intellectuals and the scholars working in the realm of international internal security and world Politics. The notion of 'Soft Security' has gained ground in the current definitions as the themes of ensuring a high and respectable position for a nation state in the regional and international human development index along with a stress on the human rights regimes, the condition of the welfare state, the state of gender norms, the themes of sustainable development and the Cassandra of Climate change have been the staple fare for the textualists of the notion of Soft Security and an attendant neo-traditional aspect of security. Also, the themes of security in the contemporary context have undergone a transience as the themes and the neo-practices of Neo liberal institutionalism, transnationalism, convergence, interdependence along with the notions of Globalization, all intertwined in the matrix of 'Internationalism' in tandem with the Dante Alligeihirie's notion of a unified 'Universal State' have become the order of the theory and practice in the cavalcade of international studies.

Another eminent International Relations observer, Jan Melissen, observers that, "The new public diplomacy has in fact become part of the changing fabric of international relations. Foreign public now matter to practitioners of diplomacy that was unthinkable as little as twenty-five years ago."[2] Thus, internationalism has come of age in the realm of international relations discourse wherein the notion of soft power and soft security very generally militate against the theme of the traditional sociologist, Max Weber's definition that "Power is the exercise of influence of one actor over the other in the realm of a relationship between two nation states or two entities and individuals[3]". Thus, International security or the sphere of security studies happens to be a norm where internationalisation has crept in and a neo-approach to security has been in the offing since the last few decades.

The recent debate on internal security involves itself with the idiom that internal security has to be equated with the theme of strife between nation states. As an instance, the inter-state conflicts, that is, the international wars have to be accepted and colluded with internal domestic conflicts and internal dissidence caused conflicts. The new sphere of international humanitarian law reflects this new concern, wherein the concerns of the state and the non-state actors within one specific state does not find a different rendering than international warfare and international conflict. This heady and intertwined notions of inter and intra state war are of immense significance for the debates and discussions on internal security. A theoretical perspective of the order of the nomenclature associated with the tenet of 'Failed States' needs to be looked at with precise and great detail. In the internal security narrative founded on individual nation's domestic polities, one needs to associate oneself with the notion of 'Failed States'.

States in which institutions and law and order have totally or partially withered away and violence has resulted as a consequence of institutional failure, are termed as 'failed' states. Ex-United Nations chief, Boutros Ghali has very aptly commented on the notion of failed states which foil the internal security stability and stolidity. One observer has commented that, "A feature of such conflicts is the collapse of state institutions, especially the Police and Judiciary, with resulting paralysis of governance leads to a breakdown of law and order[4].

Anti-National Contours of the theme of Conflict

All these threats can be enumerated with a lot of convenience as a genre of sub- nationalism or to utilise a novae linguistic terminology, the sub-nationalist threats which pervade throughout the nook and cranny of the international system. The anti-national threats as the terminology suggests might be a very arcane and a stereotypical methodology of suggesting the developments within the internal security framework of a specific nation state. Still, what needs to be mentioned and emphasised is the notion that scourges of the order of terrorism, fake currency notes, economic destabilisation, a drastic or a gradual fall and decline in the context of internal and human/ comprehensive security-all amount to a process of a general and palpable decline in the general well being and the demeanor of the nation state, wherein the scholars have been theoretically inclined to emphasise the significance related to the themes of national security or under the ambit of the internal security threats of the South Asian region or the general international system. What needs to be emphasised in the popular parlance is that such developments tend to obfuscate the growth and the general humanitarian and the welfarist make up of a nation state, especially which has recently emerged out of the mire of underdevelopment and failed national and internal parameters.

Such developments can be conjoined in a set up and a well delineated framework of the 'Anti-National Threats' or 'Sub-national threats', which tend to pervade the nook and cranny of the Indian nation state and several other fledgling, micro and developing nation states of the order of region of South Asia. The term is nation state which I intend to utilise intentionally with enough academic deliberation. The term State is more 'Kosher' as far as the theme of International Law Treaties and the International State practice is concerned. When one discourses about a nation state then it is not only the themes of Government, the Regime and the Constitution which we are referring to, but the themes of popular concerns, the inclinations of the hoi polloi and their general belief and personal practice in the ideology of nationalism and patriotism which we are definitely concerned about. What makes United States of America a near to invincible and paramount sovereign nation state of the international polity? Its civic devotion to the theme and practice of nationalism conjoined with the theme of a well designed and orchestrated national sentiment and a national edifice which runs at large in the nation state of Mt.

Sinai which cannot be compromised in any way or manner by the anti-national threats and the fissiparous threats and the 'alternate bottlenecks' of violent dissent and the foreign hand in the questioning spirit of some misguided sections and segments of the society and polity. It is herein that emerges the significance of the theme of nationalism and the spawning of the anti-national threats which are a grave cause of concern for any sane and concerned mandarin in a self-respecting nation State, India and South Asia being no exception to this unwritten rule and paradigm of a national and unavowedly universal concern.

A nation state emerges by the four themes of the Montevideo Convention, wherein the four well delineated parameters are of the order of:

1. population,
2. a Well defined Territory[5],
3. the presence of an effective Government, and
4. the capacity of the nation state to enter into a kind of relations with other nation states of the global polity[6].

One can have a look at some of the under-mentioned articles of the Montevedio Convention which phenomenally undertake to define the parameters of the nation state setting to rest the debate and discussion about self-determination, insurgency, secessionism and other attendant fissiparous tendencies and inclinations involved in the debate which have their direct ramification and reflection, to the theme of independence and the question of nationality of the myriad nation states.

Definitively, freedom, self-determination and the unhindered exercise of freedom are the iconic elements and the determiners of all these conjoined themes of nationalism, but still the theme of how to preserve the security, both internal and external of the designated and a free and a sovereign nation state, emerges as one of the fundamental parameters of sovereignty which is well established and entrenched in the internal security framework of the designated and a 'challenged' nation state. Several anti-national threats of the order of ethnic strife, divisions in the name of caste, creed and colour along with the attendant themes of the order of cross border terrorism, economic profligacy, cross border international and bilateral public opinion engendering to vitiate the self-image of a nation state are some of the threats which any nation state irrespective of its power and equation in the international polity can be faced up with. Also, the rise and the dirty upsurge of the insurgent and secessionist movements of the ilk of the Pakistani sponsored terrorism in the Indian Union along with the scourge of Naxalism are some of the anti-national and prominent internal security threats which cannot be easily encountered by any fledgling state such as Maldives or an established nation state of the order of India in the internal security rubric of South Asia. The advance of technology and the increasing dependence on technical intelligence (TECHINT) for the maintenance of internal security have given rise to new ethical questions to which no satisfactory answers have been found anywhere in the world.

According to a prominent security analyst, B. Raman, one might find him contending that, "One may cite one example of the kind of problems now faced by intelligence and investigative agencies operating internally"[7]. Public Opinion militates against the increment of the interventionist and the snooping powers of the state agencies in most of the national cultural experiences. In the aftermath of the 9/11 catastrophe, the agencies have been given the additional powers which have reached them through the myriad instrumentalities of the order of Homeland Security Act and the Patriot Act in the United States of America.

The issue of self-determination too needs to be diligently calibrated if the idea of secessionism and separatism needs to be carefully placed in the discourse. The standard comprehension of the definition of self-determination posits that freedom is true and legal only if it is attained from the clutches of colonial rule. The United Nations resolution passed in the year, 1960[8] too calls upon the oppressed nationalities and the peoples of the unfree world to be free from the shackles of imperialism.

Thus, the attendant concern emerges that freedom can be asked and demanded for only from the oppressive bludgeon of the colonial rule or even third world ethnic groups, populations and demographic stretches can claim for freedom and self-determination from the yolk of their majoritarian rulers from the same countries, too. As an attendant factoid such an approach applies itself with the Palestinian movement and other inter state movements which militate against the majority rule or any other form of repressive government in their own home nations. The domestication of national self-determination by limiting it to decolonisation has somehow seemed as too arbitrary a construct which was in a way meant to sustain the European hold over the myriad Vietnams, Combodias, Burma's and Philliplines. Thomas Franck argued that such a selective approach to the theme of self-determination is uncalled for and if the theme of self-determination were to be applied as law, it needs to be applied coherently.[9] But, the narrative gets complicated when the whole of the European Union recognises the statehood of the broken republics of Yugoslavia.

International Law wise, the Helsinki Final Act of the Conference on Security and Cooperation in Europe (CSCE) of 1975 recognised that self-determination is applicable beyond the colonial construct and conditionality too.[10] The UNGA resolution passed in the year, 1970, too contends that "In pursuit of their right to self-determination people are entitled to seek and receive support in accordance with the purposes and the principles of the Charter[11]". The narrative on self-determination contains little food for agreement between the myriad scholars. It can be emphasised as pertinent poser that it is just and legal to support liberation struggles in places such as Kosovo, Kashmir and the North-East in India and can international law's legal sanity be spawned for the definition of self-determination and its myriad interpretations. The programnme of self-determination can be questioned if the oppressive practices of self-determination such as in Rhodesia and Kashmir insurgency can become the *de riguer* and the accepted practice in the larger narrative of ethnic strife and separatism in South Asia. One perception can be of the order of the notion that national self-determination ought to serve as a justification of the narrative of a state centered international order. The need arises to look behind the veil of statehood to unearth the idea of 'What lies beneath' if the conditionality of marginalised section and the suppressed minorities has to be given prominence in the context of a situation of challenged statehood and unquestioned sovereignty.

Balraj Puri contends that "India was among those countries that had insisted on adding recognition of right of all people to self-determination to the International Bill of Human Rights which the United Nations adopted in 1976 to give a legal form to the rights set forth in the universal declaration of Human Rights[12]". In my view, the right of self-determination which India championed along with the attendant notion of disarmament has boomeranged against the national interest of the country in the context of the South Asian concerns. As a matter of fact, the national integrity and the territoriality of the nation is challenged by the instrumentalities of self-determination with the new juggernaut of the invocation of the human rights violations in the besieged State of Jammu and Kashmir. Thus, the dismemberment of Yugoslavia can be perceived as a red rag for the Indian Union, wherein in the name of localised concerns the larger ambit of a Gellenerian oneness is compromised beyond retribution.

Thus, various domestic concerns have to be rounded about if the all pervading concern of national security and nationalism have to be honestly and diligently made part and parcel of the notion of the over all security and integrity of the Indian nation state and the idea of India or for that matter the idea of any other South Asian state as an extension of its national/cultural narrative. Also, the South Asian region is seething under the cauldron of myriad centripetal and divisive trends which need to be tackled and surmounted by the Indian nation state and the South Asian region in particular, if the UN charter's idiom of 'maintenance of international peace and security'[13] has to be enshrined in the domestic lore, myth and the individual jurisdictions of the international comity of nation states and not states specially in the context of South Asia.

One can eavesdrop upon one of the themes of the order of North-East in India with some precision with epistolary evidence. The political ferment and cultural confusion in the North-East was prophesied by Sardar Vallabhbhai Patel which is evident in an epistle which he wrote to Pandit Jawaharlal Nehru in the year, 1950. Sardar Vallabhbhai Patel contended that "Let us also consider the political conditions on this potentially troublesome frontier. Our northern and north-eastern approaches consist of Nepal, Bhutan, Sikkim, Darjeeling and the tribal areas in Assam, which can be termed as weak spots, which are open to infiltration and outposts"[14]. Thus, mainstreaming of the marginalised sections of the national population tends to be a primal concern of the regime of the day which was well envisaged by the political founding fathers of India since the times of Sardar Vallabhbhai Patel.

The ethos of taking note of the idiom of secularism and communalism would also do a word of good for the national and conjoined framework of the Indian Union. What is needed is a rejection of the anti-national threats of communalism and regionalism but in a very Indian, indigenous, original and a national manner. Being a follower of a specific religion does not and ought not to embolden the detractors from branding the followers of a particular religion as being communal, sectarian and segmented in one's approach to a national and cosmopolitan life. What is required is the theme that internal conflicts of the order of asymmetric conflicts needs to be rediscovered in the idiom of a national credo which would in itself be a defeating exercise for the 'Alternate way of lifers'. Asymmetric conflicts are a part of a developing nation state's way of life, but it ought not to preclude any planning and execution on the part of the political and bureaucratic mandarins who should ideally be prepared for tackling anti-national threats of all denominations and all kinds of centripetal vagaries.

As students of security, we need to remember that internal camaraderie needs to be maintained but not at the cost of compromising with the anti-national and fissiparous inclinations of the foreign abettors who frolic with the peace, unity and integrity of the nation state. Imported extremism of any variant cannot be tolerated in the Indian nation state and the infectious impact of the failed nation states has to be subverted and constrained, as we already have a failed nation state in our neighbourhood of the order of Pakistan and Afghanistan and also another South Asian nation state needs to be in a state of great strategic repair. Thus, destabilsing tendencies of the sub-national variant have been mollycoddled in India to a certain extent and they can be brought to book in the larger context of the South Asian nation states as a regional security concern.

The Historical and Developmental Context of Failed Nation States

The 'failed states' existing at present are essentially Third World and the developing states which have been affected by a few geopolitical conditionalities:

1. The end of the Cold War led to a disunity of shadow governments leading on to allies through supplies of arms or through ideology-based power structures.

2. The heritage of Colonial Regimes which had lasted long enough to annihilate societal frameworks and the instrumentality of modernisation which led to social mobility but did not lead to a nation-building process.

Perceived through the prism of international humanitarian law, Article 3, common to the four Geneva Conventions of August 1949 relates thus:

(a) violence to life and person, in particular murder of all kinds, mutilation, cruel treatment and torture; (b) taking of hostages; (c) outrages upon personal dignity, in particular humiliating and degrading treatment[15].

A particular advantage of the rules of international humanitarian law applicable to internal armed conflicts is that, unlike human rights law, they call directly to account not only state organisations but also non-state players. However, such

Covenants are not of much use in the failing or failed states. Thus, as perceived in the South Asian region, the situations and the conditionalities of *Machtenfaltung* have been such that the security situations have turned out to be a matrix and a unique and precarious amalgamation of internal situations in nation states, which is marred by the security disparity in the internal dynamics of the receptacle nation state. The internal security precariousness caused by the dissidents or the rebels in the territory of the nation state tend to get mixed up with the neighbouring nation state's act of intentionally aiding and abetting the security situation in the tarred nation state.

In South Asia, too, the acts of LTTE (Liberation Tamil Tigers Elam), along with the Talibanists in Afghanistan and the terrorist 'sleeper cells' operating in India tend to be posited regionally and globally in the international and larger-than-region matrix of International Terrorism, wherein transnational actors of the order of Al-Qaeda and Indian Mujahideen in India in consonance with Harkat-Ul-Ansars, Hijbul Mujahideens and Lashkar-E-Toiyabbas in South-Asia all depend on the epicentre of Terrorism and insurgency from the nation states of the order of Islamic Republic of Pakistan and Afghanistan. The terror networks and the destabilisers, all tend to have an international and South Asian identity and habitat and get their funding and ideological and material support from Pakistan, thus worsening the internal security health of all the nation states in South Asia as the regional concerns are all conjoined into one narrative in the context of internationalism and globalisation. The Chinese factor, in the context of the south Asian security, too, cannot be ruled out as is evident with the recent border constructions by PRC in the context of the North-Eastern frontier with their known linkages to Nepal and the Maoist movement in India.

The much hallowed United Nations Organisations has led to the new found concern of human security, wherein the notion for intervention in the domestic state of affairs a state under the aegis of Article 39 and Article 2, para 7 of the Charter has appreciably decreased. One of the suggestions of the Commission on Global Governance contends that:

"Where people are subjected to massive suffering and distress, however, there is a need to weigh a state's right to autonomy against its people's right to security. Recent history shows that extreme circumstances can arise within."[16] The notion of internal security and keeping one's house in order need not be completely equated with the western percepts and strategic thinking as much before them the Indian people and the founding fathers believed in the notion of a welfarist non violent nation where the state can be relegated to the keel of an intermediary and a just interlocutor and not an entity which unnecessarily meddles in the upkeep and the substance and the maintenance of a stable and peaceful national polity. Freud wrote: "Homo Homini lupus. Who in the face of all this experience of life and history, will have the courage to dispute this assertion?"[17]

In the context of national security, Chidambaram contended in a news report provided by the national daily, *The Hindu*, that NCTC needs to have a larger framework to refer to different genres of terrorist violence which are mounted against the Indian nation state and the people. He further went on to mention that "NCTC thus functions on the themes of intelligence, investigation and operations. All intelligence agencies would therefore have to be represented in the NCTC."

President George W. Bush related to Donald Rumsfeld, that "I don't care what the international lawyers say, we are going to kick some ass." Institutionalists on the other hand have a contrary opinion to hold[18]. Thus, security definitions have not changed overnight but there happens to be a great diminution of the notion of security as perceived through the paradigm of 'hard core security' which partakes of the notion of Military might and the Idealist notions as advanced by Kant and President Woodrow Wilson.

The women's peace movement also pertains to the notion of a gendered security with the women victims in South Asia, as a consequence of terrorism and insurgency in South Asia have not able to come to the forefront of the international relations and the security radar of the scholars and the observers of the security studies. In the perspective provided by J. Ann Tickner, international relations looks into security issues from a structural perspective or from the prism of its decision makers. The feminist take on it refers to how world politics can contribute to the insecurity of marginalised sections of people.

India's Home Ministry establishes internal security as part of the general narrative of South Asia. Also, the theme of the idea of the creation of Zonal Councils was mooted by the first Prime Minister of India, Pandit Jawahar Lal Nehru in 1956. One of the concerns of the zonal council contends the, 'Arresting the growth of acute state consciousness, regionalism, linguism and particularistic tendencies.[19]

In the Indian firmament, the Indian Home Ministry has come out with the titles of organisations which are banned in the Indian Union, currently. The list which has been provided by the Indian Ministry includes a large number of terrorist organisations.[20]

The definitions of international security provide one with a plethora of methodologies to wade through the phalanx of approaches and dismember the obfuscation associated with the theme of international, regional and state security. The theme of 'international security' leads on to the imageries of unmitigated Armageddon, competition betwixt superpowers and the attendant practice of interstate conflict. Several scholars have defined security in a myriad varieties of terms. One can begin with the legendary name of Stephen Walt, who describes security as Security studies-the study of the threat, use, and control of military force. Terrorism and the scourges of separatism too present a strategic danger not only to the stability of democratic establishments, but also to the structural framework of the nation state.

The Internal Security Situation in South Asia

To quote, Professor S.D. Muni, "All the Southern, Eastern, Western and Central regions of the Asian sub-continent comprise the Indian Union's extended periphery. Attendant to all these developments, is the norm of the evolving partnership between India and the United States."[21]

Themes of the order of internal security also require an analysis of the theme of energy security and water conservation and sharing by the South Asian neighbourhood. Ambassador Rajiv Sikri opines in one seminar conducted under the aegis of the Institute of Defense Studies and Analysis that, "The People's Republic of China is a relatively water-starved nation state, wherein the disbursal of water is rather scanty and dismal which makes PRC very aggressive in its foreign policy for resource generation and mobilisation"[22]. Thus, such instrumentalities which have a direct and all pervasive influence on the carrying on the day to day life of the people, too, amounts to a preponderant state of policy making and academic deliberation if the larger picture of security in the region has to be addressed pivotally and incisively.

Thus, the notion of soft security or the non-traditional norm of security is being considered seriously by the scholars and think tanks at least in South Asia, particularly in India. Indian think tanks based in places in the country such as Institute of Defense Studies and Observer Research Foundation need to be taken seriously and the implementing mechanisms of the government policy departments need to be influenced by the South Asian scholars and the intelligentsia working in the sphere of security studies and foreign policy in the region as a whole. The above mentioned exchanges betwixt the scholars and workers in the field on the theme of energy security and water conservation go a long way into establishing the license of a newer and much broader framework of analysis which 'soft power or soft security' forms in the South Asian firmament and region.

In the perspective provided by Nirupama Rao, Foreign Secretary in India, "Given our shared history, we can safely assume that greater regional integration is difficult to attain. India stresses upon the future of peace, security and development of the region which has to be embedded in the paradigm of common economic prosperity."[23] India has been home to a slew of incidents of Naxal violence which has led to comments by prominent Indian observers. N. Manoharan, premised in the Centre for Land Warfare Studies, contends that "The Indian Defense establishment needs to match threats and facilitate procurements in the longer run. Indian defense spending has not crossed 2.5 per cent of the Gross Domestic Product (GDP) when India's adversaries have been allocating double that figure."[24] Thus, though the term internal security only seemingly refers to the notion of what goes on inside the nation but the externally ordained decision making pertaining to the Defense and non-Defense matters, too, needs to be accounted for as elucidated by N. Manoharan.

Instead of a Marxist perspective on the theme of suppression of the Proletarians and the teeming masses of humanity, it becomes more pertinent to recognise that a nearly existential and humanist / individualist approach intertwined with the thread of a welfarist notion of the nation state, needs, to be the call of the hour instead of a directly bludgeoning approach to rectify the rotten system with a violent revolution leading to the wrecking of the state. The South Asian nation states thus need to take a leaf out of the book of these estranged and torn states in Africa and Latin America whose internal security (soft security) dilapidations have left sores open for the imperialists of the order of their former colonial masters of the order of Britain, France and Belgium and Italy, to foment and make them fester.

Internal security in the South Asian region can be manned and maintained more subtly and with fine precision with the human security aspect of the notion of soft power in the region. In the words of Dr. Sayeed Rifaat Hussein, developments and themes of the order of Disaster risk management and Reduction, HIV/AIDS challenges and regional environmental security mean a great deal for the myriad posers present before the Regimes and the Governments of the South Asian nation states.[25]

The impact of the epidemic aggravates the vulnerabilities of the weakest groups in society including women, children and the poor. Since the detection of the first HIV/AIDS case in South Asia in the mid-1980s, the virus has infected more than five million people today.[27] In the South Asian region, new and smart managerial governmental and regimental talent is required with a persistent political will on the part of the political leaders if the need of the hour has to be met with alacrity and aplomb and the administrative legerdemain of an astute welfarist.

The security scenario in the Emerald Isle refers to discouraging themes about the charred political history of the nation. In the words of an international affairs and conflict resolution strategist, Tejal Chandan, the Sri Lankan struggle against separatism initiated by the LTTE is a kind of eye opener for all other democratic regimes of the day. Much before the fall of Jaffna and the military termination of the life of Vellupillai Prabhakaran, the following was the internal security situation in the Emerald Isle of Sri Lanka.[28]

Tejal Chandan further comments that, "Sri Lanka posits a grave human rights pogram going by the vast majority of correspondents being attacked in the Emerald Isle. The Sri Lankan economy has grown at 6 per cent for the past three years in the midst of war."[29] In the international firmament, a federal solution would bestow more legitimacy on the central government and likely increase both the amount and scope of international aid. Afghanistan is another nation state in the substratum of the South Asian political circus which needs to be delved inside if a wholesome and complete picture of the internal security situation in the contemporary context has to be analysed with pithy detail and precision. Henrik Woods, a commentator on the cauldron which erupts now and then in Afghanistan, comments upon the entire situation as the words suggest, "to expel two ministers tarnished by graft allegations is a positive sign of his efforts to improve the effectiveness of his administration."[30] Afghanistan reeks of a scenario, where-in another Iraq or Nicaragua can be replicated. Thus, these are the anti-national forces operating in the newest entrant to the

SAARC Comity of nation states and they need to be tackled and the threats posed by them should not only be conceived as merely quintessential anti-national threats but as threats to the nationality and the national ethos of the country and the region in general if further plunder of the international stolidity has to be maintained in the region irrespective of the bilateral equations between the various nations in South Asia.

Karzai, the Afghani Prime Minister, is regarded by the international community as being unreliable and ineffective. These conflict ridden regions in South Asia needs to be internationalised as the United Nations and the prominent and interested nation state actors need to be given the responsible mandate in order to make their way out of the mirage of 'troubles' (on the lines of what happens in Ireland) with an international and an institutional support to these conflict ridden nation states which have more or less become a playing field for the trials and tribulations of the eccentric and often uncalled power practices of the West. The Occident stands compromised and it needs to be maneuvered through with indigenous solutions of ushering in democracy and representation of people and power sharing at the grassroots level.

Now, the internal security threats are no longer limited to an India-centric notion of internal security as India is a traditional leader in the field of internal security and defense studies in the region. Pakistan too crops up in any discussion on the theme of internal security strife in the South Asian region with India being as always the 'cause celebre', for the South Asian nation states. In an international news portal, perturbed by the recent terror attack on the Sri Lankan cricket team in Lahore, United States Secretary of State, Hillary Clinton has said that the situation in Pakistan is threatening, as it is facing serious internal security challenges.[32] So much the so for the Occidental concern for the turmoil in the region.

The notion of internal security in the South Asian region is per se related to the theme of Systems Approach to Political

Science and International Relations. David Easton and Gabriel Almond are the classical propounders of the tenet of a systemic approach to the notion of internal security and political, social and economic disturbances in the region and in the constituent nation states as a whole. When the internal security concerns of a nation are disturbed then at that point of time, the economic domain and the socio-political domain, all of them are influenced by the themes of security in the region or a nation state on the whole.

There needs to be a differentiation between the political and the economic systems. An Eastonian distinction of the political and the economic is construed to be completely conventional as it pinpoints at the delineation of the systems for the objective of academia. In practice, no such system is autonomous or closed.[33]

So, the myriad contours of internal strife serve and function as 'Demands' on the political systems in the South Asian firmament. Also, the demands have not been amply reintegrated in the respective political systems apart from the respective and credible 'Feedbacks', which are nascent but inbuilt in the political and communicative systems in the South Asian nation states of the order of: India, Bangladesh and now to some extent in the civil societal firmament in Pakistan. Thus, the framework of the Systems approach can be deftly utilised to unearth the political turmoil and internal ramifications in the various political subsets and systems of the South Asian political situation. The anti and sub-national instrumentalities need to be tackled by the respective national mandarins of the region and the Indian Union as a whole if the state of normalcy and bonhomie needs to be restored in the Indian nation state and the South Asian Region as a whole. The forces are all vying to destabilise the Indian Applecart and such a plethora of centripetal tendencies need to be equated with the national and patriotic sanity of the Indian nation state.

These are not merely aspects of internal security and internal threats to the nation and the South Asian region as a whole but these diatribes against the Indian nation state are the add-ons which foreign forces tend to conglomerate in the Indian Union in order to foment trouble and turmoil in a vastly progressive and pacily developing India which is knocking on to the gates of super powerdom.

In a book released by the HCM State Institute of Public Administration, titled as *'Internal Security: Some Current Issues'*, a very initial but path breaking insight inside the rubric of the internal security order in the nation is referred to. It is here that a harking back to the percepts of Political science occurs, wherein man is posited as a social animal which lives and subsists in a conglomerate of people and thus a responsible intertwining of individual interests is essential if the society and the concomitant nation does not have to fall into the throes of utter chaos and anarchy.[34] Thus, the conditionality of the maintenance of utmost and people friendly law and order and not lawlessness has to be a fundamental prerequisite of the complete notion of bonhomie and tranquility in the nation which is what is also harked back to in the governmental acts of the order of Prevention of Unlawful Activities Acts, and so on.

In one of the papers, A. N. Saigal, Law instructor, Internal Security Academy, contends that, "The maintenance of public order and offences against public tranquility are dealt within the Chapter VIII of the Indian Penal Code, 1860"[35]. The Paper further contends that, "It describes the word 'unlawful assembly' in section 141 of the Indian Penal Code as an assembly of five or more persons can be dispersed by any police officer not under the rank of a Sub-Inspector or an Executive Magistrate if the intent of the unlawful assembly is found to be riotous and offending the public tranquility and bonhomie."[36] Thus, apart from the Indian Penal Code, there are several states enshrined as the saviours of the internal security scenario in the nation of the order of, Code of Criminal Procedure, MISA (Maintenance of Internal Security Act), Prevention of Seditious Meetings Act, Police Act, 1861 along with the norm of prohibition orders which are some of the legal provisions in the nation to tackle the want of lawlessness and a law and order discrepancy in the Indian nation state. Still, in my view, it needs to be fathomed that some of these legal provisions are in a scattered state of affairs and they need to be conjoined and combined together so that they could be made much more handy, easily available, understandable and comprehensible.

A. N. Saigan contends that, "The IPC too has become much arcane now and reforms in such ancient legislation have become the order of the day if the internal security establishment of the nation has to be firmed up in the larger context and a larger sense of the term."[37] He further contends that, "The nature and content of Chapter X of the CRPC needs to be widened which deals with the notion of 'maintenance of public order and tranquility"[38]. Intelligence too plays a greater role in the collection, acting upon and dissemination of the urgent information, facts and incidents which if provided in a quick pre-catastrophic mode can be made available to the security agencies and can be earnestly acted upon by the agencies in a timely manner to avert a larger catastrophe. Also, a series of light, unnoticeable incidents which are seemingly inane in nature and ramifications can be made part and parcel of a larger prognosticated picture which can sum up all pointers and sparks which might be pointing towards a big public conflagration which might be a linguistic riot, a communal conflagration or a terrorist attack. Thus, intelligence can avert many disasters as 9/11 Commission had suggested that the fall of the Twin towers of the World Trade Center was a major repercussion of a want of timely intelligence and it was the establishment's intelligence failure of the worst order.

For instance, the people of the order of can catch an incident when a cycle *rikshaw wallah* hits an old man belonging to another community and the very next day a woman squabble at the water point of the town or a hand pump turns denizens of both communities into torching each other's homes and religious buildings. If the *rickshaw wallah* incident could have been pointed out by the beat constable, who were assiduously engaged in other inane activities then the breaking of the communal conflagration could have been effectively prevented in the midst of the aggrieved township. Thus, as an attendant fact, the significance of timely intelligence cannot be overlooked and even in the age of bugs and technical eavesdropping, the significance of HUMAN IT can be overlooked or shrugged under the carpet. Thus, internal security is about the assiduous maintainance of strict and well regulated law and order in the society and the *Kotwali* and as our police personnel happen to be the primary law implementators of the nation and the attendant society, so the strengthening of the *Thana* needs to be made a theme of paramount significance which needs to institutionally strived for in an age of technological and communication advances at the doorsteps of the destabilisrers, insurgents and the terror mongers marring the tranquil landscape of the Indian nation state and 'pre se' any South Asian nation state.

References

1. Joseph Nye Jr. (2004), "The Means to Success in World Politics," (New York: Public Affairs, 2004) pp. 14-24.
2. *Ibid.*
3. Max Weber, "Essays in Sociology" (Routeledge: Byyan S. Turner) pp. 14-26.
4. See the Concluding statement by the United Nations Secretary-General Boutros Boutros Ghali of the United Nations Congress on Public International Law: Towards the Twenty-First Century: International Law as a Language for International Relations (13-17 March, 1995, New York), Documents, p. 9.
5. "Montevideo Convention and the Rights and Duties of States" (Online: Web), Accessed on 19th June, 2010, URL: http://www.jus.uio.no/english/services/library/treaties/01/1-02/rights-duties-states.xml.
6. *Ibid.*
7. B. Raman, "Random CONMIT Sweeps: Use and Misuse" (Online: Web), Accessed on 10th July, 2010, URL: http://www.southasiaanalysis.org/%5Cpapers38%5Cpaper3777.html.
8. UNGA Resolution No. 1514b (XV), 14th December, 1960.
9. Thomas M. Franck, " The Power of Legitimacy among nations" (1990) pp. 153-174.

10. CF. Principle VIII of the Helsinki Final Act.
11. UNGA Resolution No. 2625 (XXV) 24th October, 1970.
12. Balraj Puri, "Why India Should Oppose the Right to Self-determination" (Online: Web), URL: http://www.pucl.org/reports/National, Accessed on 1st January, 2012.
13. "United Nations Charter" (Online: Web), Accessed on 10th of July, 2010, URL: www.un.org/en/documents/charter/index.shtml.
14. V. Sundaram, "Abject Surrender: A Tale of Subversive Anti-Nationalism" (Online: Web), Accessed on 10th July, 2010, URL: http://www. boloji.com/analysis2/0144.htm.
15. Hans-Peter Gasser, "International humanitarian law" in Hans Haug, Humanity for All, Henry Dunant Intitute/Paul Haupt, Berne/ Stuttgart/Vienna, 1993, pp. 491 ff., in particular pp. 554 ff.
16. "The Commission on Global Governance, Our Global Neighbourhood" (London: Oxford, 1995, pp. 71.
17. Michael Bratton, "Beyond the State: Civil society and associational life in Africa," Associations Transnationals, 1991, p. 137.
18. Thomas J. Schoenbaum (2006), International Relations: The Path Not Taken and using International Law to promote World Peace and Security" (New York: Cambridge University Press, 2006) pp. 40-60.
19. *Ibid.*
20. "Banned Organisations" (Online: Web), Accessed on 11th January, 2010, URL: http://mha.gov.in/uniquepage.asp?Id_Pk=292.
21. S.D. Muni (1998), "Asian Strategic Review" (New Delhi: Academic Foundation, 1998).
22. "IDSA IIC Talk on Water Security in the neighbourhood : Cooperation or Conflict" (Online: Web), Accessed on 11th January, 2010, URL: http://www.idsa.in/event/WaterSecurityintheNeighbourhoodCo-operationor Conflict_ 091209
23. *Ibid.*
24. N. Manoharan (2010), "The Route To Reform" (New Delhi: *Indian Express*, 2010).
25. Non-Traditional Security Challenges in South Asia" (Online: Web), Accessed on 11th January, 2010,URL: http://www.rsis-

ntsasia.org/resources/publications/policy-briefs/inaugural-meeting/rcss.doc.

26. *Ibid.*
27. Tejal Chandan (2009), "The Sri Lankan situation" (Online: Web), Accessed on 11th of January, 2010, URL: http://securitywatch.csa-chennai.org.
28. *Ibid.*
29. Henrik Woods (2010), "In Defense of Hamid Karzai" (*World Politics Review*, January 18, 2010).
30. "Pakistan Facing Internal Security Threat: Clinton" (Online : Web), Accessed on January 15th, 2009, URL: C:\Documents and Settings\abc\Desktop\Int Security\Pakistan facing internal security threat Clinton.htm.
31. David Easton (1953), "The Political System: An Enquiry Into the State of Political Science" (Chicago: The University of Chicago, 1953.
32. Hari Mohan Mathur, "Internal Security: Some Current Issues" (The HCM Institute of Public Administration, Jaipur, 1976, India).
33. *Ibid.*
34. *Ibid.*
35. *Ibid.*
36. *Ibid.*

2

Posers of Internal Security: Indian Institutional Answers and the National Security Doctrine

As the order of present things stand, the answer as to how internal security is to be defined is to be one which is a consummation of a sociological, international relations approaches and which is to posit upon the soft state approach towards India as a nation state. India is a pillar of South Asia which needs to throw its weight and manage its internal security which is conjoined with the national security approach of the country in the domestic realm. Apart from the bland maintenance of law and order and rule of law, one needs to zero in upon the human security prism too, which makes it pertinent on the part of a nation state to firm up its performance in the realm of literacy, human development, gender empowerment, the human rights situation in strife torn regions and the twin threats of communalism and casteism. Still the anthem of strategic security in the Indian sphere has to be of paramount importance because internal stability and rule of law are the substratum upon which other edifices of human development can be built upon. The notion of internal security dwells at large upon the theme of anti-national threats which are being faced by the Indian nation state. The lore and practice of asymmetric warfare, low intensity conflict and internal disturbances of all kinds are posing a threat to the internal security framework of all South Asian nation states, India being no exception to the deluge of challenges that are being posited before it. They all amount to a belittlement and disparagement of the notion of internal security and the nationalistic framework as envisaged by our founding fathers, in the Indian Union which needs to be taken care of by the establishment of the Central Government and their institutional mechanisms.

The notion of internal security is deeply intertwined with the much larger pretext and the hallowed context of the theme of national security. The deficit in the Indian scenario is that there is no such well written and well delineated entity of the order of the national security document on the lines of the Draft Nuclear Policy doctrine which enshrines the utility and the rationale behind the modus operandi of, 'no first use,' and the notion of a 'recessed option'. Thus, certain externalities and the material and the tangibles of the theme of national security have already been worked upon by the Indian strategists while the human security and the soft power approach has not acquired much of a currency apart from the governmental documentation in the national capital. Thus, the incentives to the poor, marginalised and the impoverished to be patriotic and nationalistic (overtly) is very ill-defined and not adequately delineated in the national narrative of the country. What is the need of the hour is the notional understanding and comprehension that populations across the international firmament need the two square meals a day with civilian security and a visible and effective administration in order to rid the populations of their security dilemma for which the denizens of a nation state need not be residents of a strife torn or an insurgency affected region in the clear sense of the term.

Officially speaking, there needs to be the existence of a well defined national and internal security doctrine in the national establishment in the realm and the ambit of the different ministries in order to actualise the concern and awareness about the area and the strategic and human concern of human security and internal security in the country with a well nigh need for coordination between the various branches of the government. The national coordination and a strategic centralisation of all sub-spheres of national and internal security is the pertinent need of the hour, wherein all the emerging events and crises in the domestic realm can be taken care of and not only consulted upon by a centralised body comprising of all the relevant and concerned braches of governance. The idea of pre-emption too needs to be inculcated in the institutional structure of internal security maintenance mechanisms so that terror or communal crisis can be dealt with an iron hand and with enhanced specificity and efficiency so that the surreptitiousness of the crime and strife can be effectively managed on the lines of professional crisis management, wherein drills of the order of 'earthquake management' can be inculcated in the urban context of the nation state. Some more of such steps can stabilise and institutional such best preventive exercises which are being attempted since the last few years.

This centralisation with an attendant flexibility of individual performance can be the panacea for the national security ills of the nation on the whole. The population is aware of the fiascos of the order of the 2G saga, the Anna Hazare movement and the flaws in the national flagship schemata of the ilk of the Mahatma Gandhi National Rural Employment Guarantee Scheme and the attendant act which has been misutilised and ill executed by the state governments courtesy the federalism ingrained follies and miscalculations by the founding fathers of the nation state. This soft security concern too forms a concern of paramount significance for the general upkeep of the nation. Also, the founding fathers need not be solely and wantonly blamed for the want of an inspiring conditionality of internal security in the nation as the execution of the different schemes and the want of an implement ability has led to the redundancy in the theme and the conditionality of internal security in the nation.

National security in the context of United States is considered to be a sacrosanct word, wherein the denizens of the nation are kept under a sheen of restrictive way of life in terms of the themes of their travel habits, net surfing habits, sight-seeing tours and the kind of books which they read. Under the ambit of the homeland security act and the Patriot Act, all the civilian activities and ministrations of the commoners are kept under a scanner. Also, there is a consequential fall in the civil liberties of the citizens of the nation which have been made into state law as an aftermath of the September 11 attacks. The Indian scenario is much different as the people are not subject to such clandestine eavesdropping by the state even in the aftermath of the October, 2001 attacks on the Parliament in New Delhi and the Mumbai terror incident on Hotel Taj in the year, 2008.

Thus, the Indian citizen breathes a much easier air even in the light of repeated terror acts and acts of subversion in the context of the nation state of India. Still there is a much palpable difference in the context of the number, severity and the propensity of the terror incidents. The numbers are much large in India back home as compared to no incident of terror being reported in the national security rubric of the Indian nation state. Thus, a liberal national security policy with the freedom and the attendant enjoyment of civil liberties leaves the Indian nation vulnerable to "terror spectacles" of much severity which destabilises the national narrative and invigorates collective angst and a sense of insecurity amongst the citizens which manifests every now and then in the form of rebellion and political violence bring perpetrated against the political system in more strains than one.

In a way this lax implementation of curbs leads to the vulnerability and the susceptibility of the national security and leaves the nation at large under the dark shadow of the nefarious terror mongers which is not the *'best practice'* in the name of liberty and freedom in the nation. This might seem akin to an extremist diatribe against the much blood which has been shed in the country since the last twenty odd years but the notional understanding of national security apart from the creation of a separate document, deserves a pithy and informed discussion amongst the mandarins at the helm of affairs. Running the risk of being branded as a extremist libertarian, a quaint and difficult to attain balance has to be struck betwixt the notion of civil liberties to the citizens and the national security strapping and restrictions being imposed in the supreme national interest. The theme of national security if perceived in a theoretical and historical prism owes its origin to the economic performance and health of United States and the Western World in the shadow and the throes of the legendary Economic Depression of the 1930s in the post World War-II scenario.

The post September-11 age of Agent Reds, Agent Orange and Agent Greens (the threat level declarations by the US Homeland Security Department in a time bound and circumstantial manner), is a pointer in the direction of a novae approach, wherein the economic meaning of national security was expanded by the scholars and the parishioners and the resulting meaning was echoed by including the strategic health, the level of internal violence and strife in the domestic polity. The term was later on expanded further to include the notion of human and comprehensive security which comprises of the parameter of the order of the standard of living of the common people and the general well being and the sense of security being experienced by the nation's hoi polloi.

The notion and the paradigm of internal security management in India is to orchestrate peace, stability and a standard, well received universal quality of life, diving clear of the talkative and politically cantatakerous demagogues, trading interests, along with politically mispropelled regimes of the order of regional neighbours and other sub-national non-state forces and their anti-national and subversive legerdemain. The below mentioned structure of Indian national security system is of the following nature which can be delved inside with some onerous and material which is already present in the public domain:

National Security Council (NSC) :

1. Strategic Policy Group,
2. National Security Advisory Board and
3. Secretariat represented by the Joint Intelligence Committee (JIC).

The following structure stands for the framework policy making structure of the National Security Framework:

1. The Strategic Policy Group,
2. The National Security Advisory Board and
3. Secretariat represented by the Joint Intelligence Committee (JIC).[1]

The Strategic Policy Group is the core and the centrally designated decision making apparatus of the Council. The Civilian component of the national security outfit includes the instrumentalities and the governmental personages of the order of Cabinet Secretary, Foreign Secretary, Home Secretary, Defence Secretary, Finance Secretary, Secretaries of Revenue and Defence Production in the governmental establishment, Governor of the Reserve Bank along with the Director of the Intelligence Bureau.[2]

The onus of carrying out the Strategic Defence Review lies with the all important and evaluative Strategic Policy Group. The National Security Advisory Board forms the third element of the National Security Council (NSC) comprising of personages of significance and sufficient importance outside the sphere of the government with expertise in the different realms of external security, strategic analysis, foreign affairs, defense, the armed forces, internal security, science and technology and economics, to name a few of the considered spheres and fields.

The nascent, timid beginnings of the Indian intelligence scenario could be traced to the rising concerns over Russian troop deployments in Afghanistan as a base camp to launch invasion of the British India during the latter half of the 19th century under the able stewardship of quartermaster General and head of the Intelligence Department for the British Indian Army Major General Sir Charles Metcalfe MacGregor. The Intelligence Bureau is structured of official cadre from the brass of the Indian police ranging to the to the defense personnel today which has been exposed as the sticky puddle of deplorable inefficiency and pervasiveness, post Sino-Indian War was split up and led to the spawning of the external espionage wing nomenclature as the Research and Analysis Wing.

The current 17th Summit of the SAARC nation states in the Addu province in Maldives refers to developing the agenda of 'Destination South Asia' in order to encash in on the parameters of tradition, history, development and legends of the South Asian region. The other indicators refer to the internal security parameters of the particular nationalities of SAARC which include the themes of a seed bank for the region, a regional disaster management structure along with a discussion on the non tariff barriers and the various obfuscating lists of the SAFTA.[3] These regional concerns stress the respective and particularistic themes of 'internalisms' of different nations in the South Asian region which further translates in the language of national security perceived through a non-military and non-defense enunciation of the theme of internal security where the general Laskian[4] well being of the people along with the barometer of good and secure living add up to the notion of an *Indian and regional wellness*. All this discussion amounts to firming up the internal security scenarios of the national regimes in South Asia which can further translate into something akin to a realisation of the acceptable prognosis at the keel of the Addu province in Maldives and many more gatherings to be anticipated in the realm of South Asian security.

Another segment from the Blogosphere also entails upon the same sentiments which brand themselves as anti-nationalists and which definitively are seditious. The so called anti-state portals too propound Naxalism, separatism and spread disaffection amongst the people. One such excerpt runs as follows, *"Naxalwad, failta hua red corridor ab apne charam per puchega. jab yeh red corridor metro cities ko bhi apni chapet me le lega, waha junglo me adiwasiyo ko apna hak nahi mil raha hai.*"[5] The Chinese government has gone to take rasping and incisive measures against the notion of such insidious messaging and cantankerous and cacophonous content on the world wide web which is another poignant and pertinent threat to the national security make up of any ordinary and law abiding nation state. India has not been so pacily interjecting of these subversive and anti-national cyber crimes which go on to militate against the internal security stability and stolidity of the Indian nation state which is once again very true of the other South Asian nation states which too are subsisting in the age of an information technology imbued with the expanse of the matrices of an information highway.

Internationally, too, the stance of freedom of press and national security is as outdated as it is ignorant of the journalist's role and functions. Such official barriers to information gathering is inherently violative of the legal provisions which prohibit censorship .[6] One of the anomalies in the Information Technology Act in the country is that the all crimes premised upon the notional understanding of cyber crimes have been assigned under the criterion of being 'Bailable' which takes away the veneer of severity from the transgressors in the context of the cyber crimes.

In the words of V.K. Singh, "The Information Technology Amendment Act, 2008, despite having been passed on 23rd December, 2008 has not been '*notified*' yet (till 24th September, 2009) and thus any prosecutions therein are not authorised by force of law[7]". Also, the internationalisation of the frame of reference of the IT Act also lends it more teeth in the context of the cyber wars and cyber crimes being committed in the Indian nation state. The Chinese have taken great pains in fomenting stringent measures upon the perpetrators in the realm of this 'real matrix' in its domestic polity. China has made significant progress in cyber crime legislation and is putting in great efforts to strengthen it," said Man Qi, one of the paper's co-authors, in an e-mail interview.[8] Though the Chinese have internally led the international geo-economy in the context of cyber laws, the majority of the official hacking ministrations have been indulged in by the same nation in different denominations and through different maneuverings unaccounted for cyber space. Thus, what happens to be the need of the hour is the dissemination of information upon the theme of cyber crimes and the attendant transgressions by a myriad genre of post-modern perpetrators along with the international striving of spawning novae jurisprudence and precedence in the sphere of cyber crime as a new war of the order of a virtual war has to be fought in the sphere of a virtual world. It is here that the jurisdictions and the sovereign conclaves of the various national boundaries and delimitations are not clear along with jeopardising the conflict resolution in this virtual matrix of connectivity and convergence. As a parallelism, in the United States, the myriad perpetrators of computer fraud are confronted with 20-year sentences, which is a much stringent modicum to tackle the menace of this novae, synthetic crime.

Cyber Crimes : The Novae Crime

C.S. Sushita Mukhopadhyaya enumerates a stolid definition of the word, maintaining that, "Cyber crime is a crime where cyberspace is used either as a tool, target, or both. This includes anything from downloading illegal music files to stealing millions of dollars from on-line bank accounts[9]".

Historically speaking in the year 1820, Joseph Marie Jacquard, created the first loom which facilitated repetition of phases in the weaving of special fabrics. This resulted in a fear amongst Jacquards employees that their traditional employment and livelihood were being threatened. The loom manufacturer was led through different indifferent measures to do away with the novae technology. This happens to be the first recorded Cyber crime[10]".

The Historicity attached with the Ministry of Defense

According to a governmental internet source, "A military department was constituted in 1776 with its earliest role of maintaining a roster of army personnel and sifting and recording orders issued by various departments of the Supreme

Government of the East India Co[11]". The army department of the colonial era was redesignated as the Defense Department in January 1938. It was as late as the month of August in the year, 1947 that the Department of Defence became the Ministry of Defence under a Cabinet Minister.[12] During the Nehruvian years there was this non-aligned movement which led to the Indian strategic neutrality in the context which took the strategic trend away from the notion of national security building in the national superstructure though the manufacturing of missiles, rockets and avant grade weapons took place under the mechanism of decision making under the suzeziarinity of the Nehruvian government in the fifties and the sixties. It was much later in the context of the governments of P V Narasimha Rao and Rajiv Gandhi that the impetus was given to the spawning and sustenance of the national security documentation and a well defined and well delineated establishment and shibboleth of the same denomination in these days. It was the catastrophic defeat at the hands of the Chinese that the Indian re-think on the spawning of a national security establishment was initiated, rather late in the nation's existential myth and lore.

India's Loopholes in Rcegistering National Security

In the words of Subhash Kapila, "The lack of a proper strategic culture has run dry over the years ever since independence." This glaring trend has been castigated upon by international observers of repute, namely the more commonly read views of George Tanham in the RAND study for the US Department of Defence. Further to borrow Henry Kissinger's views in another context, it can be said that neither education nor exposure nor incentives existed for the Indian political leadership and civil bureaucracies to think in strategic terms or appreciate matters military.[13] Also, the role and the advent of insurgencies, separatism of different genres have to be charted in if the complete picture of the nation's security has to emerge. The new non-state actors too have to be accounted for as the days of asymmetric warfare are in and a Mahabharata styled sunrise to sunset warfare does not have to be routinised in the Indian national security establishment and the indigenous security practices and apart from that the theme of rogue players in the regional firmament has to be taken into account for in the theme of economic and other related aspects of national security in the nation.

* Arranging for independent evaluation of decisional premises and options where necessary. In conclusion, past records show that NSC should be *legislatively institutionalised* and the approach in the national security dictum needs to be not of an ad-hoc in content and style and operation but instead of it, there needs to be a continuity in the norm of national security in India so that a well defined and well delineated institutionalism can be spawned in the domestic polity in the context of tangible and intangible threats to the national fabric, one of which also happens to be the novae menace of fake currency.

Fake Currency: A Poser in the Face of National Security Mandarins

Fake and Torn Currency, Beware!!! This happens to be one of the instructions which are given to the common children at the age of ten to twelve as they learn the art of how to deal with the shopkeepers so that they begin to differentiate between the various denominations of the currency notes at a tender age and are not be fooled by the cunning and external eorld. The Reserve Bank of India, apart from doing a balancing act between exchange rates is the primary watchdog when it comes to countering the threat of fake currency and regulating the monetary policy. As per Section 25 of the RBI Act, 1934, the design, form and material of bank notes are to be approved by the Central Government on the basis of advice tendered by the RBI. Section 22 of the Act gives RBI the sole right to issue bank notes in India.[14] The cost of the foreign attained papers is not a pittance and thus it hampers a domestic printing process to ensue in the national confines itself.[15]

As an instance, Anrool Sheikh, belonging to West Bengal and Dubai Babu belonging to Tamil Nadu were two handlers,

Distinguisihing Features Between Original And IsI Sponsored Counterfeit Currency

Sl. No.	*Original Currency*	*Counterfeit Currency*
1.	Silver Bromide thread with RBI marks in Hindi and English are prominent.	The security thread (silver coated) and the logo. "RBI" in English and Hindi are hazy.
2.	Three watermarks on each note, i.e., (i) Ashoka Pillar or Gandhiji's caricature (ii) Denomination and (iii) R.B.I. are prominent.	Not prominent.
3.	Sprinkled blue dots all over the note, when seen in UV light.	Sprinkled dots not visible, when seen in UV light.
4.	The digits "500"(denomination), superimposed on the right side, when seen horizontally.	The superimposed"500" digits not visible when seer horizontally.

apprehended in Bangalore and booked under Sec. 498A, IPC for trading high denomination fake currency notes.[16] Investigations deep into the matter exposed a chain of contacts, stretching all the way from Malda in West Bengal where the notes, appearing just as good as any other legal note were distributed through unsuspecting people.[17]

What all this pinpoints is at a need to properly harness the various agencies of the regime of the day and make them coordinate adequately and effectively with the functioning style and format of the coast guards along with the custom officials in key and strategically sensitive conduits all across the passage points in the international border in the country.

Investigation Of Fake Currency Cases

State of the art equipment is the need of the hour for the immigration, customs, border and airport authorities to keep that crucial one step ahead of the counterfeiters. Many private corporate houses too have been roped in order to partner with the security and the economic agencies in order to counter the counterfeiters in the domestic sphere and the strategic backyard of the South Asia. Technology is a must run-in-mechanism, in the ceaseless striving to enhance the notion of tackling the threat of a steady and stealthy running-in of the fake currency in India. To a novice's eye, the scourge of counterfeiting cannot be caught, such technologically advanced devices can be utilised at Banks and other significant conduits of monetary transactions in order to dwindle this new found threat to the nation's economy. The Institutions and the establishment too have now woken up to the menace of internal security (as anti-national threats) and stability as being posed by the scourge of fake currency notes in the Indian Union.

Internal security is a novae theme which is being discussed in academic circles in the contemporary context. The new idiom of internal security refers to both the exogenous and the endogenous threats to the nations in the South Asian sub-continent. Internal security can be conveniently juxtaposed against the theme of the telling foreign relations/ bilaterals and the multilaterals which nation states have to contend with the exercise and the upkeep of internal security in their respective nation states. The notion of keeping one's own house in prim, proper and Kosher order is a primary concern of the internal security mandarins of the nation states in South Asia as all the nations in the regional and the internal context belong to the idiom of growth oriented and potentialed states of the developing genre in the larger regional and international firmament.

In the Indian context, the Prime Minster chaired Conference of Chief Ministers is a utilitarian instrumentality to re-order the internal digress in the social-political and economic grid of the Indian nation state. The Prime Minster in the Conference of Chief Ministers on internal security in the nation, contended that, "The year 2010 saw a decrease over the previous year in the numbers of incidents and causalities of security personnel. The civilian casualties have been augmented. Chhattisgarh, Bihar, West Bengal and Jharkhand continue to be a cause of concern[18]".Thus, the casualties of the security personnel seem to have decreased but the collateral damage to civilian life and pelf has been on the rise largely due to the ministrations of the scourge of Left Wing Extremism in the nation.

Thus, ethnic violence, communalism and terrorism still remain as the primary threats to the upkeep of tranquility in the nation state but the menace of left wing extremism can be safely perceived as the single most dangerous threat to law and order in the Indian nation state. The positives in the pantheon of terrorist and other destabilsing incidents were earmarked further by the Prime Minster in his speech, "The response to the Ram Janma Bhoomi judgement by and large was mature, respectful and dignified. Otherwise also, no major communal incident was reported from anywhere in the country in 2010."[19] Thus, despite the sensitive nature of the law suits in the nation's judiciary, the Indian hoi polloi remained calm and peaceful which foresees the positive and tranquil state of affairs which can be expected in terms of communal camaraderie in the Indian nation state. Border management too happens to be a foremost concern of the people in New Delhi, wherein the process and the external stratagem of illegal immigration from the neighbouring South Asian states needs to be tailored down in the light of the demographic and political challenges which they pose before the nation state, with the victimised party being India.

The Prime Minister was of the view that, "In order to secure our borders, the work on the integrated check posts at Attari, Raxaul and Jogbani is progressing well. The coastal security initiative gathered good momentum in 2010 with 71 out of 73 coastal police stations being made operational."[20] Thus, border management has emerged as a gargantuan imperative at the hands of the security agencies in the nation along with the combined efficacy of the practices of technological and human intelligence.

Linguistic diversity and the language divide too can serve as a cause of concern and a thorn in the flesh of the internal well being and the health of the nation states in South Asia. It has been a major factor in shaping ethnic relations in multiethnic societies of Asia.[21] The non-Burman nation has adopted Burmese as the national language to mitigate the notion of differentials aimed at them.[22] The nation state of Pakistan too decided to embalm Urdu as the national language which initiated the corpus of ethnic strife in the region, as the Bengalis and Sindhis, perceived the stratagem as a policy of privileging some ethnic groups over others.[23]

The Indian North-East too needs to be comprehended as a cause of concern as the hoi polloi in this segment of the nation state seems to be in the quagmire of not being mainstreamed in the larger context of the mainland nation that is India. Dipankar Banerjee contends that, "The region presents a mixed and varied population of diverse linguistic groups, each group having a distinct life-style and heritage, and even aspiring for a separate political identity. An estimated 483 different tribes with varied dialects populate the region[24]". Thus, the notion of ethno-centrisms and castigating the different person from a different racial stock easily breeds the culture of 'the other' and 'the inner circle person' in the socio-cultural narrative of the North-East at some sublime level, when the homogenisation of the North-Eastern or India's Far East is taken into cognizance in the context of larger conjoined concern of the Indian nation state and their repercussions in the country's 'Look East Policy'.

To Conclude if so, this is also the right time to consider the following questions: Would it be advisable to have a separate adviser for internal security working in the PMO? The positions of the Intelligence, Homeland Security and National Security establishments ought to be very clearly defined and articulated in order to meet up with the thematic and practical threats of insurgency Naxalism, cross border terrorism and the threats posed by fake currency in India, which need to be subverted by our national security establishment in tandem with the attendant theme of human development which takes a backseat when the menace of neighbourly subterfuge comes rolling in its fullest ambit and deluge. Then, as a *sine qua non*, there needs to be a notional existence of a written and drafted National Security Document which can be earmarked for reference and action at a crisis time in the grand and an all ebullient national interest.

References

1. Ministry of Home affairs website.
2. *Ibid.*
3. See *Indian Express*, 12th November, 2011.
4. See Harold Laski in "Grammar of Politics".
5. *Ibid.*
6. "Harakah dua kali sebulan" *Berita Harian*, 2 Mar, 2000, Ministry of Energy, Communications and Multimedia. (Online: Web), URL:http://www.ktkm.gov.my/, Accessed on April 14th, 2010.
7. V.K. Singh (2010), "Indian information Technology Amendment Act 2009 in the Pipeline," (Online:Web), Accessed on April 4th, 2010, URL: http://cyberlawsinindia.blogspot.com/search/label/INFORMATION %20, TECHNOLOGY%20, ACT%20, 2000.
8. "As Hacking hits Home: China Strengthens Cyber Laws", Accessed on April 18th, 2010 (Online: Web), URL:http://www.

cio.com/article/492317/As_Hacking_Hits_Home_ China_ Strengthens_Cyber_Laws.

9. "Cyber Crime and Cyber Terrorism: The Need to Know Cyber Laws," (Online: Web), Accessed on April 18th, 2010, URL: http:/ /www. caclubindia.com/articles/cyber-crime-cyber-terrorism-the-need-to-know-cyber-laws-5153.asp.
10. *Ibid.*
11. "About the Ministry", (Online: Web), Accessed on April 18th, 2010, URL: http://mod.nic.in/aboutus/body.htm
12. *Ibid.*
13. "India's National Security Council: A Security Review"(Online: Web), Accessed on April 18th, 2010,URL: http://www.southasia analysis.org/papers2/paper123.html
14. "RBI Bulletin", (Online: Web), Accessed on 17th July, 2010, URL: http://www.rbi.org.in/scripts/BS_View Bulletin.aspx? Id=11104.
15. *Ibid.*
16. Times of India Correspondent, "Fake Currency Notes Racket Busted in Bangalore" (New Delhi, *Times of India*, 16th July, 2010).
17. *Ibid.*
18. Prime Minster's Address in the Chief Minister's Conference on Internal Security in the Year 2010.
19. *Ibid.*
20. *Ibid.*
21. For details, see, M.E. Brown and Sumit Ganguly (eds.), Government Policies and Ethnic Relationsin Asia and the Pacific, MIT Press, Cambridge, 1997.
22. Burmese was the only language allowed in the Union Parliament and regardless of a legislator's proficiency in his dialect or language or his fluency in English, he was required to speak in Burmese. *The Nation*, August 8, 1950, p.1; *The Nation*, March 14, 1959, p.1; *The Guardian Daily*, March 14, 1995, p.1.
23. Many Pakistani historians have admitted that this policy was wrongly adopted. See Hasan Zaheer, The Separation of Pakistan, Oxford University Press, Karachi, 1996.
24. Dipankar Banerjee, Myanmar and North-East India, Delhi Policy Group, New Delhi, 1997, p.11.

3

The Notion of Conflict and its Nature of Operation

The free Online Dictionary defines conflict as,

"A state of open, often prolonged fighting, a battle or war,

2. A state of disharmony between incompatible or antithetical persons, ideas, or interests, a clash;

3. *(Psychology)* A psychic struggle, often unconscious, resulting from the opposition or simultaneous functioning of mutually exclusive impulses, desires, or tendencies;

4. Opposition between characters or forces in a work of drama or fiction, especially opposition that motivates or shapes the action of the plot.[1]

The notion of conflict can be defined through a prism of the sociological variety also and also through the politico-strategic mould in the general sense of the term. Management gurus and the media commentators have gone on to contend that conflict can be managed once its root causes have been defined and comprehended in the larger sense of the term. This requires the need to simulate scenarios dealing with the sociological and security conflicts in the context of both an internal security situation within a nation or an eminent Armageddon betwixt two distinct nation states. Still the mythical, imaginary and finally the sociological roots of any internal or external conflict cannot be ruled out permanently as it is within the origin of the society that the genesis of both domestic and international conflict lies.

Conflict can be of different genres. It can be international in nature, where in two nation states are battling it out with each other with a full fledged military confrontation involving battle tanks, G.I. Joe skill sets and fighter jets of the recent genre. Conflict can be internal in nature, where in a less accoutered State Actor is pitted against the non-state actor and the non-state component has been aptly nomenclatured by the State instrumentalities. The non-state actor is consequentially at the receiving end, as it is less resourced and it is not able to withstand the standard "*Fourth-Estate*" propaganda mechanism of the other state actor which is the government of the nation state[2] and all the access to the governmental resources in tandem with its practice and instrumentality of sovereign concerns in the strict Austinian sense.

Conflict is a condition of opposition and painful tension set up by a clash between opposed and contradictory impulses.[3] However, that very example went on to show how and when this conflict became violent with the widespread destruction of infrastructure and livelihoods and their associated suffering, grief, trauma, anger and bereavement and how it became difficult to see the opportunities for a fairer, safer future.[4]

Types of Conflict

Straitjacketing variants of conflicts is an arduous task considering the fact that conflict itself is an amorphous term. However, we suggest for the sake of practical convenience, four categories one of which is surface or latent conflict. The causes of conflict can be sociological in nature.

Surface conflict: This has shallow or no roots.

Open conflict: This conflict is very visible and has deep roots, sometimes over several generations. Both the causes and the effects need to be addressed.[5]

Latent Conflict

This is conflict below the surface. It might need to be brought out into the open before it can be effectively addressed. Thus, conflict studies has a well defined and well discernible sociological aspect attached to it which can serve as a reminder that our familial concerns, community concerns along with the attendant national concerns-all go a long way into spawning a conglomerated and aggregated existence within which undercurrents of conflict and separation subsist together, which finds an ample reflection in the South Asian context, too, with its multi-ethnic, multi-religious and multi-party zealotry. Also, the notions of internal conflict can be dealt with a certain amount of academic satisfaction when one studies and delves inside the attributes, origins and nature of conflicts within the confines of these South Asian nation states[6].

Sometimes, the notion of internal conflict can go on to have an international dimension as it occurred during the liberation of Bangladesh in the year, 1971. The independence of Bangladesh went on to become a part of a national defeat in Pakistan. One commentator in the IDSA portal has commented that, "Unfortunately, in our country's history, there is no victory against our name. We always faced defeat and disgrace. The incident of 16th December in which the Dhaka Platoon laid down its arms is the worst defeat in our history."[7] The Indian intent to intervene in the internal conflict in East Pakistan refers to the notion that India was interested in Bangladesh due to the ten million odd refugees which had taken shelter in the states of Assam, West Bengal and Tripura with Tripura's refugee shelters being the biggest of the lot which had created a grave humanitarian crisis for the Indian Union. A great deal of economic stress was heaped upon the Indian exchequer courtesy the influx of the Bangladeshi refugees and not much can be attributed to the Bengal-Bengal camaraderie which has been cited by some scholars as the cause of Indian intervention in East Pakistan which some still perceive as an internal conflict within the ambit of the nation state of Pakistan.

South Asia too is a variegated network of diverse communities, where in different ethnic groups have their leanings and their individual cultural and political priorities in the majoritarian conceived political systems of the different South Asian states. A report of the United Nations Institute for Disarmament Research observes that, "Within states, the ethnic and religious composition of the population is also very diverse. In other words, state boundaries do not contain closed, ethnically and religiously homogeneous regions."[8] This in the author's perception can be the root cause of internal and ethnic strife in the South Asian region which is multi-faceted and demographically heterogeneous in all its conceived ramifications.

Apart from the apparent military threats posed by the non-state actors, human crimes of the order of human trafficking, drug venturing and displacement coming to the fore as a consequence can pose a national threat to the diffused populations across borders. The UNIDIR Report observes that, "Displacement due to smaller internal conflicts is largely unrecorded in international systems of reporting. Hence, the total number of displaced people is likely to be larger than the estimates cited above[9]".

This adds on to colour of sub-nationalist threats which endanger the individual nationalities of the respective South Asian nation states. Conflict strewn in the framework of the 'anti-national emphasis and colour' is ridden in the South Asian society. When the partition of the subcontinent took place, the Indian nation state was spawned along with the Islamic Republic of Pakistan with the attendant gory vitiations of violence, bloodshed and gore. The trains full of dead bodies, traversed the charred landscape of Indian and Pakistani Punjab along with the agony and frenzy of the citizens of a now-extant British India which was undivided into India and Pakistan. Also, the conditionalities of violence were a consequence of the conflict between the Indian and Pakistani populace which was engendered by the British Policy of Divide and Rule. This conflict between two communities was further prolonged by the Government of Pakistan which created a 'Political Bugbear' out of the Indian nation state which was nothing but a continuation of the Hindu-Muslim conflict and divide in the subcontinent which forms the core region of the South Asian region in the Mackendarian and Mahan's idiom of core areas during a geo-strategic trend of domination and territorial conquest.

In the words of David Zurik, South Asia's political and ethnic turmoil began in 1947, following the withdrawal of British colonial administration, tearing the region asunder with over 40 ethnic struggles till date that are yet to be resolved.[10] The conflict in South Asia was a cause of the British colonial rule which was the master of the South Asian land mass before the different nation states began attaining their independence and freedom. The colonial rule itself was replete with and all about anti-national contours which seems to have permeated the nook and cranny of internal security dilemmas in the country and in the South Asian region.

South Asia is home to several world religions, over 30 major languages, a thousand dialects, and innumerable castes and sub-castes which adds to the colourings of anti-national forces and emboldens them to soften up the region and the Indian nation state.[11] Such differentials and differences impart fissures to the body politique of the South Asian region or any other conjoined entity. Such differentials ought to have led to the ethos of unity in diversity but they sometimes lend an air of 'differentials' and 'fissures' to the region on the whole and the Indian nation state in particular with the light of the nation state of Pakistan with its turmoiled North-West Frontier regions along with the tedium of incessant and blood curdling political violence in the Malakand.

The theme of conflict, per se, can be theoretically and thematically tackled as there are myriad definitions of conflict doing the rounds. In the words of an eminent think tank based in New Delhi the Institute of conflict Management, 'The core areas of research ought to include: Continuous appraisal of internal security and the state's responses in all areas of existing or emerging conflict in South Asia; Planning for development and security in India's North-East and administrative reforms[12]". Thus, internal security conflicts in the regional polities form a core area of research amongst the academicians in India and in South Asia in general. The notion of security has often been misunderstood as the act of securing one's borders and external frontiers which can be related to the notion that unless one keeps one's house in good order, one cannot be aiming successfully for the international overarch. Thus, the theme of governance needs to be inculcated in the rising tide of debate on internal security in India.

In the context of the notion of conflict, a definition of the RAND/MIPT database project has been chosen[13] which states that, "Terrorism is violence, or the threat of violence, calculated to create an atmosphere of fear and alarm. These acts are designed to coerce others into actions they would not otherwise undertake, or refrain from actions they desired to take. All terrorist acts are crimes.[14] It is the ethos of nationalism and a commonly felt conjoindtedness which can stem the tide of these fissiparous trends and inclinations.

The Regime Theory[15] contends that there ought to be cooperation and coordination betwixt the nation states in a regional polity otherwise there is a pertinent danger that the region might slide into a perennial state of confusion, anarchy and pandemonium. Also, attendant to these concerns, the thought which needs a paramount and pertinent consideration is an ever present state of anarchy in the surrounding international system. Kenneth Waltz has very rightly conceded that all the nation states in the World Polity tend to be war mongering as international polity happens to be power centric. It is a Neo-Realist notion straight from the realm of International Relations Theory which pinpoints towards the concern that nation states are involved in a 'Zero-Sum Game,' wherein the nation states are involved in an incessant striving in order to win a game of one-upmanship.[16]

The Conflict in India with their Attendant Ramifications

Internal conflicts are very difficult to contain and then their efficient resolution is a stiffer challenge to the states concerned. India still grapples with Jihadi terrorism, Pakistan is at crisis crossroads in the tune with its Af-Pak issues and it called for a complete war like operation to fizzle out the LTTE dissent in Sri Lanka. In recent years, internal conflict has also become closely linked to such things as the international drugs trade, piracy and, perhaps most dramatic of all, to the rise of international terrorism.

The myriad rounds of negotiations and intermittent ceasefires which have been the common state practice with an on and off response from the rebels in India, have not led to a creation of a secure and safer region and an Indian nation as it can be observed in the context of the Indian North-East. Peter Jones and Iann O' Flynn write, "For example, having recognised that they are in a mutually hurting stalemate, the parties might decide to compromise for the sake of peaceful co-existence. Even so, their main concern may be to concede as little ground as possible to the other side in order to secure that goal."[17] Thus letting low the various dispute settlement mechanisms and political negotiations which take place between the state and the rebellious non-state actors in the various national, regional and international contexts. There might be another angle to the fungibility and the success of the peace processes and negotiations. Shane O Neil contends in a paper that, "It must also be remembered that peace agreements will also affect those who do not want to shape their relationship to the polity along ethnic line[18]".

Thus apart from the majority of sticklers for ethnic unison and with people adhering to the life blood ethnic ties, internal conflicts also have a novae group which partakes more of a gender and a class wise indemnificatory process. It is contended that, "In the ethnic conflict literature, it is generally agreed that any workable compromise must include both moderates and hard-liners."[19] Thus, most of the conflicts fall apart because the negotiators in the peace process are not able to amalgamate the different concerns of the hawks and the doves amongst the rebels. Bernard Crick observes in the same context that, "Contemporary Northern Ireland, Israel with Palestine and South Africa are each places where normal political compromises do not work, or where the price to be paid if the current South African negotiations are to be successful is far, far higher than either side supposed when it went into the process"[20] Such disparate strife torn regions have a different story to tell and it is one of the approaches while the internal conflict is going on to nomenclature the non-state actors as the anti-national or sub-national actors in the larger comprehension of the term.

There are three main sources of internal conflict in India exacerbated by anti-national/sub-national inclinations and forces in India. First, there are long-running separatist movements in several north-eastern states (Assam, Manipur, Nagaland, Tripura), all of these states have been classified as 'lagging' for the purposes of this report. Since 2005, ULFA has been in a process of indirect negotiations with the government via a People's Consultative Group. However, they continue their campaign of violence, and did not respond to a unilateral ceasefire announced by the government in 2006.[21]

A series of peace accords with various Bodo groups culminated in the formation of a Bodoland Territorial Council.[22] There are also several militant groups claiming to represent the interests of specific ethnic groups. For instance, the Kuki National Front (KNF) wants a separate homeland for the Kukis, the Zomi Revolutionary Army (ZRA)[23].

The second source of internal violence in India comes from incidents perpetrated by leftwing extremist groups (Naxalite movements) in many states of India which is an emerging anti-nationalist threat. The third source of increasing violence in India stems from the incidents of terrorism in India's cities which is another of the anti-national threats spreading its dreaded tentacles in the nation State. Many of the terror attacks are suspected to be orchestrated by fundamentalist groups, such as the Lashkar-e-Taiba (LeT), Jaish-e-Mohammad (JeM) and the Students Islamic Movement of India (SIMI).

The Concept of Self-determination: A façade For Anti-national forces or a 'Just Cause'.

The right to self-determination remains one of the most intractable and difficult problems to be addressed by the international community which has tainted the discourse of nationalism and integrity in the Indian nation state and elsewhere. Many legal formulas have sought to define the existence of the right to self-determination, to define who constitutes a people and who has a right to a separate existence. The subject has been the basis for contention and multitudes of warring scenarios and conflict unencumbered. Some of the insurgent groups putting up the façade as protestors of independence and freedom militate against the theme of sovereignty of the nation states as all demand for a sequestered political existence cannot be entertained as it might lead to Balkanisation of even stable and legitimate nation states in the global polity.

In a comprehensive analysis of the right to self-determination, Aureliu Cristescu wrote:

It is clear that the relevant provisions of the Charter have been interpreted in an increasingly progressive spirit over the years. Today, it is generally recognised that the concept of self-determination entails legal rights and obligations and that a right of self-determination definitely exists (Special Rapporteur..., 1981).

References

1. "What is Conflict," URL: http://www.thefreedictionary.com/conflict (Online: Web), Accessed on 19th December, 2011.
2. Smith, Anthony D., The Ethnic Revival in the Modern World, 2005, Cambridge: Cambridge University Press.
3. "What is Conflict?: Peacebuilding with our Communities," (Online: Web), Accessed on January 27th, 2009, URL: http://tilz.tearfund.org/webdocs/Tilz/Roots/English/Peace-building/Peace_Esection1.pdf.
4. "What is Conflict?: Peacebuilding with our Communities", (Online: Web), Accessed on January 27th, 2009, URL: http://tilz.tearfund.org/webdocs/Tilz/Roots/English/Peace-building/Peace_Esection1.pdf.
5. *Ibid.*

6. Gibert. Paul, Terrorism, Security and Nationality, Routledge, London, 1994, p. 156.
7. "We haven't learnt anything from history and again we are killing our own people: A.Q. Khan," URL: http://www.idsa.in/pup/Dec12-18, (Online: Web), Accessed on 11th January, 2012.
8. "Internal Conflict and Regional Security in South Asia: Approaches, Perspectives and Policies," URL: http://www.unidir.org/pdf/ (Online: Web), Accessed on 11th January, 2012.
9. *Ibid.*
10. David Zurick (1999) "Land of Conflict in South Asia," (Focus, January, 1999).
11. Raju G.C. Thomas (1996), "Competing Nationalisms: Secessionist Movements and the State" (Harvard, Harvard International Review, 1996).
12. "The Institute of Conflict Management an Introduction" (Online: Web), Accessed on January 26th, 2009, URL: http://www.satp.org/satporgtp/icm/index.html.
13. "RAND Corporation/Oklahoma City National Memorial Institute for the Prevention of Terrorism" (Online: Web), Accessed on January 14th, 2009,URL: http://db.mipt.org/rand_tc.cfm.
14. Ghosh, SK, Terrorism, Ashish Publishing House, New Delhi, 1998, p. 45.
15. Robert Keohane (1984) "After Hegemony: Cooperation and Discord in the World Poltical Economy," (Princeton: Princeton University Press, 1984).
16. Kenneth Waltz (1954), "Man, State and the War," (New York: Columbia University Press, 1954), pp.56-76.
17. "Internal Conflict, the International Community and the Promotion of Principled Compromise," URL: http://www.ucl.ac.uk/spp/seminars/political-theory-downloads/, (Online: Web), Accessed on 1st January, 2011.
18. O 'Neill, Shane (2003), "Justice in Ethnically Diverse Societies: A Critique of Political Alienation," *Ethnicities*, 3(3), 369-92.
19. *Ibid.*
20. Crick, Bernard (1990) The High Price of Peace', *History Today*, 40(10), 7-9.
21. Guha, Biswajeet Ed., Conflict and Violence in Indian Society, Kamushka Publishers, New Delhi, p. 326.

22. The central government and the government of Assam signed accords with the All Bodo Students' Union in 1993 and the Bodo Liberation Tigers (BLT) in 2003, and a ceasefire with the National Democratic Front of Bodoland (NDFB) has been in operation since 2004.
23. Handerson, Harry, Global Terrorism, Jaico Publishing House, Mumbai, 2003, p. 234.

4

The Twin Threats of Casteism and Communalism in India

Anti-nationalism is a sentiment and a legerdemain which is not only foisted upon India through external nefarious and centripetal contributions but is something which is internally hewn and spawned through the socio-political and cultural baggage and the diverse construct of the Indian nation State. The scholars and strategic affairs analysts have been harping upon the themes of cross border terrorism and the influx of 'sleeper cells' in the Indian security and political dynamic. What needs to be underscored is the factoid that the threefold threats of casteism, caretelisation of religion in the form of communalism and the now au-currant threat of regionalism, have taken a toll of the Indian integrity and the ingrained sentiment of oneness and nationalism.

Internal security is a paradigm par excellence and all the more a necessary arsenal in India's state doctrine in the face of daunting, consistent challenges, some of which have manifested themselves as attendant security threats of the order of Naxalism, talibanisation of the indian polity, insurgency in secessionist movements and the threats to tranquility and order through the mechanisms of foreign hands, cross-border terrorism, rearing up their ugly heads in India. India too is faced with other attendant challenges of the order of casteism, communalism and regionalism in the national polity which amount to a deleterious and stultifying impact on the domestic polity as security and well defined defense challenges.

The menace of casteism is a threat to the all intertwined national fabric and the attendant unity and integrity in the Indian Union. Caste in the grave form of curtailed freedom has always been a bone of contention and has had an imminent impact on the state of egalitarianism and the patterns of regional development and electoral politics in India. Politicking and Politics goes on unabated in India. The ethos of Harijans which was espoused by the likes of Mahatma Gandhi and Dr. Bhimrao Ambedkar, they have been let down by the populist leaders, threatening the true ethos of Dr. Ambedkar. As a contradiction, it might seem fashionable to stymie the charismatic impact of the leaders of the order of Lalu Parasad Yadav and Mulayam Singh but they have led to a twin pronged attempt to develop the lives of their downtrodden brethren and also objectify developmental parameters for the browbeaten people.

The strict and straightforward ethos of the Indian Varnashrama Dharma can be divided ideally into the segmented cleavages of the order of: Brahmins, Kshatriyas, Vaishyas and Shudras in the Indian polity and society, primarily meant to uphold and sustain a freewheeling, irrational and exploitative system in one view of the term and the complete caste narrative in the Indian nation state. Also, the other perspective on the caste fold in the rubric of the Indian Union contends otherwise. This notion holds the attendant rationale that the spawning and the sustenance of the caste system had a functional significance in the national societal rubric as the division of the social structure into different caste echelons led to a stability and operationability in the society as the divisions were vocation based premised upon the functional and professional differentials in the society. The societal concern is to delve inside the overlapping ramifications of caste violence and caste wars which make one person look up with disgust and dismay and view these threats as the perennial threats to the peace, tranquility and internal security of the Indian nation state. Apart from the stereotypical defense and security threats from within and from external actors, one needs to perceive these threats as being severe fissiparous tendencies amounting to a distinct and stultifying sub-national threat to the unity and integrity of the nation. The question of ethnicity and the race posers also fall in the same realm as the menace of caste based discrimination in the Indian society and the attendant political firmament.

Human rights abuses against Dalits are in common parlance, and should not be accepted and socially regularised definitely, as part of the national lingo. An international news report goes on to contend that, "Dalit boy beaten to death for plucking flowers"; "Dalit tortured by cops for three days"; "Dalit killed in lock-up at Kurnool"; "Dalits burnt alive in caste clash"; "Dalits lynched in Haryana", "Dalit woman gang-raped, paraded naked," "Police egged on mob to lynch Dalits[1]". Thus, the state of caste violence still remains a staid reality in the rubric of the Indian nation state and much after the Temples of India revolution and the superimposition of the nation over the international firmament, the clamour of international power status does not run well for the aspirations of a rising India in the South Asian and the larger international context.

The notion of caste system and caste diversity if understood and comprehended in a positive sense underscores the factoid that India is a cornucopia of 'Unity in Diversity' which can be embellished as a 'Unique Whole' going by the desires and trendsetting examples of our equitous, egalitarian and unadulterated notions of our Founding fathers. Also, we need to have a critical look at the anti-national practice of dividing people in the name of caste and creed which has become part and parcel of some of the Political mandarins of the day in the name of Vote Bank Politics. This practice of Caste based Politics, is very much 'inimical' to the general national and comprehensive interests of the nation state that is the Indian

Union. These politically mischievous and deleterious trends need to be construed as anti-national threats akin to the external security threats of the order of 'Cross Border Terrorism, Influx of Illegal migrants in the Indian Territory', apart from the notion of national security as it is understood in the stereotypical understanding by the security experts in the country.

The same news report adds that, "Dalits are not allowed to drink from the same wells, attend the same temples, wear shoes in the presence of an upper caste, or drink from the same cups in tea stalls[2]". Such trends of defoliating the nationalistic and the conjoined ethos of the Indian Union need not be taken lightly by the scholars, intelligentsia and the Political leaders of the day and the times. Going by the nationalistic and conjoined socio-political culture of the Indian nation state, we need to decipher out the threat of casteism as a national security threat to the Indian Union, which is a hidden but a flagrant violation of the Indian constitution and the attendant ethics of an ideally and inherently just Indian nation state.

Speaking and writing about Untouchability, is not a leftist discourse being construed as an anti-nationalist threat. It is a matter of national concern as Caste Violence being perpetrated in myriad parts of the Indian state perpetuates a sense of apathy and disaffection amongst the suffering lot and makes them militate against the nationalistic and conjoined ethos of the Indian nation state. Such a threat needs to be categorically calibrated as an anti-national threat to the body Politique of the Indian nation state. India's Untouchables are relegated to the lowest jobs, and live in constant fear of being dehumanised by upper-caste people purportedly to keep them in their place. Merely walking through an upper-caste neighbourhood is a life-threatening offence in some interior regions of the nation. Nearly 90 per cent of all the poor Indians and 95 percent of all the illiterate Indians are Dalits, according to figures presented at the International Dalit Conference that took place May 16 to 18 in Vancouver, Canada.

A Delving Inside the Category of Crime Against Dalits

Statistics compiled by India's National Crime Records Bureau indicate that in the year 2000, the last year for which figures are available, 25,455 crimes were committed against Dalits. "There have been large-scale abuses by the police, including raids, beatings in custody, failure to charge offenders or investigate reported crimes[3]". Do we write about it all as state apathy or the general rot in the system?

There are web portals which have assiduously connected the torn data entries and cumulated a convincing fact base to protest against the violence in the rural hinterland of the Indian Union as we stay in the secure confines of the Urbania oblivious to the ground realities engrossed in our own saga of foibles and dreary routine lives. In an incident which was widely reported in the national daily, *The Hindu*, the news report runs thus, "According to Sakunthala, a widow, a gang armed with pipes and stones attacked her house. Spitting vengeance, it started breaking television sets, electrical fittings, utensils, steel cots and almirahs[4]".

The issues of land rights, the last vestiges of the Zamindari system goes on to contend that the day to day fracas of distribution of water sources in the village community along with the theme of clearing the way of dirt and the allocation of village pathways for the running of marriage processions and deity processions happen to be the points of conflict in the Indian rural context whether be it the dustbowls of the colorful state of Rajasthan or the gangetic plains in the hinterland of Bihar bypassing the places of Supaul and Jamui. In southern India, too, apart from the scourge of caste wars, organised crime is on the rise in Chennai recently, with the befalling of five gangsters in the city which have either been a fallout of inter-gang rivalry or mercenary killings. A social worker was murdered recently in broad daylight and according to reports, the victim had mobilised public opinion against local goons and reportedly paid the price for it. Organised Crime too can be conveniently construed as an anti-national threat to the Indian state that it beckons a 'Law and Order' problem in the rubric of the Indian nation state. Organised Crime is not attached to any specific ideology, political party or a specific religious group but it still shatters the peace, tranquility and general well being of the States in a profound and gradual manner as the rot of civil unrest tends to set in the system in the Indian Union.

Recent killings have shown that gangsters are rather meticulous in their operations. One need not be surprised. A Doctoral thesis titled as, "Organised Crime — a study of criminal gangs in Chennai," studied 59 criminal gangs and 341 criminals who share 1351 police cases between them. The author goes on to contend that, "Chennai may not be as bad as Mumbai, where the mafia has a large presence. It is a fact though that many gangs have emerged in Chennai in the last few years."[5] These gangs have a well defined functional structure much on the lines of the Ghetto structures in United States and other Urban dwellings in the Western nation states. They indulge in crimes of the order of theft, robbery and burglary and run 'departments' for surveillance, planning, organising and execution. The crimes also include the notion of crime and isolated killings of old people in sequestered bungalows in cities such as Delhi which are home to floating and recipient populations from the neighbouring states and the most of the crime committed in the Urban landscape is associated to these people, wage labour forces belonging to these neighbouring and adjacent populations near the capital city of the anointed nation. Skin Trade is too rampant lending an amoral air to the urban existence. Community Policing can serve as an appropriate to this internal security challenge which is very much institutional in nature. Drug peddling and utilising patronage from the local politicians also enumerates the other tardy elements of this unholy nexus. These non-Dalit crimes are also related to the same societal superstructure which lies embedded in the casteist rubric of the Indian nation state. These general imbalances in the general law and order and tranquil state of affairs in the Indian nation state can be construed as an ever present genre of anti-national threat which needs to be clubbed as a 'Law and Order' problem being faced by our nation as a whole.

In the context of caste strife in India, Arvind Koshal reports that, "The lives of Dalit leaders like Kanshi Ram, Ram Vilas Paswan and Mayawati have one thing in common all of them have an older member of the family who broke away from conditions of village poverty."[6] Thus, the leadership provided by these neo leaders in the societal and political make up of the states in India is phenomenal as at least the lost souls of the society can have recourse to practical and state succor in the light of the years of marginalisation and sequestration which they have faced since the hallowed days in the country civilisational history.

The same author further contends in a write up in the *Times India Network* that, "Labourers crowding the roofs of trains from Bihar and UP to Punjab during harvest bear witness to abject poverty of the landless in the Indian countryside. The money order economy too has its roots in the trouble of internal instability"[7] In a news report, which appeared in a well circulated and well received internet portal, "More than 200 recruitments are alleged to have been made by a bank by submitting fake caste certificates."[8] Thus, the recruitment of populations emanating from the village yards leads to the notion of furthering anarchy and pandemonium in the national urbania especially in the cosmo-joints of Mumbai and Delhi. Thus, the politicisation of social issues happens to be a obfuscatory role playing instrumentality in the national political firmament which tends to delimit the free and open ended welfarist role of the state by painting the state's affirmative action in political colours.

There are some commentaries which tend to blame a certain sect of the nation's mandarins, further divide the nation state into enclaves of, 'higher' and 'lower castes' which is another negative development for the body politique of the Indian nation state. Such casteist divisions create and spawn further discrepancies within the notion of nationalistic concerns, ethos and the social unity and integrity of India. These caste wise demarcations are not only operational in the rural hinterland of the nation but the biases and prejudices still remain embedded within the rubric of the cosmopolitan make up of the Indian nation state, if, perceived in the Urbanized millue in the Indian nation state. Thus this sub-national narrative of casteism is not only in operation in the village republics in India but also in the cities and metropoles of the country. The same national cleavage can be said to be reminiscent of an anti-national threat when the political leaders and the misguided and indoctrinated populations of the various Indian states clamour for separate States and Autonomous Councils in the name of autonomy and regionalist concerns or based upon the developmental raison D'Etre or premised upon the linguistic understanding of collective living. These regionalist threats too fall in the same category whether it be the Telangana theme of separate statehood or the North Eastern demand for autonomy.

The Gujjar-Meena Turmoil in Rajasthan: A New Northern Naxal and Sub-National Outburst?

About the minority rights in South Asia, we need to remember three idioms:

Firstly, the countries of South Asia have a unique social history based on the societal realities of their own as caste plays a major role. Second, the nation states of South Asia have a large number of people belonging to dominant groups regarding the validity of 'minority rights' as separate from the all and perennially understood notion of 'human rights'. In most of the nation states in South Asia, the minority rights are getting pushed back because of the increased role of Majoritarianism along with the glaring incidence of religious fundamentalism.[9]

In the last few years, Meenas and Gujjars, both belonging to the scheduled castes and tribes of the state of Rajasthan have been embroiled in an insidious fracas in the state of Rajasthan. Still, what has become a rankling aspect now is the notion that these people have begun to confront each other as the Gujjars and have not been able to be accorded reservation status in a particular category in the state of Rajasthan. Rajasthan was known to be a very liberal and composite entity which was known for its collective and caste neutral and non-violent way of living. In the aftermath of the First World War and from the time of the formation of the League of Nations, the concern of the Minorities particularly in the context of Europe was on the agenda of the League of Nations. Fransesco Capotori, Special Rapporteur of the Sub Commission on Prevention Discrimination and Protection of Minorities on the Rights of Persons belonging to Ethnic, Religious and Linguistic Minorities (1977), proferred the following definition of a minority group:

"A Group numerically inferior to the rest of the population of a state on a non-dominant position whose members being national of the state possess-ethnic, religious or linguistic characteristics differing from those of the rest of the population."[10] The Constitution of India is very clear in this context. The objective of the Republic is to "secure to all its citizens; justice, social, economic and political, liberty of thought, expression, belief, faith and worship, equality of status and opportunity and to promote among them all fraternity assuring the individual and the unity and integrity of the nation".[11]

In a news report which appeared in the national daily, *The Hindu*, it so transpired that, "Lack of employment opportunities, dearth of good educational institutions, deficiency of civic amenities and an abysmal poverty spawn the continuing rivalry between the dominant Meenas and rebellious Gujjars."[12] Rajasthan was home to political violence and violent dissent for over a month and it is scaringly true that the scourge of these caste wars can become an annual event, serving as a precedent for the next, like in the processions marred with violence in Ireland over a few decades. The Delhi-Jaipur Highway may not have witnessed a war in the conventional sense, yet during the agitation there was nothing to differentiate the Highway from a War Zone.[13]According to one perception of the caste quagmire, the Gurjar revolt is also propped up by the theme of having a Meena dominated bureaucracy in the state of Rajasthan which is the point of ire and acrimony between the Gurjars and the Meenas. Also, the infighting between the Gurjars and Meenas is an apt instance of the marginalised classes toughening their own playing turf as this runs truant to the motif of marginalised unity in the Indian nation state and in the country's societal and political make up. The State of Rajasthan has been an aggregation of small city and sub-regional economies within the larger context of an underdeveloped and lagging behind economy of the nation. It needed help right from the day, the Princely States were amalgamated in as the hesitant constituents of an Indian independence and the much fought and sacrifised for Indian freedom.

Thus, the Princely pantheon of Rajasthan where the moolah was dominated by the royals and the corporate local-traders, it was always a ripe ground for the mutilation which the state has faced at the hands of the caste wars. The marginalisation and the *Estragruffen* felt by the poverty ridden hoi polloi will always raise its head in the context of a poor, impoverished, geographically impoverished, poorly rainfed, and unindustrialised belt of India with the very true attributes of a *Bimaru* state in the northern part of the nation. Paul Brass refers to another instance, wherein he studied the context in a sub-region of the State of Uttar Pradesh. Paul R. Brass, contends that, "To determine, how the Congress functioned in a context, wherein Hindu-Muslim relations had been embittered as a consequence of the presence of the Aligarh Muslim University in the City. The intervening violence was striking."[14]

As related by V.S. Vyas, "The same feudal past influenced social organisation, essentially characterised by a hierarchical orientation, sharp differences between the elite and masses, strong paternalistic organisation of the families and low status accorded to women."[15]

The rivalry in Rajsthan can develop into something similar to the threat of Naxalism, a primal fear for many strategists and national security persons. The caste warriors this time were the Gurjars in Rajasthan, traditionally a shepherd community, now engaged in a violent agitation demanding Scheduled Tribe status. One report by Rohit Parihar in *India Today* mentions the notion that, "The Gurjars are already listed as Backward Class, but seeing the employment advantages and political power that Scheduled Tribes (ST) like Meenas have earned in Rajasthan, they too have been demanding ST Status."[16] Thus, the ensuing scuffle betwixt the twin groups in the state of Rajasthan metamorphosed into a real security quagmire for the enforcing and the monitoring quagmire.

The Telangana Issue: Rise of Regionalism in the South. Is it an Anti-national Threat to the Conjointness of the Indian Union

It is commonly perceived fact of life in India that federalism is a mixed bag in the country and what remains to be seen is the notion that does the unitary bias as elucidated by the likes of Durga Das Basu and Wheare led to a notion of the states ending up as sacrificial lambs in the dilemma of the Centre and the State divide. The concurrent vows of the concurrent list and the attendant separation of powers between the Central power denomination and the receptacle smaller and largely dependent states has been the bone of contention since the attainment of independence by the nation. Linguistic states came up as a consequence which have been stabilised after recurrent slights at the unified contexts in the same Indian states.

One region of the Indian Union has a unique distinct from the rest of the nation state in the name of linguistic reasons and other differences of culture, traditions and norms. In such a scenario, some political leaders and outfits, contend themselves to be able to harness the regional resources for the development and betterment of their own sub-regions as an instance, the regions can be of the order of Telangana in the Southern part of the country. The novae entrants of the order of Uttarakhand, Chhattisgarh and Jharkhand are a result of similar movements in the northern and central parts of the country but still what separates them is the factoid that their mother states of the order of Uttar Ptradesh, Madhya Pradesh and Bihar had not to contend with the birth place movement of Naxalism which separates out and sanitises the issue and the corollary demand of Telangana in the State of Andhra Pradesh. Such states exist in the Indian Union as India can afford them separate federated developmental parameters along with the notions of a linguistic and cultural identity. The trouble begins when such state movements tend to defy the Constitution of the land and they take up a violent and vituperative mechanisms, wherein the law and order and the unity and integrity of the Indian Union can be harmed, compromised and destabilised.

It is here that the notion of sub-nationalism and not the commonly bandied about word, sub-nationalism comes into play and the political class and the civil societal activists have to take up cudgels against the notion of 'hidden separatism' ingrained within the rubric of such notions of selective Regionalism. We are living in a globalised world, wherein the cross national currents and convergence of the currency markets and corporate chains seem to be the order of the day. Such a fast unifying world must not be enchained by the parochial concerns of the regional satraps who grind their axes for the petty political and electoral gains. Telangana is one such instance of 'Regional Separatism' in the auspices of the Indian land without tarnishing the tenet of federalism in the Indian polity.

In the context of Telangana, K Chandrashekar Rao (KCR) has attempted every possible gimmick to carve an image of an"Ultimate Warrior of Telengana[17]". Some scholars have contended that, "The list is endless. Breaking the country into such smaller units increases regionalism in Indian politics. Further it is a multi-crore task for the government and funds for the formation of so many states cannot be accommodating in the forthcoming budget[18]". The formation of newer states and with weak administrations and a palpable want of resources will enable the foreign states to destabilise the internal and national security of the country even more.

Sammer Hashmi writes in one of the Internet web portals, "The two big questions that need to be answered before creating the new states are-(1) Is the government moving in the right direction by creating smaller states (& 2)[19]". Thus, we are mired in the aftermath with a discussion and a narrative on the norm of federalism in the Indian Union, wherein the practice of unitary bias runs supreme and is the idiom of the Indian nation state. Federal concerns surmount the national concerns. Smaller states can in a way tide over the lopsided results and consequences of development in the different states of the nation. Dr. Harihar Bhattacharya contends that, "The strategically most significant effect of globalisation, from the viewpoint of national unity and integrity, is the growth in inter-state and intra-regional disparity in development."[20] The reasons of the order of the Central apathy in involving the states in the policy making and the decision making exercise and the Central competency in spawning the macro economic policy framework for the entire nation are some of the pointers in the direction of blaming the unitary bias of the nation's developmental pattern.

Akin to these factors, the different political coalitions in the states all across the length and breadth of the nation also curtail some of the devolution of power with inhibited politics ordained decision making in New Delhi. The constitution of the land has ample provisos for the creation of new states in the direction of devolution of more autonomy and individual and a more focused and a targeted developments of the grey regions which still are mired in the morass of under development in the nation as peripheries. Ramchandra Guha writes that, "'Regionalism', to give the sentiment a name (or academic label), has come in different forms and been accompanied by varying degrees of violence. The legitimate kind of regionalism has demanded a separate space or state of one's own, within a space or state within India".[21] It can be further elaborated that linguistic sub-nationalism does not satisfy the want of the separate states and they further hanker after a greater pie of the Center's share in terms of allocations and planning. Thus, if the protest is limited to a fast or a democratic protest than the conditionality of a law and order floatation does not arise but political violence attached to the regional activism can mar the social and political landscape of the nation state irreparably and is definitely unconstitutional. The demand for an equitable pie along with the notion of an autonomous existence need not be tampered by the politics of regionalism.

The Centre and state divide also rests on the allocation of financial resources which is premised in the various constitutional lists. J Dasgupta contends, "The states, on the other hand have been assigned taxes, as a consequence, the states of other federations, like the USA can meet about 70% to 80% of their expenditure from their own resources, Indian states can only meet about 40% of their expenditure."[22] Thus, the fiscal allocation and the division of the national exchequer happens to be a significant bottleneck in cordial and smooth Centre-state relations. Shefali Jha in another argument refers to the ordinariness of the centre -state disputes. She contends that, "The Supreme Court has proved to be the defender of the states against the Union's arbitrariness. In the Bommai case, for instance, when the petitioner questioned the imposition of President's rule[23]". Thus, the Judiciary in the country too has been involved and enamoured of the context of the federalism and regionalism narrative in the country since long.

There are various ethnic groups like the gorkhas, karbis, bodos etc., demanding for a separate state. There are people who are not satisfied with a separate state called as Telangana but they clamour for a tribal state to be carved out of Andhra Pradesh which though with its *pros*, would breed fissiparous tendencies as such states will not be able to sustain themselves and might fall prey to the external forces and Indian foes and other destabilsing movements of the order of Naxalism.

The decision to carve out a separate state of Telangana, which will take the total number of states in the Union to 29, comes at the end of a 40-year-old struggle for a distinct identity. This comes after a gap of nine years when three new states were carved out. Jharkhand split from Bihar on November 15, 2000 to become the 28th state while Uttarakhand split from UP on November 9 and Chhattisgarh was created on November 1 the same year out of Madhya Pradesh.

The threat to internal security can be comprehended in a more robust form if we delve inside some current media reportage of the Telangana movement in the context of the political fracas and the attendant political violence. The scourge of regionalism is nothing but abatement to the breakaway tendencies in the Indian Union which might deteriorate into a pseudo-Naxal movement and might be aided and abated by the Naxals themselves if they foresee an opportunity to destabilise the State of Andhra Pradesh.

Reports in the national daily, Business Standard, too sum up the threat to internal security through these new and nascent states as part of a kind of compromise with the country's internal security and thus, this rationale rules out the reasoning behind the creation and spawning of a new state in Andhra Pradesh. The news report contends that, "Even if there is a legitimate case for the creation of a separate Telangana state, violence, mayhem and political blackmail cannot be the midwives of the new state's birth."[24] Thus, political violence in the name of rendering of political and developmental justice cannot be a correct panacea for the realisation of egalitarianism and the just distribution of resources in the beleaguered State of Andhra Pradesh.

The newspaper report contends that, "With the architect of the Congress party's victory in Andhra Pradesh, YS Rajasekhar Reddy, no more, the party itself is offering varying interpretations of what that verdict means for the question of Telangana's statehood[25]". Another threat associated to the demand of Telangana is the notion that Maoism which might hijack the agenda on the premise of the claims of equitable distribution of resources along with the themes of malgovernance and maladministration in these politically tricky terrains of the state of Andhra Pradesh. The city of Hyderabad might suffer as the corporate hub of the state which might shift quarters to the novae business corridors of a neophytic Telangana, which might further exacerbate the conflict with the theme of counter rebellion by the entrenched elites and the populace of the rich regions of the State of Andhra Pradesh.

Thus, countervailing measures need to be the call of the hour in the ambit of the whole debate.

The recent advent of the demand for the Awadh Pradesh too can be a pointer in the direction of the debate of a federated existence which now confronts the Indian Union in its true and bright light. The antiquity attached to the notion of Awadh Pradesh cannot be swept under the carpet but the spawning a state in the name of elegance and the tradition attached to it is no replacement to the rationale of good and convenient governance. Thus, creating new states in the name of living up to the myth and lore of the locality and the region cannot be an authentic motive for the division of the well established and older states. Federalism already provides the nation with several states which have been carved out of the larger existing ones and this need not be the sewing rationale for a new state.

One can genuinely conclude that India is faced with these threesome threats of Communalism, Regionalism and Casteism which have to be taken into consideration as segmented threats to India's national and internal security which lead on to a centralised monolith of a problem. India has progressed by leaps and bounds but the notion of attaining some semblance of sobriety and peacenik approach to the domestic polity has to be of the paramount concern as these are a few numbered non-defense and security threats which pervade the nook and cranny in India. If these regional movements remain in the realm of acceptable political behaviour one can contend that such notions are very much amenable to the internal security and the nationalistic ethos of the Indian nation state. Still, if they delve inside the case study of South India, the Naxal movement is of utmost significance and these regional disaffections can be conveniently converted or strategically co-opted to a new genre of anti nationalist movement or a regional protest which might tend to become violent in nature in the later on context of the Indian nation state. Thus, in summation one can contend that without giving any political colouring to the threesome anti-national threats of Casteism, Communalism and, Regionalism, the notion of they impinging upon the nationalistic candour and flavour of the Indian nation state cannot be revoked quite convincingly. Thus, all the well defined security, strategic, social and political dimensions have to be surmised under the ambit of the internal security and national integrity in the Indian nation which have a decided sub- national dimension attached to them.

References

1. Hillary Mayell (2003) "India's Untouchables Face Violence, Discrimination," URL: http://news.nationalgeographic.com/news/2003/06/0602_030602_untouchables.html, (Online: Web), Accessed on April 18th, 2010,
2. *Ibid.*
3. *Ibid.*
4. A.V. Raghunath, "Dalit Houses Attacked in Salem Village," (Online: Web), Accessed on April 21st, 2010, URL: http://www.hinduonnet.com/stories/2002050202950400.htm
5. *Ibid.*
6. Arvind Kaushal, "Missing the Benefits of Education" (Online: Web), Accessed on April 21st, 2001, URL: http://deccan.com/regional.
7. *Ibid.*
8. "Bank Recruitment on Fake Caste Certificates" (Online: Web), Accessed on April 21st, 2010, URL: http://www.ambedkar.org/News/News032102.htm#news4.
9. James Massey (2008), "Minority Rights in the South Asian Countries with Special Reference to India" (Alpjan Quarterly, Vol. VIII, October 2007, March 2008, Nos 1 and 2.
10. Fransesco Capotari, " Study on the Rights of Persons Belonging to Ethnic, Religious and Linguistic Minorities, (United Nations, New York, 1991, p. 96, Para. 568).
11. The Constitution of India, (As on Ist June, 2009).
12. Mohammed Iqbal (2008), 'Meena-Gujjar Rivalry : A major Issue in Karauli' (Chennai: *The Hindu*, 2008).
13. *Times of India*, New Delhi, June, 2, 2007.
14. Paul R. Brass (2007), "Organised Riots and Structured Violence in India," (Chennai, New Delhi, August 23, 2007).

15. V.S. Vyas (2010), "Rajasthan Moving towards the Maisntream" (New Delhi: Seminar, 2010).
16. Rohit Parihar (2007), 'Caste in Conflict" (New Delhi: *India Today*, 2007).
17. Mentioned in "The Telangana Issue and the Rise of Regionalism," (Online: Web), Accessed on April 22nd, 2010, URL: http://www .merinews.com/article/the-telangana-issue-and-rise-of-regionalism/15790350.shtml
18. *Ibid.*
19. Sammer Hashmi, "The Telangana Dilemma," (Online: Web), Accessed on April 22nd, 2010, URL: http://behindindia.com/india-news-stories/article/telangana-15-12-09.html
20. "Globalisation and Indian Federalism: Current Trends," An in-house seminar presentation at the Institute of Federalism, Fribourg (Switzerland), 16 May, 2007.
21. Ramchandra Guha, "Feeling Left Out" (Online: Web), Accessed on 3rd January, 2012, URL: http://www.indiatogether.org/2007.
22. J. Dasgupta, 'India's federal design and multicultural national construction', in A. Kohli, ed. *The Success of India's Democracy*, 2001, p. 70.
23. Shefali Jha, "Democracy in India: The State Institutional Domain,"URL: http://www.democracy-asia.org/qa/india/Shefali%20Jha.pdf (Online: Web), Accessed on 3rd January, 2012.
24. News Agencies, "Talking About Telangana," (New Delhi: *Business Standard*, 7th Janjuary, 2010).
25. *Ibid.*

5

Red Star Over India: Naxalism Revisited and a Few other Concerns

Naxalism: A Menace to be tackled for the Indian National Security Concerns

The tenet of rebellion runs in the bloodstream of humanity whether it be the steppes and the Urbania of a Czar tortured Soviet Union or the charred hinterland of the Indian Union. Reasons abound for the antipathy to the state but still the sores are there to be seen all across the length and breadth of the national polity. The images provided by cinemascopes of the order of Hazar Chaurasi Ki Maa, etc. can provide one with what transpired in the seventies in certain tracts in the country which is witnessing further but interconnected fulmination now in the contemporary context. Naxalism with its advent has made the people eschew their tribal innocence and if one goes by the 2010 Bollywood flick's ditty, the, one can concentrate upon the theme song, "Sasural Gainda Phool" which refers to the peace and tranquility of the life in the hinterland of the state of Chhattisgarh, wherein, the people are alive to the natural rhythms of sequestered life away from the Urban cacophony. Enter Naxalism and the innocent verve along with the tranquil village republics go off for a six and the rigmarole of security forces involved in seizures and the Maoists blowing up of public vehicles becomes the staple fare of life in the land of God and the heart of India.

Naxalism has turned out to be a significant irritant in the back for the Indian Republic, which has a proud history of secular and socialist credentials, as enumerated in our Preambular narrative. Naxalites have never been a potent force in India, but with the persistence of the Maoist movement in Nepal, they have been able to develop a meandering corridor in the Indian Union which is referred to as the 'Red Corridor'. The failed land reforms in the country, being a significant reason for the movement's upswing. The dreaded **'Red Corridor'**[1] cuts through a swathe of Indian territory across the states of Bihar, Jharkhand, Orissa , Chhattisgarh, and finally the mother state of the movement in West Bengal, where it has lost much of its relevance in the contemporary world. The Indian polity still suffers from the scars of a bloody and violence instigating movement which is based entirely on an anti-state argument and dialectic, akin to the Flower children movement in the West in the times of personages like Timothy Leary and Martin Luther King.

The history of the Naxalite movement can be traced all the way back to the People's War Group (PWG).[2] The details of the PWG have been profusely provided by the anti-terror research portal, South Asian Terror Portal. The objectives for the PWG was established deserves a closer look and delving inside. The Ministry of Home in the country too regards the Naxal unrest as a mixed bag. In the report released by the MHA, in the year, 2006, it contends that, "Naxalism continues to be an area of concern. Naxalites typically operate in a vacuum created by inadequacy of administrative and political institutions, espouse local demands and take advantage of the prevalent disaffection."[3] Thus, the human security idiom of the Naxal problem was realised late by the national establishment and the violence in the garb of the killings going on unabated. In a 2006 release, the following figures provide a perfect picture of the insurgency in the Naxal affected regions in the country:

Head	*2003*	*2004*	*2005**	*2006*
No. of incidents	1597	1533	1608	1509
No. of civilians killed	410	466	524	521
No. of policemen killed	105	100	153	157
No. of naxalites killed	216	87	225	272[4]

The figures reflect the notion that the number of security personnel who have been annihilated in the Naxal violence has dwindled during the years but the number of collateral damage done has been on the rise, which is a cause of concern for the internal security officials of the nation. Another government policy directive makes for good sense which can have a significant impact on the rising expanse of Maoism in the nation, which is a kind of: "Naxalism being an inter-state problem, the states will adopt a collective approach and pursue a coordinated response to counter it."[5] Thus, a coordinated approach to counter the Naxal internal security threat can go a long way in decimating the scourge of the Maoist violence, wherein the myriad political denominations have to rise above their immediacy orientated political gains and the rites of political one-upmanship.

Dr. P. Vara Vara Rao is the prominent ideologue amongst the Naxalites[6]. The major agenda refers to the withdrawal of the official governance, wherein none too clandestine Kangaroo Courts are functioning parallel to the paralysed state apparatus in the rural hinterland of the Indian Republic. It scavenges upon the loyalties of the citizens by making them aware about the excesses of the regime and also, as the root cause of their all harsh life, misery, poverty and an all pervading underdevelopment. It amounts to a debatable theme where the state has no other option, but to make its ameliorative presence felt in the Indian Dominion, in the comprehension of some authors and observers of Indian affairs.

The Law and Order Problem: The Sub-nationalist Narrative

Do police matter? Can they prevent crime—or, for that matter, terrorism? The long-prevailing view of the police department's role in society was spelled out in the famous 'Principles of Law Enforcement' of Sir Robert Peel, the founder of London's Metropolitan Police (Scotland Yard). "The basic mission for which the police exist," Peel wrote in 1829, "is to prevent crime and disorder." Accordingly, Peel proposed that the test of police efficiency should be the absence of crime and disorder, not the visible evidence of police action dealing with them. Thus, the police service in any nation is the closest to the undercurrents and the seamier side of what all ails the nation.

Nationalism is an entity which is not to be unearthed by the investigators of the state at all but it happens to be a norm and a practicable entity rather than being an intangible narrative which appears goody-goody only in the books and the heightened corridors of the class elites. The nation state is a barometer and a container for the keeping intact of the conditionalities of a conjoined existence which tends to be bartered away by the foreign forces and the human development indicator challenges in the country. The police service in India is a sub-culture in itself which runs very close to the seething undercurrent of the sub-nationalist challenges in the nation, and as an intermediary and the service provider, the police officers have to serve as national managers in order to keep intact the procedural efficiency of the service. It is they who maintain a clean and perforce image in front of the public, so that the public faith in the conundrum of anti-national narratives being bandied about by the alternate way followers and the rebels of the day who function in the rural hinterland of the country, can be effectively stymied. The separatists in the strife torn regions of Jammu and Kashmir along with the sequestered confines of a non-mainstreamed segment of the North-East, too, suffer from the similar regular security challenges.

The police service in India in a paramilitary role is charged with the responsibility of maintaining law and order in the country and apart from the apparent crimes being social-political and economic in nature, a different genre of crime syndicate has evolved in the nation which can be surmised in the definition of, 'Asymmetric threats.' Also, the notions of how far the police are savvy enough to tackle such a new variant of a hydra headed and technologically sophisticated crime, is also a concern for the mandarins of the police administration in the country. One of the primal challenges present before the law enforcers happens to be that of Naxalism which has earned a bad name for itself in the context of the theme of coercion which is some tense and critical situations a paramount conduit and instrumentality of law enforcement in India when the investigation process and the special situation demands its usage. Internationally speaking, new theorists posited that crime was the result of collective "root causes" like social injustice, racism, and poverty runs true in the tackling of the instability and anarchy caused by the advent and operation of Maoism in the nation.

The practical implication of such root-cause theory was that crime could only be prevented if society itself were radically changed. These views became memorialised in President Lyndon Johnson's Commission on Law Enforcement and Administration of Justice and became the virtual dogma of criminal-justice thinking. The problem of asymmetric threats requires specific targeting as the scourge of terrorism is not incident oriented but needs to be taken in as a 'problem' in general and 'the broken windows approach,' entailing the notion of tackling poverty, youth angst-all leading up to general public disorder need to be the primary movers in the direction towards evolving a strategy against the sub-nationalist narrative in the country which raises its ugly head in the form of Naxalism, Terrorism, insurgency, ideological indoctrination of the youth, appearance of gangster sub-cultures in the nation and other related challenges.

The Ideology behind the Movement

The move was an international ramification of the Sino-Soviet split in the 1960s, which divided the Indian Communist scenario. The people who call themselves as Naxalites, derive their fundamental rationale from the Maoism of the Chinese ilk. As reported and commonly comprehended, the significant objectives include the annihilation of the regime which has become disfigured due to the nepotism, and the utter nonchalance of the government of the day leading to an all ground neglect of the poor and the downtrodden citizens of the country.

The time-tested experience of the 'International' communist movement and the left sectarianism and ultra-left adventurism is a by-product, and contains within itself the seeds of rebellion for an enlightened and aware civil society. The origin of the Naxalite movement can be traced to Europe, Asia and America, when new "radical and popular" movements were characterised by the Marxian dogma, and a redefinition of the idea of revolution in order to lay down one's lives for a cause célèbre. These developments were reflected in the National Liberation struggle of the Vietnamese people and concomitantly in the civil rights and anti-war movements in the USA and also in the varsity protests in Western Europe along with the cult of Che Guevara's[7] sacrifice in the Bolivian forests along with China's Cultural movement[8]. This trend was initiated for curbing governmental red tapism and to exonerate the wounded psyche of the exploited class. It was a clean up exercise to terminate state tyranny, in all its sordid forms. The Indian government made preparations to curb the menace which is very much Frankeinstienian[9] in nature. We are facing a blowback effect, similar to the one faced by United States in the realm of counter-terrorism and its Global War on Terror (GWOT).

Naxalite Movement in India: A brief delving inside the tenet of Revolution

The Naxal movement is much more than the theme of thick black spectacles along with a Hare Rama Hare Krishna dress thrown in, very much in line with the tenet of Flower Children of the Timothy Leary variant, thrown in to complement the revolutionary skill set in the Indian context. This might be pictorially very exciting, still the Naxalite movement involves a pantheon of activists and ideologues inherent in its founding myth. The Naxal activist, Charu Mazumdar, was apprehended from Kolkata. As an aftermath of the initial thrust, the 'Naxalite surge' received a setback. In the post- Emergency era, there was a revival of the Naxal trend at the hands of various human rights groups in India and abroad. The current activism in our 'Red Corridor' is a significant threat to our national democratisation process, which has been marred by other attendant ills like nepotism, License Quota Raj and the incorrigible want of a single sinew 'National Character' despite the country having entered into an age of globalization and cosmopolitanism. Here, the infirmities of globalisation have taken their toll on the conjoined rubric of 'Bhartiyata'. There has emerged an unholy nexus between these fissiparous forces and the international terror mongers who exploit the youth in the name of the much tom-toommed rubric of 'Alienation' and in state inflicted by 'Underdevelopment and Corruption'. Quoting Edmund Burke, "A Revolution is very harmful for the Rule of Law in the longer run, whether it is aimed at Public Welfare[10]".

The attendant traumatising tenet of violence in the name of 'Freewill' is a misleading and misplaced concoction which annihilates instead of purging the ills of the polity and the nation at large. The Indian hinterland has created a mammoth and myriad mélange of songs, literature and movies which have had an indelible impact on our national consciousness. The regime's so called incapacity and the inflexibility of the internal security apparatus at tackling this reinvented *razzmattaz* of terror in our rural hinterland has been questioned by the authorities and the hoi polloi alike. In the aftermath of the arrest of Maulana Naseeruddin[11] in Gujarat, Naxalites began supporting the Dasargah-e-Jehad-e-Shahadat's call for the release of the accused. The Naxalites are fast turning into India's 'Fifth Columnists,' more than willing to join hands with external forces that have been trying to undermine India's territorial integrity. The intellectual class of the nation tends to support some of the strains of Naxal movement and if the government of the day honestly partakes of the instrumentality of the developmental paradigm in its truest form and shape, then, it will go a long way in stymieing the current of disillusionment and disgruntlement with the governance and ruling mechanism of a state stoutly painted in the colour of black. Laxity and nepotism are the twin bottlenecks in the body rubric of the realisation of good governance in the nation. The media and the intelligentsia ought to lament the absence of all goodies of governance, which are being rendered at the people's doorstep but the outright rejection of the state apparatus need not be the bone of contention and the commonly bandied out refrain of their jottings, perceptions and outpourings as the nation is still a democratic entity and much good has accrued the way of its plethora of polices and schemes for public welfare and the running sours ought not to become the primal barometer of judging the nation as 'a failed democratic experiment' as yet. That would be a very pessimistic reading of the whole rebellion oriented narrative in the Indian nation state.

Also, if India stands as 'failed,' then what kind of consideration will earmark the distressed nationalities of entities of the order of Pakistan and Afghanistan. Doesn't the 'drive-out-all-annihilation-line' of the Naxal ideology bespeaks a great deal of the days of the 70s emergency heaped upon the country where trains used to run on time and the *babus* used to reach the offices at nine in the morning, but all at a cost of a threatened reprisal by the state. A *Juntaisation* of democracy is not what the political doctor has ordered for and an attendant justification for the realisation of political correctives need not occur with the individual liberty and the freewheeling nature of individuals being clobbered at the altar of a monotonous uniformity and 'stately subscription' to a specific ideology as the grand Indian political prescription.

The Curious and Strange Case of Kobad Gandhi: Part Deux of Naxalism

One needs to apprehend that one stand out example happens to be that of Kobad Gandhi, who was never disenfranchised akin to his impoverished Indian masses but still he took up cudgels against the brasstacks of the establishment and the statal apparatus. The elites only are known to talk and firm up their intellectual fiefs if an incident of injustice is heard of or witnessed in the near vicinity, but the people need to realise that there are some public school alumni who think beyond their regular Pindari Glacier school trips and the Vivekananda rock visits during the summer holidays and do not merely cock a bear can to the teachers. Thus, this can be a light hearted account of the elite sympathy with the cause of the Naxalites. They also wish to change the way the things run in the surroundings. One such personage happened to be Kobad Gandhi. Though the damage that ensues to the national security apparatus is also a factor which deserves a great deal of genuine concern. The Indian Express reported that, "The Delhi Police arrested Gandhi based on an intelligence tip-off. The People's Union for Democratic Rights has asked the Union Home Ministry to come clean on Gandhi's arrest[12]". They have also revealed that Mr. Kobad Gandhi headed the publication division of the CPI (Maoist) and also its sub-committee on mass organisations. The civil rights groups and organisations defended Mr. Kobad Gandhi against the threat to his life, contends the general public opinion of the alternate media.[13]

A known journalist, Suvojit Bagchi of BBC Bengal met him once. The following are excerpts from his interview:

"Has the Maoists' emphasis on educating the poor contributed to their rise in Chhattisgarh?

"Why do you think so? We have a clear-cut definition of development. We think the society is in a semi-feudal, semi-colonial state and there is a need to democratise it. There is a need to distribute the land to the poor in the villages.[14]

The Salwa Judum Movement: Is it a Panacea for the masses in Chhattisgarh?

The Salwa Judum is one such movement which was initiated by the state Government of Chhattisgarh in order to ameliorate the state of general law and order Salwa Judum was established and conceptualised by the government which festooned itself soon upon the political landscape and the firmament in the tribal state of Chhattisgarh. Salwa Judum was also helped by politicians such as Mahendra Karma, which also served as 'a return modicum,' for the government of the day, who had become insignificant later on in the state of Chhattisgarh. The Ministry of Home Affairs in its annual report in the year, 2005-2006, delineated three categorisations, wherein the anti-insurgency maneuvers will be activated. These three regions of operability happen to be:

1. The local capacity building of the affected states in terms of intelligence gathering and training police forces for effective military action;

2. Making the administrative machinery more responsive, transparent and sensitive for effective dealing with public grievances; and

3. Encouraging peace dialogues between the affected states and the Naxal groups.[15]

A report of the National Commission for Women reported that as part of the Salwa Judam happenings, one member had to be sent to each person residing there. This points towards a spontaneous people's movement with a modicum of state enforcement. The tribals were completely living a parasite existence being dependent upon the supplies by the Chhattisgarh government. The report further reported that most of the special police officers were of a junior age, who could not take up any occupation and only followed the 'counter-annihilation line[16]". These developments have been opposed by various civil society groups in the hope that the occupation of being counter killers at a nascent and an immature age of life is a gross violation of the fundamental tenet of human rights and natural justice in the country. This is one perception and a figment of analysis doing the rounds in the general narrative of the nation. It's a tricky terrain to take sides.

Tanto Paggio, Tanto Megilo, are the twin tenets of the revolutionary mind which sustain their diatribes against the state and anything which faintly resembles the status quo, has to be eliminated. According to one observation, "Telengana too suffers in the sphere of developmental parameters,"[17] thus, establishing another rationale for the Naxal movement in the scarred region.The subjects face a strange but severely felt security dilemma. People are left with two alternatives. Either they have to fight along with the state police forces and become martyrs or they have the ubiquitous choice of joining the ranks of the rebels and continue to be in the good books of the local warlords who provide aid and succor to the Naxal elements operating from clandestine locations.

In a rather incisive and engaging rendition of the *'Other India,'* Sudeep Chakravarti combines political history, extensive interviews and individual case histories as he travels to the heart of Maoist zones in the country: Chhattisgarh, Jharkhand, West Bengal, Karnataka and Andhra Pradesh. His enunciation includes rendezouses with Maoist leaders and sympathisers, policemen, bureaucrats, politicians, security analysts, development workers, farmers and tribals and all the other gentiles and ruffians, who constitute the actors and the audience in this war being fought in the developmentally challenged 'Village Republics' all across India.[18] What emerges is a sobering picture of a deeply divided society, and the dangers that lie ahead for India.[19] The same theme has been elucidated in another work by him titled as, 'Red Sun: Travels in the Naxal Country' which has been published by Penguin India. Professors in JNU, Kamal Mitra Chenoy and Anuradha Chenoy also have penned down a work on the theme of Maoism and other armed conflicts in India, which is an eminent read, sheds light on the culture of this rampant strife in India and imparts an empirical study of the phenomenon of Naxalism and other armed conflicts in the nation[20].

Gone are the ideal references to the Jawaharlal Nehru University's Chandrasekhar of the days of yore. The present day Naxals are trainees from the middling dusty terrain of India with a bit of technical wizardry being made part and parcel of their seemingly pliant paraphernalia of debilitation and destruction for the annihilation of the civil government. Now, with fresh recruitment coming in, one cannot safely conclude that the sacrifices of Hemant Mandavi (a police official who laid down his life in Orrissa),[21] have limited the menace to the states of West Bengal, Andhra Pradesh, Bihar, Karnataka, Maharashtra and parts of Tamil Nadu. The advent of the Maoists in the Hilly Billy Kingdom of Nepal, too, leaves the Indian government stranded on its feet, as the Prachanda led outfit formally eschewed violence only in the recent past and leaves behind a legacy of bloodcurdling violence and maiming since the year of 1996 when the Maoists initiated their campaign against the Nepalese Royalty.

The constitution of the country needs to be amended, and a separate section on 'National Security[22]' and internal security appended in the text to spawn a national establishment to deal with internal security threats above the partisan palaver of the politicos in the country. Otherwise, the nation state will lurch on a wretched and shaken state from one failed '*Salwa Judam*'[23] to another in the places which bear the heart of our motherland. They intend to wound the heart and soul of civility and the nation.

The Supreme Court, too, asked the NHRC to look into the human rights strictures of Salwa Judum in the state of Chattisgarh. The '*bleeding-white stratagem*', being a tertiary stratagem, unleashed by them to uproot the Naxal movement all from the civil steeds. The Supreme Court in a March 31st, 2008, statement contended that the state ought not to provide arms to fight insurgency. Chief Justice, *K G Balakrishnan* and Justice Aftab Alam opined that there could be no objection to an independent enquiry into Salwa Judum as demanded by subaltern scholars of the order of Ramchandra Guha and Nandini Sunder.[24] The civil society activist group, People's Union of Civil Liberties, refers to Salwa Judum, as "a state when state makes war against its citizens[25]".

A report of the Human Rights Watch released in the year 2008, has reported that, "In the Salwa Judum run 'relief camps', only a few villagers reside in the camps. Those, that refused to leave their villages have apparently been forced by Special Police Officers (SPO), militias from the Salwa Judum campaign that did not hesitate to use coercion and threats."[26]

"... Life conditions in the 'relief camps' are close to inhuman..."[27] Such internal refugees do not have a certitude about their ration cards and they do not know whether they will be able to return to their homes[28]".

These seem to be some excerpts which make us take notice of the plight of the people in these tarred regions. Taking sides might not be the core concern for the civil society and the academia, as far as Naxalism is concerned, but it is the amelioration of the impoverished masses which ought to be the professed mandate of the national establishment. Voice of America, the American News Agency reported that, in April, 2006, an Indian News Agency reported that India cannot negotiate with the Naxals until they surrender.

Thus, the rationale and the functioning of the Salwa Judum camps have been questioned in the above exchange which necessitates the need for a genre of transparency and consistency in the functioning of the state government, as per one stipulation ensconced in a view.

The Naxal spread and the grand overarch in India has been referred to the want of the land reforms in the country. In the presence of land egalitarianism, Naxalism will face a challenge in the nation state. Land needs to be distributed for the poor hoi polloi and there has to be a spawning of a physical infrastructure in the form of communication, power networks, motoarable roads and a proper framework and a timetable of the implementation of the governmental schemes.[29] Another aspect which needs to be delved inside, happens to be that the multinational organisations do not have a valid rehabilitation policy. The Central Regime has around 300,000 crore investments from the SEZs and it intends to spawn around 3-4 million new works. In the contemporary context, more than 48,000 hectares of land has been acquired for the SEZs.[30]

Some observers contend that the theme of India being besmirched by a lot of peddlers from the Naxal wing has been beaten for too long a time and there might not be all truisms in the state allegations in the context of the case of Dr. Binayak. BBC has reported that, Dr. Binayak Sen, was arrested for helping the Naxals in the State of Chhattisgarh and he was raising the issue of human rights violation of tribal who were victims of police atrocities.[31]A BBC report informed that Dr. Sen was garlanded with the Jonathan Mann Award, for serving the tribal communities in the nation.[32]Does support to the Maoists warrant a life time imprisonment? This has turned out to be a rankling question in the context of the arrest of Dr. Binayak Sen. One Times of India report contends that, "The bulk of the judgment by the Raipur sessions court that sentenced doctor-activist Binayak Sen to life imprisonment, labours over Sen's links with Maoists, that legal experts say, even if proved, attract a lesser punishment[33]". Thus, a hornet's nest has been seemingly opened with the kind of judgment which been rendered for Binayak Sen. Is it time to take sides and earmark our fences?

As measures to tackle the surge of Naxalism, the Central Government has partaken of financial assistance of the order of Rs. 2, 475 crores for 55 affected districts in the nine states of Andhra Pradesh, Bihar, Chhattisgarh, Orissa, Jharkhand, West Bengal etc. under the rubric of the Backward Districts initiative (BDI).[34] The scheme includes a quantum of Rs.15 crore, which has been distributed to each district to help improve social infrastructure. The Scheduled Tribes (Recognition of Forest's Rights) Bill, 2005, was introduced in the ambit of the national legislations.[35]

Current Naxal Attacks: A Cause For Concern

Commentators can be prominent translators of developments and socio-political events which happen around us. It happened in the month of April 2010, wherein personnel of the Central Reserve Police Force in Chhatisgarh have witnessed a watershed and has been nomenclatured by Shekhar Gupta as a kind of insurgency in India which is very much similar to a 'Bell Curve'. Shekhar Gupta further contends that, "We are accosted by a Leviathan[36]". He further cited the instance of Mrs. Indira Gandhi that in the year 1975, the Mizo rebels infiltrated the police headquarters when the entire top brass, namely Inspector General of Police, Arya, his DGP Sewa and his special branch official, Panchpakesan were holding a meeting.

Around 72 CRPF personnel were annihilated by around 1,000 odd insurgents and later on in the tenor of Periclean patriotism, the insurgent group claimed through a release that around 300 odd revolutionaries were involved in the incident and it was a release by a Naxal cadre, Rammana, which contended that the Dantewada reprisal was aimed at rousing the commoners against the regime of the day.[37] P. Chidambaram, too, confessed in the same vein.[38] In another news snippet in the same national daily, the West Bengal Chief Minister referred that, "This is not the time to blame anyone or blame each other but is the time to work together collectively"[39].

The notion of the security dilemma rules the roost in the firmament of international politics. There is a rational choice before the citizens of our nation. Either, amalgamate yourself with the rubric of the security forces and end up as a martyr, or end up on the other side of the fence along with the terrorist and the insurgent outfits, wherein the personage is likely to and up a casualty with his family, kith and kin being uncared for in the event of any casualty. Thus, the rational choice lies in the hands of the citizens as was very well postulated in a point and a matter-of-fact manner by the ex-Police Chief of Punjab, K.P.S. Gill in the tumultuous days and the ferment of the Khalistani insurgency in the hey days of the Punjab state's terror spectacle.

Cyber/ Technological Training of Insurgent and Anti-National Outfits in India

Apart from the scourge of Naxalism in the Indian hinterland, it is pertinent to delve inside the technological usages by the Naxalites which enables them to carry on elaborate and well planned attacks on the institutional establishments in Chhattisgarh, Andhra Pradesh and West Bengal. Though Andhra Pradesh is a success story, with the Naxal rehabilitation being a significant achievement of the establishment. The current Maoists attacks pinpoint and strongly posit the factoid that the Maoists are a well oiled outfit with their international *connexions* which make them successfully circumvent the governmental machinery and the state and central security forces.

Linkages have been deciphered and unearthed by the security agencies in India. Naxal outfits in Chhattisgarh move around in small groups and they sleep and survive in tents made of Blue Plastic. They have one person specially deputed to operate a laptop which is normally a dilapidated piece of machinery but it is fully operational. Also, the Maoists have a printer and they download loads of literature from anti-governmental and anti-regime websites which are even contraband in some nations. Thus, along with the moving and roving Naxal parties in the state of Chhattisgarh, they are reasonably provided with computer technology which is further enabled by access to Internet. The activists have to inculcate a regular reading habit which is further augmented by regular lecture visits by ideologues from the regional and zonal committees.

The Chinese connection in the light of the whole of developments cannot be sighted out, totally. The Chinese ring is present in the region of Sichuan and it might be probable that, "the Chinese government approved of the spying," one New York Times report informed. The same news piece contends that, "Intruders pilfered classified and restricted documents from the highest levels of the Indian defense ministry." The literature titled as, 'Shadows in The Cloud: Investigating Cyber Espionage 2.0', was written in the University of Toronto.[40]

The newspaper DNA Daily reported in a piece that, "The profile of documents recovered suggests that the attackers targeted 'specific systems and profiles of users'. Some papers 'constitute of clandestinely kept knowledge in the national security council secretariat relating to the scenario in the states[41]". The China Post reported that, "The Chinese hackers attempted to break into Indian government computers and the computers of Ministry of External Affairs personnel worldwide. The U.S. web sites were attacked by the Chinese computer nerds, and the size of the Chinese government too harbours more non-establishment computer hackers[42]". The Indian officials contend that the Chinese carry on asymmetrical warfare, through their cyber brigade. The same Chinese newspaper reports that, "The Taiwanese are very advanced technologically and anybody sitting anywhere in the globe can truncate anybody's cyber operations, especially the Taiwanese[43]". The Chinese have also singled out the western organisations like NATO. In a report which appeared in Rediff news, it was stated that, "NATO reports that the Chinese are cyber-wise aggressive and the propensity of attacks has been augmented over the past few months[44]". As mentioned earlier, the Naxal surge has been accompanied by a terrorist like reliance to both crude and advanced technology which poses newer challenges for the internal security mandarins of the country.

As a solution, good governance can be a novae approach to the crisis of Naxalism in the country. The failed administration and the attendant administrative apathy can be cause of popular unrest and youthful angst as a large plethora of unemployed rural and tribal youth feel suffocated within some sections of a system which amounts to a non-rewarding and corrupt political and administrative systems. The *Annas* of the commoners have to rise to the occasion and the institutional fiasco which India has witnessed within its rural confines despite the grand quadrilateral highways, and the themes of mainstreaming the North-East has left the hoi polloi with a bitter taste in their mouth, thus emphasising the Developmental aspect of the rising tide, if Naxalsim in India and the state of Andhra's success at the rehabilitation policy of the Naxalites, can serve as a pointer in the direction of the much needed administrative reforms. Also, the 11th Five Year Plan categorically pinpoints the threat of Naxalism as a significant national worry and stipulates the governmental strategy to tide over the ruckus.

Along with the theme of the *Force Majore* nature of the debate on Naxalism, the failure of governmental schemes in the rural hinterland of the country in the form of the clouds cast on the Mahatma Gandhi National Rural Employment Guarantee Scheme (MGNREGA) seem to be the opportune movements to render apart the nature of state dysfunction in some regions of the nation. It has become a primary concern of the rural development apparatus to delve inside the rubric of the MGNREGA implantation in the naxal affected states and regions of the country.[45] The delay in wage payments along with the corruption in the local banks and post offices has led to the negatives of MGNREGA, which is primarily a demand for work driven scheme.[46] Some of the probable workers in the states of Orissa and Chhattisgarh do not opt for MGNREGA and prefer to work for the privately owned bigger farms as at least timely daily wage is assured to them in order to make their two ends meet.

Still, the argument for political violence against the state need not be a solution for the poor and impoverished in the nation as the nation happens to be of a democratic denomination and constitutionally inviolable tenets have to be respected by all and sundry in the country, whatever might be the corpus of rebellious distrust and apathy. Violence in the land of Gandhi is simply inadmissible and in any phoenix form is acceptable for the general up-keep of internal security in the nation.

In one of the recent security successes in the month of November in the year, 2011, ambit of countering naxalism and LWE (Left Wing Extremism) in the nation, Kishenji has been annihilated in a CRPF operation. The Lal Mati, it might seem, has had enough of him as he was killed in a fierce gunfight in West Bengal, his area of operation in the current context. The state's notion has been construed by some of the observers as the notion of letting open the door of development through the intruding feet of security, as according to some observers, the route to development can only be prepared and adequately trajectoried when and if the common denizens of the hinterland of the Indian nation can be allowed and permitted an air and more than an aura of security. It is possible only in a secure environment that the conditionalities and the instrumentalities of development can be assured to the people at large, which happens to be the official refrain.

In a recent narrative, it has been deciphered out that the practice and the exercise of fighting a rebellion in the nation can be equated with the notion and praxis of cutting a soup fluid with a knife. Also, in a recent interview with a national daily, Vijay Kumar, the Director General of Central Reserve Police Force (CRPF), contended that the contexts of theories of Ink Blot and the Triangular approach[47] of the forces are tantamount to the notions of security, development and the political narrative needs to be a three pronged approach in order to combat the menace of naxalism in India and he also added that CRPF happens to be the biggest force in the nation fighting insurgency in its territory.[48] Thus, even the security forces and the grand Indian establishment agree that the heady mix of rooting out distrust from amongst the people in the affected regions and getting along the local youth can lead to the bringing of the Veerapan brigands to the book. Attendant to these concerns, an observer might be drawn to harbour the notion that the iron hand approach of a Vietnam, Malaya or a Philippines like fix might be a tall order for the establishment in the country, but a steady soft power approach could change the tide in the favour of the country.

Also, the argument that all security forces are the bad guys and the idea of a nation is inherently and fundamentally flawed needs to be given a re-look by the people adhering to the notion of the grand alternative narrative as life and socio-political systems have always been functioning and existing in the myriad shades of 'greys'. Vijay Kumar commented in an interview that the security forces cannot throw away their guns in the bushes like the Naxals and thus cannot mingle with the tribal hoi polloi, so the security forces cannot camouflage themselves like the rebels and thus the visible strength of the 'state' becomes an inevitable weakness which runs open for violent attacks on their lives and selves. Thus, the *Vietcong advantage* is there to be strategically enjoyed by the Maoists, which renders the turf a far more difficult one for the security forces in the affected regions. Also, the domestic and the chameleon like quality of the Naxal attacks leaves the scenario far more difficult to be negotiated by the security personnel and the primal planners in the security outfits.

Also, the tinkering that too a forceful one, with the symmetry of the nation's political system can go a long way in undoing the national and the collective fabric of the nation which was much wishfully undertaken and sewn together in the days of the independence struggle. Also, as an attendant approach to soft and human security in the Naxal affected regions, the local collector of Dantewada has taken promising initiatives in the direction of the education of the people in the region which can be replicated in the larger context of the affected regions, and apart from that, the communitarian model as perfected by likes of Wajahat Habibullah can be made the core operative concern of the Naxal affected region, so that a people centered approach can be driven home and attempted to be implemented in the context of State of chhattisgarh.

Outtorching the light of rebellion can be an inconvenient task when the defense forces and the Maoists eat from the same *Chai* shop in the vicinity of a Dandakaranaya, then how can the people differentiate as to who owes them what. In a recent incident in February, 2012, Gadchiroli can serve as a reminder of the notion that if policy implementation can take place in a more human and public spirited manner, the hoi polloi and the effected masses can summon courage to lead a normal life. The local elections in regions of Wardha and Gadchiroli have been appreciated by the domestic media in the nation and people have turned out in numbers in order to cast their valuable and decisive votes in a terrain marred and charred by the waste of a system which is facing a question mark in some parts of the nation.[49] The scenario appears glum but is not irretrievable, keeping in view the responses of the electorate in the regions of Gadchiroli, Wardha and the surrounding regions. The recent electoral successes of the Maoists in the elections in Orissa are being perceived both as a cooption of the insurgents inside the political system and also akin to the ingress being made by the Maoists in the political culture, so that the final putsch can be visualised and further prcaticalised against the Indian state. Still, the notion of mainstreaming of the Maoists also needs to be given a chance as the success of grey hounds in the State of Andhra Pradesh along with the notion of the surrender and rehabilitation policy, draws essential attention away from the dry, sundry and direct law and order solutions to the Naxalite problem. It is only a humane institutional approach which can be best surmised with a carrot and stick policy, which can serve as afirmed foundation of an approach to a solution to the Naxal quagmire in the country. The securitisation approach too cannot be ruled out as part of the 'stick' but the dangling carrot of 'development" with the practicalisation of an 'appropriate appropriation' of the natural resources of the hinterland with an emphasis upon the indigenous management of nature and its coveted gifts, can too serve as 'an ideal mismatch' of a policy framework to render to the nation what belongs to it. There are no easy solutions, but the difficult road has to be traversed instead of following and trudging along the much beaten tracks.

References

1. The term "Red Corridorr" refers to a swathe of Indian territory across the States of Bihar, Jharkhand, Orissa, Chhattisgarh, and finally the mother state of the movement in West Bengal, where it has lost much of its relevance in the contemporary world. The terrain of the Red Corridor runs through from the Hindu Emprer's auspices of Kathmandu all the way down to the hardlands and badlands of Kanniyakumari.
2. The People's War Group was formed in southern Indian State of Andhra Pradesh on April 22, 1980 by Kondapalli Seetharamaiah, one of the most influential Naxalite leaders in the state and a member of the erstwhile Central Organising Committee of the Communist Party of India—Marxist-Leninist, (CPI-ML). Seetharamaiah was later expelled from the group.

He died unsung on April 12, 2002. The PWG's operations commenced in Karimnagar district, in the North Telengana region of Andhra Pradesh, and subsequently spread to other parts of the state as well as in other states.

3. Government of India, Ministry of Home Affairs, *Annual Report*, 2006-2007, Departments of Internal Security, States, Homes, Jammu and Kashmir affairs and Border management.
4. *Ibid.*
5. *Ibid.*
6. *Ibid.*
7. Jon Lee Anderson (1997), "Che Guevara: A Revolutionary Life," (New York: Grove Press, 1997).
8. Michael Schoenals (1996), "Cultural Revolution, 1966-1969: Not a Dinner Party," (New York: M.E. Sharpe, 1996).
9. Frankenstein is a European legendary monster who was created by a doctor who wanted to have supreme control over human life by stiching together various parts of human remains. But, he intended the new artificial human construct to follow his orders but the monster turned out to be a docile human being, fell in love with another human being and went on to prevent the physical transgression of his lady love who had become the centre of attraction for his creator.
10. Edmund Burke (Online: Web), url: http://plato.stanford.edu/entries/burke/, Accessed on 1 November, 2011.
11. After spending five years in Ahmedabad, Sabarmati Jail and facing trial for his alleged involvement in former state home minister Haren Pandya's murder, Hyderabad cleric Moulana Mohammed Naseeruddin has been granted bail by the Supreme Court. A division bench comprising Justice M Katju and Justice Ashok Kumar Ganguli granted bail to the Moulana after a seven month long proceeding in the apex court.
12. "Naxal With a Rich Past Arrested in Delhi" (Online: Web), Accessed on March 28th, 2010, URL: ttp://www.expressbuzz.com/edition/story.
13. "The Press Statement To Release Kobad Gandhi" (Online: Web), Accessed on March 28th, 2010, URL: http://ajadhind.wordpress.com/2009/09/27/produce-mr-kobad-gandhi-senior-maoist-leader.
14. *Ibid.*

15. Medha Bisht (2007), "Securitising Development and Naxal Threat," (Online: Web), Accessed on May 10th, 2008,URL: http://www.idsa.in/publications/stratcomments/MedhaBisht120207.htm
16. "Naxalism in Chhattisgarh" (Chennai: *Frontline,* September-October, 2007).
17. Ashok Das (2000), "An Eye for an Eye" (New Delhi: *Hindustan Times*, March 12, 2000).
18. From the Newspaper Desk,"Gandhi and Education" (Bangalore: *Deccan Herald*, September 27, 2007).
19. Sudeep Chakravarti (2007), "Red Sun: Travels in Naxalite Country," (New Delhi: Penguin Books, 2007).
20. See, " Maoism and Other Armed Conflicts in India".
21. Editorial (*Indian Express,* 27th February, 2008).
22. National security refers to the requirement to maintain the survival of the nation state through the use of economic, military and political power and the exercise of diplomacy and tact. The concept according to an American definition entails the territorial integrity, sovereignty, and international freedom of action of the United States. Intelligence activities relating to national security encompass all the military, economic, political, scientific, technological, and other aspects of foreign developments that pose actual or futuristic threats.
23. *Business Standard Reporter* (2008), "Supreme Court Asks National Human Rights Commission on Salwa Judum" (Delhi: *Business Standard*, 15th April, 2008).
24. "Campaign For Peace and Justice in Chattisgarh" (Online : Web), Accessed on June 15th, 2008, URL: http://cpjc.wordpress.com/2008/03/31/government%E2%80%99s-support-to-salwa-judum-amounts-to-endorsing-vigilantism-says-supreme-court.
25. 'When State Makes War on Its own People" (Online : Web), Accessed on April 4th, 2010, URL: http://www.pucl.org/Topics/Human-rights/2006.
26. "Facts Finding Reports on Salwa Judum" (Online: Web), Accessed on April 4th, 2010, URL: http://cpjc.wordpress.com/reports-by-fact-finding-teams-on-salwa-judum.
27. *Ibid.*
28. *Ibid.*
29. *Ibid.*

30. S.M. Bhatnagar (2007), "Special Economic Zones: Law and Procedure" (New Delhi: Centax Publications Limited, 2007).
31. "Dr. Binayak Sen: The Tribal Doctor" (Online: Web), Accessed on June 10th, 2008, URL: http://news.bbc.co.uk/2/hi/south_asia/7397734.stm.
32. *Ibid.*
33. Binayak Sen Case, "Support to Maoists Doesn't Warrant a Life Term" (Online: Web) URL: http://articles.timesofindia. india times.com/2010-12-28/india/28223321_1_sessions-court-b-p-varma-piyush-guha, Accessed in October, 2011.
34. "Backward Districts Initiative: Rashtriya Sam Vikas Yojana, The Scheme and Guidelines For Preparations of District Plans," (Online: Web), Accessed on June 15th, 2008, URL: http://www.planningcommission.nic.in/plans/stateplan/guid_rsvy.pdf. The excerpt of the scheme: *The Backward Districts Initiative under the Rashtriya Sam Vikas Yojana has been initiated with the main objective of putting in place programmes and policies with the joint efforts of the Centre and the States which would remove barriers to growth, accelerate the development process and improve the quality of life of the people. The scheme aims at focused development programmes for backward areas which would help reduce imbalances and speed up development.*
35. *Ibid.*
36. Shekhar Gupta (2010), "The Buck Starts Here" (New Delhi: *Indian Express,* 10th April, 2010).
37. *Express News Service* (2010), "P M Rejected PC Offer to Quit", (New Delhi: *Indian Express*, 10th April, 2010, Page No. 1).
38. *Ibid.*
39. *Express News Service*, (2010), "It's Time to Work Together not Blame Each Other says Buddha" (New Delhi: *Indian Express*, 10th April, 2010, Page no. 7).
40. "Shadows in the Cloud: Investigating Cyber Espionage 2.0" URL: http://www.nartv.org/mirror/shadows-in-the-cloud.pdf (Accessed on October, 2011).
41. *DNA* Correspondent, "Did China Govt. Okay Cyber Attacks on India" (New Delhi: DNA, 7th April, 2010).
42. "India Suspects China Behind Cyber Attacks" (Beijing: *The China Post*, 21st January, 2010).
43. *Ibid.*

44. "Chinese Cyber Attacks Give NATO Sleepless Nights," (Online: Web), Accessed on 21st July, 2010, URL: http://news.rediff.com/report/2010/mar/08/china-has-declared-cyber-war.htm
45. Proceedings of a "National Workshop on Empowering people through MGNREGA: The Reform Agenda" held by the conjoined Ministry of Rural Development and United Nations Development Programme on 14th November, 2011 in the India International Center, New Delhi.
46. *Ibid.*
47. See *Indian Express*, 29th January, 2012.
48. *Ibid.*
49. See *Indian Express*, February, 2012.

6

The Volatile Vortex of Extremism and Inundation in Pakistan

The notion of Pakistan is co-terminus with India and the nation state of Pakistan is a strategic neighbour but it strangely dabbles in sub-national threats to the entire South Asian region as a whole as part of an internal systemic socio-political and ethnic collapse. This negativistic visage of Pakistan does not necessitate a pessimistic approach towards the nation in the context of the relationship with India and such an assertion does not necessitate war mongering or lay a conflictual foundation for the twin neighbours of India and Pakistan. This is no cheap rhetoric but any empirical study of the defense casualties, the collateral damage as part of the terror running modules in India and the three wars fought between the twin nations has repeated with noxious profundity. But, this does not paint the neighbour in a debilitating light but definitively places the nation in the wide eyed distrust of India. Since the British Policy of divide and rule was initiated in the colonised sub-continent, since then the promulgation of the Indian Independence Act along with the division of the Indian sub-continent between India and Pakistan, the twin nation theory came into being as propounded by Mohhamed Ali Jinnah, the first governing head of Pakistan. Pakistan since then has been foisted upon the South Asian region as an American sponsored 'Frontline State' which has made a part and parcel in the central pillar of its foreign policy to counter India now and then by raising the bogey of self determination and the secessionist theme of the State of Jammu and Kashmir. Still, all is not about external security in the South Asian region, the factors impinging upon the notion of internal turmoil and security in Pakistan too have taken a toll of the civic life of the Islamic Republic of Pakistan. It would be no understatement to make that in the name of an anti-India foreign policy along with the notion of extremism and fragments of fundamentalism in Pakistan, the internal stability and the general well being of the commoners has been sacrifised in the larger run which too reflects in the U-turns it makes in the realm of foreign relations with India and in the larger South Asian context. Thus, the internal security of the Islamic Republic of Pakistan is challenged by a benumbing talibanisation of the North West Frontier Province (NWFP) and the SWAT territory in Pakistan which have a bitter future for the State of Jammu and Kashmir once the Americans retreat from the badlands of Afghanistan and the unemployed talibanists might be diverted inside the Indian North to scalp a few and maybe more innocent lives. Conflict is discernible but Pakistan's inside tale is rife with similar strife and obfuscation in the name of identity and the race question in South Asia.

Religious extremism and fundamentalism in the nation state of Pakistan was bound to occur due to the all pervading and the timeless nexus between the Military Junta and the Democrats there, who have been puppets in the hands of the Military Junta in Pakistan. Then, when the Military rule predominated in the country in the form of Ayub Khan, Zia-Ul-Haq and General Pervez Musharraf then too, the religious seminaries and the Deobandi school of education and civic life in Pakistan predominated[1]. This nexus has led to an obfuscation of civil society in general in Pakistan and it no more thrives as a vibrant democracy but more as a 'Failed Nation State,'[22] much due to the internal failings of its domestic polity and the segmentations in a volatile society.

It was during General Zias' regime that the religious right in the Islamic Republic of Pakistan received an impetus in the political firmament in Pakistan's internal security dynamics. Also, the PPP in the aftermath era of Zulfikar Ali Bhutto received downsizing of its political agenda and its political influence in the light of the radicalisation and Islamisation of the Pakistan polity. It has contended that, "Once the social character of Islamisation is placed in its proper historical and contemporary perspective it becomes a reality to pin down the origins and the fountainhead of the idiom of Islam in the Pakistan Polity[3]". The author further contends that, "Hence Zia's efficient use of state repression, despite its monstrous proportions must be seen together with its concerted policy of building bridges in civil society, as part and parcel of the process of ideological repression and reproduction."[4] It is these fangs of insidious institutionalisation which led to the sponsoring of terrorism and insidious strategic designs against a neighbour with which the Pakistani nation state had fought three wars and the history of bilateral volatility was further exacerbated by the internal instability and the institutionalisation of a specific variety of state procedure and way of life which translated into the idiom of state sponsored terrorism. This is not an allegation but an empirically evidenced fact of life for South Asia which mars the internal security of many a nations in the volatile vortex of the region.

In the current context, Imran Khan, the cricketer turned political leader has contended that the days of the Army are numbered in Pakistan notwithstanding the ravenous royal candor of the Army in the nation state of Pakistan.[5] The Army thus holds a more than a significant steed in the political firmament and the comprehensive pantheon of the internal security scenario in the country. In the context of current history of Pakistan if it is being written, then, the people in Pakistan have been witnesses to the theme of the Prime Minster in December, January, 2012 reaching out to the hoi polloi and staking the claim that democracy is once again being threatened by the Army and the Rawalpindi establishment. It was thus reported in the Reuters that, "Prime Minister Yusuf Raza Gilani went hammer and tongs after Army Chief General Ashfaq Kayani and the director general of the Inter-Services Intelligence agency Lieutenant-General Ahmed Shuja Pasha for filing court papers in a case involving a mysterious memo that has pitted the military against the civilian government."[6] Thus, the internal strife and political equations have fuelled the general situation of instability in this prominent South Asian nation which lives a challenged and vitiated existence in the light of the Western disturbances and the over-weaning presence of the US forces in the neighbourhood.

The report further added that, "In an interview with Chinese media, Gilani said the filings were 'unconstitutional,' infuriating the military's high command, who issued a stern press release."[7] It is this facet of radicalisation of the Pakistani polity which pervades throughout the nook and cranny of the receptacle nation state. Thus, the nation state of Pakistan unwittingly finds itself within the engulfment of an aggressive and self suicidal bilateral policy which adduces to itself a great iota of ill luck and strategic dangers of the highest order in a rather peacefully inclined South Asia. The radicalisation of the Pakistani nation state began in right earnest in the form of the statement of Pakistan's first foreign minister, Zaffaraullah Khan who deciphered the first instances of the radicalisation of the Pakistani polity. Text books were also rewritten and history reinvented to suit the interest of the Regime. For instance, the University Grants Commission of Pakistan made Islamic study and Pakistan study compulsory subjects for all students at all levels.[8] Thus, akin to the so called saffronisation of the Indian education-debate, the parallel sub-set of greening the landscape of the Pakistani polity remains a core and primal reality of life and politics in the nation state of Pakistan.

Arun Shourie too in his work, "A Tree Mildewed by Rust" has too referred to very many of the same instances, wherein, a hob goblin status of a marauding and a hegemonic and a demonic state is attributed to the Indian state right from the lessons which are imparted to the primary school children in the Pakistan's educational system which marauds and militates against the notion and the regional picture perfect world of a South Asian Enclave to meet up to the rising tide and wave of globalisation and convergence. Still the internal destabilisers in the form of terrorism, insurgency and the Gobbelesian propaganda heaped against each other denudes the white cloth of peace off the South Asian camaraderie and the notion of a conjoined ethnic and social entity which the sub-continent is definitively is but is lost amidst the smokescreen and strategic debris of political one-upamnship in the telling bilateral betwixt the twin nation states of India and Pakistan.

Also, the twin nation states of the order of India and Pakistan, have been blood brothers in the truest sense of the term but the internal political polarisation betwixt the telling political foes in the internal dynamics of political stalemates in both the nations leads to a subversion of a conjoined ethos despite what has been recalled in the first paragraph by the author. The Pakistani Army has a great role to play in this debacle of internal mutations which manifest themselves in the tarred diplomatic terrain betwixt the twin nation states.

The foreign Policy intertwined with the rubric of the Pakistan's intelligence policy and the policy of aiding abetting and supporting the scourge of terrorism in the Indian Union leads up to an amounting of an anti-national threat to its besieged neighbour and the attendant South Asian region which has a telling impact on the internal security situation in the Indian nation state which is also bedeviled with the sobriquet of being a Benign Hegemon by some of the South Asian observers. The Pakistani nation state aided and ably supported the scourge of insurgency and terrorism by its intelligence agencies serves to act as an "asymmetric internal security threat" to the nation state of India. The internal turmoil and the political and the civil decadence in the nation state of Pakistan can serve as a genre of sympathising factor for an internally disturbed and 'failed' nation state of Pakistan, but the infectious impact which the Pakistani translucence has on the Indian security and national ethos are themes to be sincerely and seriously pondered over without actually fracturing the theme of an envisioned and imagined, South Asian unison and camaraderie.

The question that arises is that if a militant theology is more often a consequence than a cause for militant orientation, then what leads religious groups towards militancy in the first place? Why did religious groups choose violence to improve the lot of their institutions and constituents, resisting repression and gaining political power? One scholar contends that one reason could be that religious societies follow the policy of competitive fanatical violence, clearing their path of any detractors by furious vengeance. Deobandi patronage by Zia for instance, led to the rift with the Bralvis[9]. The Crisis States Research Centre defines a 'failed state' as a condition of 'state collapse'.

Failed States: Is There Any Barometer?

Since the year, 2005, the United States think-tank, the Fund for Peace and the magazine *Foreign Policy*, has been publishing the annual *Failed States Index* of sovereign entities (determined by membership in the United Nations[10]. Several territories whose political grade is under question in international law, as for example, Taiwan, the Palestinian Territories, Northern Cyprus, Kosovo, and Western Sahara are not included in the list, even though some are recognised as sovereign states by some nations. Ranking is based on the total scores of the 12 indicators.[11]

A few social, economic and political indicators have been ascribed to the failed states, wherein the notion of ill governance becomes the dominant idiom of the day all in the context of the internal security threats in the Islamic Republic of Pakistan. Those first 32 nation states in the list are considered as 'failed nation states' by some international relations observers in the following tabular representation.

Pakistan definitely falls in the categorisation of the failed nation states even if we rule out the human development

	Country I-1	*I-2*	*I-3*	*I-4*	*I-5*	*I-6*	*I-7*	*I-8*	*I-9*	*I-10*	*I-11*	*I-12*	*Total*	
1.	Somalia	9.8	9.9	9.7	8.5	7.7	9.5	10.0	9.9	9.9	10.0	10.0	9.8	114.7
2.	Zimbabwe	9.8	9.1	9.1	10.0	9.7	10.0	9.8	9.8	9.9	9.7	9.5	7.6	114.0
3.	Sudan	9.0	9.8	9.9	9.0	9.6	7.0	9.8	9.5	9.8	9.7	9.5	9.8	112.4
4.	Chad	9.3	9.4	9.8	7.8	9.3	8.3	9.8	9.6	9.5	9.9	9.8	9.7	112.2
5.	Dem. Rep. of the Congo	9.7	9.6	8.9	8.1	9.3	8.3	8.6	9.2	9.0	9.7	8.7	9.6	108.7
6.	Iraq	8.7	8.9	9.7	9.1	8.6	7.6	9.0	8.4	9.3	9.7	9.6	10.0	108.6
7.	Afghanistan	9.3	8.9	9.6	7.2	8.4	8.3	9.8	8.9	8.8	9.9	9.1	10.0	108.2
8.	Central African Republic	8.9	9.0	8.6	5.7	9.1	8.4	9.3	9.3	8.9	9.6	9.5	9.1	105.4
9.	Guinea	8.5	7.1	8.2	8.6	8.9	8.7	9.8	9.2	9.0	9.4	9.2	8.0	104.6
10.	Pakistan	8.3	8.6	9.6	8.3	8.8	6.4	9.1	7.5	8.9	9.5	9.6	9.5	104.1
11.	Ivory Coast	8.6	7.8	9.0	8.4	8.1	8.3	9.1	8.0	8.5	8.5	8.5	9.7	102.5

(Contd.)

(Contd. Table)

	Country	I-1	I-2	I-3	I-4	I-5	I-6	I-7	I-8	I-9	I-10	I-11	I-12	Total
12.	Haiti	9.3	5.8	7.3	8.6	8.2	8.9	9.2	9.5	8.5	8.4	8.3	9.8	101.8
13.	Burma	9.0	8.8	8.9	6.0	9.5	8.2	9.5	9.0	9.0	8.4	8.7	6.5	101.5
14.	Kenya	9.0	9.0	8.6	8.3	8.8	7.5	9.0	8.0	8.2	8.0	8.8	8.2	101.4
15.	Nigeria	8.5	5.3	9.7	8.3	9.5	6.6	9.2	9.0	8.6	9.4	9.6	6.1	99.8
16.	Ethiopia	9.4	8.0	8.2	7.7	8.8	8.3	7.9	8.2	8.5	7.5	8.8	7.6	98.9
17.	North Korea	8.5	6.0	7.2	5.0	8.8	9.6	9.8	9.6	9.5	8.3	7.8	8.2	98.3
18.	Yemen	8.8	7.9	7.7	7.4	8.9	8.2	8.3	8.5	7.7	8.4	9.0	7.3	98.1
19.	Bangladesh	8.9	6.9	9.4	8.4	9.0	8.0	8.5	8.0	7.6	8.0	8.9	6.5	98.1
20.	East Timor	8.4	9.0	7.3	5.7	6.8	8.4	9.4	8.4	7.0	9.0	8.8	9.0	97.2
21.	Uganda	8.7	9.3	8.0	6.5	8.7	7.6	8.0	8.0	7.7	8.2	8.2	8.0	96.9
22.	Sri Lanka	7.5	9.3	9.8	6.9	8.5	6.1	9.0	6.6	8.5	9.2	9.2	6.1	96.7
23.	Niger	9.5	6.4	8.5	6.3	7.6	9.2	8.7	9.5	8.2	7.4	7.1	8.1	96.5

(Contd.)

(Contd. Table)

	Country	*I-1*	*I-2*	*I-3*	*I-4*	*I-5*	*I-6*	*I-7*	*I-8*	*I-9*	*I-10*	*I-11*	*I-12*	*Total*
24.	Burundi	9.2	8.1	7.5	6.5	8.4	8.0	7.5	9.0	7.6	7.3	7.7	8.9	95.7
25.	Nepal	8.3	6.8	8.7	6.0	9.3	8.5	8.0	7.4	8.7	8.1	8.4	7.2	95.4
26.	Cameroon	8.0	7.5	7.2	8.0	8.9	6.9	9.2	8.0	8.0	7.8	8.7	7.1	95.3
27.	Guinea-Bissau	8.6	6.5	5.8	7.0	8.5	8.5	8.6	8.7	8.0	8.5	8.0	8.1	94.8
28.	Malawi	9.3	6.3	5.9	8.3	8.5	9.1	8.3	8.8	7.5	5.6	7.8	8.4	93.8
29.	Lebanon	7.0	9.0	9.2	7.2	7.4	6.3	7.8	6.2	6.9	9.1	9.1	8.3	93.5
30.	Republic of Congo	8.9	7.8	6.5	6.1	8.0	8.0	8.6	8.8	7.9	7.8	7.1	7.6	93.1
31.	Uzbekistan	7.9	5.3	7.4	7.0	8.7	7.2	9.0	6.6	9.2	9.0	9.0	6.5	92.8

(Contd.)

(Contd. Table)

	Country	I-1	I-2	I-3	I-4	I-5	I-6	I-7	I-8	I-9	I-10	I-11	I-12	Total
32.	Sierra Leone	8.9	6.9	6.6	8.5	8.4	8.6	7.4	8.7	7.0	6.1	7.7	7.3	92.1
33.	Georgia	6.4	8.3	8.5	6.0	7.5	6.0	9.0	6.3	7.5	7.9	8.9	9.5	91.8
34.	Liberia	8.6	8.0	6.1	6.8	8.5	8.2	7.0	8.5	6.7	6.9	7.9	8.6	91.8
35.	Burkina Faso	9.0	6.0	6.1	6.5	9.0	8.2	7.9	9.0	6.5	7.5	7.6	8.0	91.3
36.	Eritrea	8.6	7.0	5.8	6.5	6.0	8.6	8.6	8.6	7.9	7.4	7.7	7.6	90.3
37.	Tajikistan	8.2	6.4	6.9	6.5	7.3	7.5	8.9	7.6	8.6	7.5	8.4	6.5	90.3
38.	Iran	6.5	8.5	7.6	6.8	7.4	5.5	8.3	6.0	8.9	8.6	9.1	6.8	90.0

Source: Fund For Peace Organisation.

indicators in the country. The quantum of political instability, vortex of violence along with the theme of sectarian, inter-state, inter-religious and ethnic violence even going in the Pakistan Occupied Kashmir, namely, the AJK (Ajad Jammu and Kashmir) and in the regions of Gilgit and Baltistan, need to be the cause of concern for the international community. Pakistan might be a failed nation state but the impact and the strategic and political fallout which this political and economic instability has on the neighbourhood comprised by the Indian nation state and other South Asian nation states, needs to be comprehended in its truest practical and tangible colours. Thus, Pakistan has always served as a threat to the stability, stolidity, prosperity and profusion of a multifarious ways of life in the Indian sub-continent. It might be a policy position or a scapegoat mechanism for the authorities in Islamabad but it does accentuate mutual distrust despite several rounds of talks between the two nations at different levels. It is not only India which is always surreptitiously and now openly castigated as being the benign transgressor, but also the theme of international peace and peaceful co-existence is too threatened and marred by the advent of Pakistan as an unstable trouble spot right in the neighbourhood of India courtesy both internal and external factors. These transgressions of violence need not spell the end of a peaceful relationship between the twin nations but an ad hocism in the bilateral talks ought to be discarded and a time table of over a year with multi level interactions under the shadow of trade benefits for the twin nations can be bulwarked as a ruse for bilateral rapprochement.

Asif Ali Zardari, the leader of the Pakistan People's Party (PPP), presides over Pakistan's first civilian government since Pervez Musharraf seized power in 1999. Prior to his election, Zardari served 11 years in prison on charges of corruption[12]. Both Zardari and Musharraf have faced difficulties in balancing the often conflicting interests of their people and the country's largest foreign donor, the United States. The Pakistani military is among the best-equipped and best-trained in the region[13]. The Pakistani civil service is also corrupt and vitiated in the general sense of the term.[14] One can only remember the days as have been mentioned in Stephen Cole's book, Ghost Wars who was an old CIA operative that in the days of the war against the Soviets in the western parts of Pakistan, United States was doling out a great deal of aid both in the form of military equipment and the stress on economic funding.[15]

The Pakistani Inter Services Intelligence had to prove to the American dole out agencies that they were making a comprehensive and optimum usage of the various funding and equipment. Whenever, the Central Intelligence Officers used to send their officers to check up on the spending by the Pakistani receptacles, the Pakistani ISI used to build makeshift camps as movie sets, wherein the training modules, trainers and the lumbering up fake trainee Mujahideens used to be presented before the American inspectors and the American people used to go back satisfied that enough had been done and justice had been done with their money and equipment which later on *boomeranged* against the Uncle Sam's establishment in the form of the America led 'War on Terror'[16]. The rest in the aftermath of the American escapade in Abottabad is a tale which has been told many a times over in the international media and academia. The ides of the terror have been indicated in the book much before the real confrontations took place. It is excerpted that, "Murad's idea is that he will board any American commercial aircraft pretending to be an ordinary passenger, then he will hijack said aircraft, control its cockpit and dive it at the CIA headquarters. There will be no bomb or any explosive...."[17]

What are the Further Attributes of Failed Nation States

The health of states (based on their ability to deliver the political goods) can have the following barometer and the attendant yardsticks:

- Strong States yield good governance and services to their citizens. They perform well in GDP per capita (and the growth of this),[18] the UNDP's Human Development Index, Transparency International's Corruption Perception Index, and Freedom's House *Freedom of the World Report*.

- Thus, if a nation falls within these parameters of being a failed nation state, then, one can have a look at the impact which such a fractious and unstable state of affairs will have on the realm of regional security and to be more precise the realm of internal security in India which is inextricably intertwined with the rubric of the notion of nationalistic concerns of India and the whole of the South Asian region.

How can the Scenario of Failed Nation States be Prevented from Hsappening?

External intervention in the form of intrusions from the Great powers buttressed by the dominance of non-civil societal forces along with the theme of destabilising and militating agencies of religious fundamentalism are the internal and external security threats which need to be delved inside. Such a fractious internal security situation being strengthened by the rampant upsurge of the anti-national forces tend to destabilise the entire nation state along with the internal security scenario in the entire region. Herein, the case being that of South Asian region as it struggles against 'Asymmetric threats' in the regional firmament. Apparently, it is much less expansive to stop a state from failing than to reconstruct it after it has failed or collapsed. Iraq, being a case in point, in the quaint name of the paradigm of democratisation and the liberalisation theme of the Occident in the larger sense of the term.

Ashraf Ghani and Clare Lockhart raise certain indubitable themes in the context of collapsing nation states in one of their works, titled as, *"Fixing Failed Nation States: A Frame work for Rebuilding a Fractured World"*. The authors posit the failure of the state system in the outmoded thinking developed post World War II: relatively independent, unified states that control markets and rely on authoritarianism when necessary.[19] Thus, it is rather unfortunate that the twin populations in India and Pakistan are part and parcel of a larger societal and anthropological design, but the narrow political considerations have led to the conjoined narrative of the Punjabi and Sindhi milieu getting marred through the exigency of partition and the subsequent spawning of the tradition of belligerency betwixt the twin nation states which can serve as a receptacle of peace and successful co-existence through the floodgates of unison such as *Khokrapar* and *Munabao* and the *Wagah* interludes.

Incessant gun culture and the spreading tentacles of narcotics-based corruption, particularly since the war in Afghanistan, too mar the societal landscape of Pakistan[20]. Thus, narcotics trade in the Islamic Republic of Pakistan also emerges as a kind of anti-national threat to the body politique of the Pakistan. This saps up the national energy of the nation and it creates a negative public image of the visage and the national contours of the domestic polity of the Islamic Republic of Pakistan as it militates against the Pakistan's incessant and repetitive declarations that it is an internationally law abiding and a peace favouring normal denizen of the Global Polity.

Some scholars contend that, "In the early 1990s, the Afghans were too preoccupied with their own concerns to agitate along the frontier, and the Soviet Union, which had long had adversarial relations with Pakistan, had fragmented into a number of self-absorbed states."[21] Thus, the nation state of Afghanistan since the time of Najibullah had witnessed political violence and then the sectarian and ethnic strife mixed up the sides and variegated fences in the Af-Pak region as the American strategists term the region as President Barrack Obama has nimbly nomenclatured the Afghanistan-Pakistan frontier as the world's most dangerous place, a kind of American Wild West. Yet Pakistani officials lambasted the US for conducting a 'transactional relationship' with Pakistan; they demand that it shifted towards a strategic alliance. Thus, though the Americans have always hyphenated the Indo-Pak relationship along with the notion that Pakistan still remains the de-facto frontline nation state in the region despite the elimination of the 'Evil Empire threat' from the region of Af-Pak.

Al-Zulfiqar was all for international cooperation in tackling international terrorism, Pakistan now has no second thoughts about supporting secessionism in the Indian Union, some of whom were engaged in activities that can only be described as terrorists.[22] This is a sad state of affairs despite the fact that once the twin cities of Delhi and Lahore were imbued with the same Gandhian fervour against the British colonial rule. In a news report which appeared in the year, 2002, it was mentioned that, "In a significant signal of its change in course, Pakistan has begun to disperse two major units of its powerful intelligence service bearing close associations with Islamic militants in Afghanistan and Kashmir."[23]

The recent angst in the end of the year 2011 betwixt Pakistan and United States points to the idiom that Uncle Sam cannot work without maintaining the status of 'Frontline state' with the Islamic Republic of Pakistan though the Pakistani military and the Regime led by Asif Ali Zardari has worded very strongly its qualms about the United States carrying on Drone attacks in the Af-Pak region. The internal community and the general sentiment in Pakistan are critical of the Americans flouting of its territorial integrity and sovereignty which was earlier on reflected in the SEAL attack on Abottabad. All this has a far reaching impact on the internal stability and the internal security situation in the realm of Pakistan, which has been lurching from one bomb attack to another and from one internal security crisis to another. The rise of the MMA, (Muttahida Majlis-e-Amal) in the 2002 hustings and the national polls in the Pakistani polity can be earmarked with the rise of the phenomenon of talibanisation in the nation state of Pakistan. The Wahabi movement lead by Syed Ahmed Barelvi ignited the tractions by contending that India is the land of war (Dar-ul-Harb), thus the principality of Pakistan began to ply weapons against the Indian nation state.

Most of the political parties in the North-West Frontier Province were in a political conclave along with the people in the Taliban and served as Taliban's political and ideological mentors. Maulana Fazlur Rehman spun the web of the Madarssas in the North-West Frontier Province so that they could serve as resource centers for the powerful and the in-favour political parties to undertake the respective election campaigns for them in the local and the SWAT's political context[24] thus paving the way for a Pakistani boomerang phenomenon akin to the American Frankenstein in the manner of the international terror apparatus sucking back on the American establishment in the manner of the September 11 run down. As an instance Maulana Sami-ul-Haq attributes the capacitiousness of the Talibanists in the North-West Frontier Province to the notion of these men and personages being trained and educated in the seminary of Akora Khattak. Even the religion of the Talibanists as attributed to the denizens of Afghanistan has been attributed ultimately to the teachers in Akora Khattak and not to the region of Afghanistan which happens to the primary and staple playground of the Taliban in South Asia.[25]

The Plight of Judiciary in Pakistan: An Eminent Internal Security and an Anti-National Threat

The Judiciary in the nation state of Pakistan too has been turmoiled and challenged by the twin institutions of the Military and the Dictatorial framework festooned upon the country of the likes of General Pervez Musharraf. These twin segments of the order of the Military and the Regime of the day in Pakistan needs to serve the purpose as the keeper of the well being of its people and its other institutions. But, Pervez Musharraf acted as a retarding and degenerating force element by subverting the Judicial apparatus of the Pakistani nation state by deposing a laureate of the order of Iftikar Ahmed Chaudhary which is the generally understood comprehension and understanding of the situation in the political system in Pakistan.

If we delve inside the logistics of the theme of confusion and the prevailing anarchy in Pakistan then we can have a delimiting view of the state of Judiciary in Pakistan since the past two years[26]. An American establishment's report contends that, "The judicial system comprises a Supreme Court, provincial high courts, and Federal Islamic (or Shari'a) Court. The Supreme Court is Pakistan's highest court. The President appoints the chief justice and they together determine the other judicial appointments."[27] The report further contends that, "The judiciary is proscribed from issuing any order contrary to the decisions of the President. Federal Sharia Court hears cases that primarily involve Sharia, or Islamic law, which got its mandate cleared by a legislation moved in 1991"[28]. This leads to a straightforward imbecility and a state of disempowerment for the hallowed and much respected institution of the Pakistani Judiciary.

Wajahat Ali in *Altmuslim* briefings contended that, "In the year 2007, Chief Justice Iftekhar Chaudhry was removed with 60 other brother judges. Some of the TV stations were shut down and the Regime of the day apprehended activists, dissidents and lawyers."[29] The news report further related that, "Asif Ali Zardari utilised the canard of democracy and initiated institutional intent to immediately reinstate Chaudhary, but, the National Reconciliation Ordinance stymied his efforts to do so."[30] Muneer Malik wrote that, "I am trying to make myself scarce to reach Lahore by tomorrow to join the long march. I was arrested yesterday and released late last night. I don't know if I will be arrested again". The National Reconciliation Ordinance of Pakistan can serve as a hope for the law, order and the concerns of normalcy in the Islamic Republic of Pakistan. Zardari's concerns have been to choose his compatriots in his governing team rather than looking at the matter of reinstating the big Judge as he had promised during the run up to the elections in Pakistan. That issue remains a pivotal bottleneck in Zardari's throne and he needed to take prompt action on that front in order to win the confidence of the Pakistani hoi polloi. Five cases are running against Asif Ali Zardari and he along with Nawaz sharif had vowed to put the last nail in the Musharraf's political coffin but that did not actually materialise as planned and the rhetorical nature of this political palaver remained the cornerstone of the democratic effort in Pakistan so as to contend likewise. In the times of

Pervez Musharraf, the Pakistani establishment initiated rounding up opposition politicians despite calls from Washington and other Western allies not to take authoritarian measures."[31] Several lawyers were detained, too.

Defense forces blocked entrance to the Supreme Court and parliament and a great deal of civil pandemonium ensued. All this while the local newspapers and opposition leaders cried hoarse over the limbo-including key Musharraf rival Benazir Bhutto, akin to the situation in the Tinanaman square in the People's Republic of China, much earlier. In his television address, Musharraf said he hoped democracy would be restored following parliamentary elections[32]. "But, in my eyes, I say with sorrow that some elements are creating hurdles in the way of democracy," said Musharraf.

The British Broadcasting Association further reported in the context of the Pakistani Judicial crisis that following was the controversial text of the Musharraf's Emergency Proclamation, "Whereas there is visible ascendancy in the activities of extremists and incidents of terrorist attacks, including suicide bombings, and IED explosions, rocket firing and bomb explosions."[33] Musharraf also contended indirectly as part of his effort to legitimise his clampdown on the judiciary that some of the judges have overstepped the limits of judicial authority have taken over the executive and legislative functions and it is they, he contended, who harp upon the notion of accountability and transparency.

On 22nd of August, 2009, a notice was duely served to General Pervez Musharraf which was widely televised throughout the complete expanse of the national and international TV channels. Later, there was another onslaught on the ongoing democratic system of governance. The answer lies in the institutional cohesiveness of Pakistan's military establishment and the civil societal mandarins of the country.

The Army angle in the Islamic Republic of Pakistan

Usually the Army of a nation state serves as a conduit for the sustenance and maintenance of internal security in the rubric of any country. The nature of developments since the independence of Pakistan point towards a different way and a different interpretation. The Military apparatus since long in Pakistan has been operating as a kind of subversive threat to the internal security of the nation state which it intends to protect. The protector itself is playing into the hands of the religious fundamentalists which have destabilised Pakistan since the recent past. The Military appears to be in a handshake with the terror elements and they in a way are disfiguring the tenet of peace and tranquility in Pakistan. The nation state and the conscience of its civil societal apparatus needs to militate against such a set up, wherein the protector itself is acting as a spoilsport in the internal security and the nationalistic framework of the Islamic Republic of Pakistan. Democratic elements in the State of Pakistan have been relegated to the backburner and the general visage and the imagery in Pakistan still remains that Pakistani Defense forces are associated with a great deal of glory, royalty and chutzpah which will go a long way in letting low the eternal foes of the nation and lead to the unified entity that Pakistan is and has become after the vast sacrifices of its founding fathers. Thus, the royal pantheon of the Army and the hallowed tradition attached to the notion of a all protector Army need not turn into a charade in royal ethos and all empty and self-suicidal gung-ho which does not actually yield any dividends for the nation in any international or domestic setting of significance.

In a contradiction to what has been stressed earlier, *stratfor*, recently pointed out that the army happens to be the instrumentality that holds the state together. Therefore, the collapse of the state would come about only if the military establishments were to fracture.[34] Thus, despite of the fact that Pakistan has had the experience of knowledgeable and charismatic people serving the stead of power since the last few decades in the form of Yahya Khan, Zulfikar Alki Bhutto, Zia Ul Haq and Pervez Musharraf, still the individual role of singular personages does not have a long standing impact on the general lore and practice of governance of the nation.

The Army of Pakistan views itself as the guardian of republican value, and there being virtually no civilian oversight over the military — the army exercises nearly complete control over the nation's treasury. What needs to be understood is the notion that the army does not have a clearly defined control over the people of the Jihadi fold though at some places it does have interfaces with the fundamentalist elements in Pakistan. Also, the people of Pakistan still have unwavering faith in the army despite the free for all great game of the SWAT genre which goes on unabated in the North-West Frontier Province in the confines of the Af-Pak region as it is nomenclatured by president Barrack Obama as part of the American 'War on Terror'.

The Demographics and Anti-Nationalism Trends: A Mapping of the SWAT and the NWFP

The majority of the Pakistani demography is centered around the region of the Indus River, which runs from the Karakoram/Western Himalayan/Pamir/Hindu Kush mountain ranges in the North to the Arabian Sea in the South.

Most of Islamism is constrained to the Pashtun areas — the tribal areas, the eastern districts of NWFP and the north-western corridor of Balochistan province which is populated by the people with a very orthodox and conservative cultural capital.[35] What the State of Pakistan seems to be suffering from is the neighbourly infectious impact of the turmoil in Afghanistan which needs to be surmounted by an independent internal security policy to be pursued by Pakistan in the Af-Pak region of the turmoil. The want of a conjoined and well thought out strategy coupled with the American intent worsens the scenario of separatism and jihadism on the ground in the nation state of Pakistan[36]. Repeated political violence along with the assassination of Benazir Bhutto also seemed to mar the ground for Pervez Musharraf and made life tough for the upkeep of a tranquil internal security scenario in the neighbourhood and not only Pakistan, in the terms of the complete collectivity of South Asia in general.

PAKISTAN

Source : Strat for : Global Intelligence.
URL: http://www.stratfor.com/weekly/jihadist_insurgency_pakistan

There are too many disagreements going on in Pakistan right now in the running year, 2012. It was Nawab Akbar Bugti who was caught and assassinated in the Baloch province of Pakistan in the year, 2006. Though the cauldron of insurgency and turmoil was brewing like genie infected vermin wine in the neighbouring Afghanistan, still the 'troubles' in Pakistan were accentuated as a state and a national crisis since then to a larger extent. According to the Human Rights Commissioner of Pakistan, at least 675 women and children were murdered in the first nine months of the year 2011 for the cardinal crime of harbouring illicit relationships. Violence can be deciphered in the political culture itself as Zulfikar Ali Bhutto was hanged in the year, 1979. President Zia-ul-Haq died in the year 1988 in an aeroplane incident and as a recent 2007 incident Ex-Prime

Minister, Benazir Bhutto was blown away to smithereens in the country's territory during an election rally. As reported in *Indian Express*, according to the Committee to Protect Journalists, the persistent violence makes Pakistan as the deadliest nation in the whole global context.[37] A foreign journalist commented on the factoid of the terrorist attack on the naval base in Karachi and the subsequent incident at Abotabad where the army was shown as the lax party, and he too was murdered.[38]

The condition of the city hub of Karachi is not conveniently placed in the practical sense of the term. The threesome balmy gangsters of the political outfits of the order of Muhajir Qami Mahaz, the muslims of Indian descent, the PPP with a Sindhi base of support and finally the Pashtuns who control the transport business in and around the commercial citadel of Karachi, have led to the besmirching of the urban bonhomie in the targeted city which definitely has seen better and prosperous days. The gangster culture seems to have taken over the urban firmament in the nation which if continued unimpeded can go a long way in souring the turf for the peaceful common denizens of the nation state of pakistan. The American war syndrome might still be a factor in the human recession in the SWAT valley and the general socio-political and economic landscape of Pakistan but the federal bias which is being felt by the province of Balochistan in being given only 9% of the Central funds is also a sore theme which can be revisited in the general security and developmental framework of the nation. Thus, the SWAT insurgency can also be attributed to the lop sided developmental gradient in the sphere of accountability, central alacrity and the fund disbursal for the general uplift of, the strife torn region which now poses more than an internal security threat to Pakistan.

The army happens to be the Praetorian guards of the Pakistani polity which owes, their origin to old and archaic Greek mythology, wherein the elite guards were recruited by the Royal Emperors to look over the royalty both during peacetime and the time of warring in the context of the general upkeep of internal security in Rome. The following statement can run as an advertisement for the army in Pakistan, "Book us for two weeks. If you aren't completely happy with the service we provide, after 7 days you can cancel and don't have to pay us a penny"[39]. In the same vein, the Pakistani polity is known to keep the army Generals and the Americans as the Praetorian guards but which on the final summation seem to be the spoil sport in the context of the internal security Bazzar in the South Asian region and the custodians of pelf and prosperity in Pakistan play the pristine politics and indirectly cause tumult in the internal security situation in the bedeviled Pakistan on.

The Trouble in Pakistan: A Reading of the Insurgency and Sub-Nationalism in Pakistan

The notion of ethnic insurgency cannot be simplistically deciphered as a kind of internal security to the Islamic Republic of Pakistan. The ethnic cleavages of the order of Swat valley fractions and internal conflict can be earmarked as sub- national threats to the nation. These ethnic cleavages can be construed as an anti-national threat to of Pakistan as Naxalism and the terror modules being spawned in India are concerned. These internal security and insurgency threats amount to a modicum of anti-nationalistic trends and inclinations which need to be subverted and strategically dealt within internal and national security firmament of the Pakistani.

In the current context, Kayani is all too aware of the need to overhaul the country's intelligence system.[40] Praveen Swami in his academic work has spawned a novel and informative picture of the strategic and internal security framework in Pakistan and generally in the whole of South Asia. He goes on to contend that, "Drawing on new material, including classified Indian intelligence dossiers and records, Praveen Swami shows that jihadist violence was not, as is widely assumed, a phenomenon that manifested itself in Indian-administered Jammu and Kashmir only after 1988."[41] Thus, the roots of terrorism hark back to the political expediency and the radicalisation of the Pakistani.

India is regarded as 'a perennial bugbear' to Pakistani and goes on to paint and taint India as the only and the single most dangerous flashpoint within the rubric of internal and national security.[42] According to one reading and perception, all the domestic failures at the front of the developmental paradigms are directed towards the hegemonic and the expansionist tendencies of the 'Imminent Threat from the Neighbourhood'. The, sole rationale for the failure of the Pakistani establishment in ensuring an acceptable standard of living in the country's hinterland has been directed down the hegemonic pretensions of India which is labeled as a Realist, belligerent and aggressive nation state in the Government's educational mouthpieces and even conduits of Primary education in the country. Going by the standard motif of the Pakistani Government, the military's typical strategy of 'out-terrorising the terrorist,' was being followed for a while but the model was flawed. The army would do an excellent job of clearing Taliban-held areas but was reluctant to maintain a presence in them afterward[43].

Harking back to the NWFP in Pakistan, initially Operation Sherdil was launched in the locale of Bajaur, a tribal area that adjoins Afghanistan and was a hub of the Taliban, where the forces were ordered to roam around the streets and worked with tribal lashkars (militias) and jirgas (councils) to identify and capture *irreconcilable* Taliban. What the Pakistanis indeed need to do is to spawn a broad consensus amongst the political forces in Pakistan apart from generally militating against the nexus betwixt the Defense forces and the fundamentalists. The military too has failed to block escape routes during actions on the Taliban's mountain hideouts. Thus, the Pakistani operation in Bajaur which was the starting norm against the Mujahideens in the Af-Pak region has not been much of a success and unless and until the nexus betwixt the Pakistani Military and the Fundamentalist forces is subverted, the real notion of peace and tranquility in the body rubric of Pakistan perceived through the internal security prism cannot be achieved in totality. Thus, the internally unstable situation of Pakistan remains a cause celebre for the terror mongers and a major debilitating factor for the achievement of great power status by Pakistan and the much needed status and bargaining space which India has achieved since the ushering in of the 1991 era, Liberalisation, Privatisation and Globalisation paradigm and the attainment of Nuclear power status by the neighbouring rival India which is always depicted in the Strong nation/ Weak nation paradigm in the systemic positioning of the twin nations in the context of South Asian security.

However, any US fears and apprehensions could be allayed by the Pakistan military's emerging counterinsurgency model, which places the Taliban at the top of Pakistan's threat assessment. The Swat valley turmoil serves as a sub-national threat to Pakistan as it is an internally destabilsing factor to the political and social health of already failing nation state or otherwise. The nation is itself facing a boomerang phenomenon. As it has aided and abated trans border influx of terrorists in the Indian territory and it has commanded and commandeered the rebels in the denomination of anti-national elements in Indian Kashmir (the whole ought to belong to India so, the same trained Mujahideens and terror modules having their disparate religious and ethnic interests have bedeviled the state of internal security in the Indian Union and in the larger context the same troupe of armed rebels have fomented a long simmering but hidden and dormant ethnic and sectarian cleavage in the North-West Frontier Province of Pakistan which can be definitively characterised and straitjacketed as a sub-national threat to the South Asian State of Pakistan.

USA and NATO have so far failed to defeat the Taliban in Afghanistan. A scholar, Saqib Khan contends that, "The leadership of the insurgency should be totally eradicated and then one ought to target the foot soldiers. If the leadership of a group or a terrorist organisation is wiped out completely, the bottom falls quickly"[44]. A.K. Verma contends in a book review, "Within Pakistan, ISI is often referred to as the 3rd Estate, sometimes getting promoted to the status of Second Estate when it has supplanted the entire bureaucratic establishment."[45] Thus, the Inter Services Intelligence of Pakistani always plays a suicidal role in ending up destabilsing not only India but the internal security scenario in Pakistan as a consequence of its and the Pakistani military's amalgamation with the fundamentalist elements in the body politique of Pakistan.

Saqib further compares between the terror stricken milieus in Ireland, India, United States, and other nation states in the goblet of strife through the anti-state terror apparatus. He goes on to contend that, "It took United Kingdom sixty years to fight IRA terrorists but at the end, it had to negotiate peace with the IRA. Basque terrorists of Spain Red Brigade of Italy, Maoists of India and Nepal, Assam's separatists, and the Khalsas' of India."[46] Here, one is not looking at the number game but still the conditions of operation of the myriad anti-national groups spread all across the regional polity in South Asia, and the international firmament in general need not be the only mode of operation against these genre of terror groups. The 'kill-capture model', was the wrong way forward as it ended up making more new enemies than killing old ones. Only when the military changed its strategy to protecting the population did the war in Iraq take a turn for the better. Another mode of the order of the 'leave-depart model' could be adopted in the Af-Pak scenario, which involves the conjunction of the Pakistani military apparatus with the Mujahideens of the region in South Asia thus added on to general norm of anarchy and pandemonium which apart from normalcy in the region has become the driving idiom of the age in this mutilitated and tarred region in the South Asian sub-continent. But, on second thoughts, why to posit the sole blame at the Pakistani establishment, the Americans too had a greatly dubious role to play in the context of insurgency and secessionism in the South Asian region, earlier. As it is mentioned in the book, "Fulcrum of Evil,"[47] the American establishment spawned a tradition of creating a 'Greater Nagaland' immediately after the Indian victory in the 1971 conflict against the State of Pakistan. This percept has been named as, 'The Palm Theory', which validated the unity of all the separatist elements in the North-East and then to unify all the seven sisters in the format of an independent and a separate nation state much on the lines of,

'Greater Nagalnd,' as demanded by the North-Eastern insurgents of all ilk, genres and denominations.

One of the pieces in the *Indian Defense Review* contends that, "The violence which afflicts Pakistani society is slowly reaching endemic proportions and turning the situation around may soon cease to be a possibility. There are clashes between security forces and militants."[48] In the current context, the threat is far more worse for Pakistan and the jury is out on whether Pakistan will implode or not, which might be a too pessimistic but a realistic appraisal of the situation in the country, which needs to be read in the light of its ramifications on India and the whole of South Asia in general.

References

1. Vries, Hent De. 2002, Religion and Violence, Maryland: Johns Hopkins University Press, pp. 456-458.
2. A failed Nation State is a state which is not able to maintain the optimum law and order and the conditionalties of peace, wellbeing and the welfare of its people in the context of matching up to the minimum human development indicators in the country and its domestic and Foreign Policy are both in the shelter of a bigger foreign power. Also, the term failed state is often used by political commentators and journalists to describe a state perceived as having failed at some of the basic conditions and responsibilities of a sovereign government. In order to make this definition more precise, the following attributes, proposed by the Fund for Peace, are often used to characterise a failed state:

- loss of physical control of its territory, or of the monopoly on the legitimate use of physical force therein,
- erosion of legitimate authority to make collective decisions,
- an inability to provide reasonable public services, and
- an inability to interact with other states as a full member of the international community.
- Often a failed nation is characterised by social, political, and economic failure.

3. Reference to Dr. Pasha in 'Mathew, Joseph C. Ajay Darshan Behera, "Pakistan in a Changing Strategic Context," (New Delhi: Knowledge World, 2004) pp.186-187.
4. *Ibid.*
5. See *Indian Express,* 2012.
6. "Pakistani Army Chief Calls PM's criticisms divisive," URL: http://www.reuters.com/article/2012/01/14/, (Online: Web), Accessed on January 21, 2012.
7. *Ibid.*
8. Mubarak Ali, " Pakistan's Search for Identity," in Paul R. Brass and Achin Vanaik, "Competing Nationalisms in South Asia," (Hyderabad, Oreint Longman, 2002).
9. Dr. Muzzaffar Iqbal, "Glimpses of a Distorted Culture," *The News*, 01 May, 2000, Sec. Agenda, p. 6.
10. "Failed States FAQ" the Fund for Peace, (Online: Web), URL: http://www.fundforpeace.org/web/index.php?option= com_content&task=view&id=102&Itemid=327., Accessed on 2007-08-25.
11. *Ibid.*
12. Rosenstock, Joshua, "Zardari's Election as President of Pakistan and the Dangerous Road Ahead", Washington Hotlist, available at http://www.washingtonhotlist.com/zardaris-election-as-president-of-pakistan-and-the-dangerous-road-ahead.
13. *Ibid.*
14. Ali Wajahat, (2010), "Pakistan's response to terrorism: A broad overview" *Conflict and Peace Studies*, 3(3):101.
15. Steve Cole, "Ghost Wars", (New York: Penguin, 2004).
16. *Ibid.*
17. *Ibid.*
18. Gerald B. Helman and Steven R. Ratner, "Saving Failed States," Foreign Policy, LXXXIX (winter 1992–93).
19. Daniel C. Esty et al., "The State Failure Project: Early Warning Research for U.S. Foreign Policy Planning," paper on the Failed States website, Purdue University (West Lafayette, February 25–27, 1998).
20. Gurr, Ted. 1970, Why Men Rebel, Princeton, NJ: Princeton University Press.

21. "Security Threats To Pakistan," (Online: Web), Accessed on April 24th, 2010, URL: http://www.fas.org/irp/world/pakistan/threats/index.html
22. *Ibid.*
23. Douglas Jehl (2002), "Pakistan Cutting It's Spy Units Ties to Some Militants," (*The New York Times*, 20th February, 2002)
24. See *Dawn,* January 10, 2012.
25. See *Friday Times*, August 10, 2002.
26. Iqbal, Nasir, "CJ Suspended, Escorted Home: Justice Iftikhar Summoned by SJC on 13th for Reference Hearing," Dawn, 9 March, 2007, http://dawn.com/2007/03/10/top1.htm.
27. US Department of State, "Background Note Pakistan," URL: http://www.state.gov/r/pa/ei/bgn/3453.htm (Online: Web), Accessed on April 30th, 2010.
28. See http://www.state.gov/p/sca/rls/rm/2007/96566.htm (Online: Web), Accessed on April 30th, 2010.
29. *Ibid.*
30. "US Warns Pakistan's Musharraf Over Military Aid: Diplomats," *Agence France Presse*, November 17, 2007; Paul Haven, "Pakistan Rejects Calls to End Emergency," *Associated Press*, November 18, 2007.
31. "Musharraf Suspends Pakistan's Constitution" (Online:Web), Accessed on April 30th, 2010, URL: http://www.cbsnews.com/stories/2007/11/03/world/main3448594. shtml? source= mostpop_ story
32. Paul Alexander, "Pakistan's Government Threatens Media," Associated Press, December 19, 2007.
33. "Text of Pakistani Emergency Declaration," (Online: Web), URL: http://news.bbc.co.uk/2/hi/south_asia/7077136.stm.
34. Startfor, "The Jihadist Insurgency in Pakistan" (Online: Web), Accessed on April 4th, 2010,URL: http://www.stratfor.com/weekly/jihadist_insurgency_pakistan
35. Shane, Scott and Eric Schmitt "In Pakistan Raid, Taliban Chief Was an Extra Prize," *New York Times,* Asia Pacific (18 Feb 2010), Web. 18 Feb., 2010.
36. Roberts, Mark, "Pakistan's Inter-Services Intelligence Directorate: A State Within a State?" *Joint Force Quarterly* 48 (2008): 104-110, Web. 15 Jan., 2010.
37. See *Indian Express*, February 17th, 2012.
38. *Ibid*

39. "Praetorian Guards" (Online: Web), URL: http://www. praetorianguards.co.uk/, Accessed on 1st November, 2011.
40. Wendy Chamberlain and Marvin Weinbaum, "Pakistan's Best Chance" (op-ed), *Washington Post*, December 29, 2007.
41. Praveen Swami (2008), "India, Pakistan and the Secret Jihad: The Covert War in Kashmir, 1947- 2007", (New York, Routledge, 2008).
42. Laurie Goering, "As Pakistan Boils, India Watches," Chicago Tribune, December 30, 2007.
43. George Friedman, "Pakistan and Its Army," *Stratfor*, November 6, 2007; Shahan Mufti, "Pakistan's Final Arbiter: The Army," *Christian Science Monitor*, November 9, 2007.
44. Saqib Khan, "Insurgency in Pakidstan," Accessed on April 5th, 2010 (Online: Web), URL: http://pakistan thinktank. org/v2/article-archives/188-insurgency-in-pakistan
45. M.K. Dhar, "Fulcrum of evil: ISI, CIA-Al Qaeda Nexus", (New Delhi: Vedam Books, 2006).
46. *Ibid*
47. M.K. Dhar, "Fulcrum of evil: ISI, CIA-Al Qaeda Nexus," (New Delhi: Vedam Books, 2006).
48. Major General Dhruv C. Katoch, "Will Pakistan Implode?" (New Delhi: *Indian Defense Review*, November, 2011).

7

Afghanistan Besieged: Security Imperiled

A beleaguered nation for the past several decades, Afghanistan has come a deplorable long way from its grand, old and hallowed days of the past and ever since then, after a great deal of diplomatic pandering has been bestowed with a full-fledged membership of the South Asian Association of Regional Cooperation and a Regime which under the leadership of Hamid Karzai is making way for a graft free process and a system in the besieged nation state of Afghanistan. The frontier nation in its heydays was renowned across the sub-continent for its upstanding, chivalrous men laden with insurmountable valour much like their distant neighbours, the Rajputs of the Indian state of Rajasthan. The myth, lore and the royal practice of the state of Afghanistan reflects the courage, valour and the proud diffidence and not the haughty arrogance of the denizens of Afghanistan which now stands vitiated by the unending fissures within the ethnic lines of the country, and the political terrain being further muddied by the corpus of international great power and neighbourly interventions. The clarion call and the sensitive dirge of the Kabuli Wala still evokes memories of an conjoined South Asian past where Afghanistan has always been a lost and forlorn frontier for the Mughals and the variously subsequent Delhi denominations. Thus, the Burmese venturings of the Indian traders and the Afghani travails in India have become since time immemorial stories and lullabies which have kept intact the conjoined ethos of an effervescent and colourful India and a bold and chivalrous Afghanistan.

Since the fall of the Soviet Union, the nation has been at the centrestage of incessant, asymmetrical fighting between its extremist factions espousing its supposed nationalistic ideals and the Freedom Alliance spearheaded by the United States of America in its Operation Enduring Freedom. While it is another thing that the divinatory Osama bin Laden and his cohorts have been wiped out from the face of the earth, the Taliban-Al Qaeda multi-headed Medusa continues to elude while being holed up in the inaccessible terrain of the highlands in the country's border with Pakistan.[1] This external intrusion as an extension of the great game in the nation state of Afghanistan leads to the upsurge of anti-national and delapidatory elements. Still, Afghanistan happens be a separate ball game altogether as it is a nation state being imperiled by the shenanigans of the ethnic and sectarian strife which cannot be directly straitjacketed into the rubric of sub-nationalism, as several ethnic groups are charging out to make a melee out of the South Asian nation State of Afghanistan, though not in the same mould of self determination debates and narratives which have witnessed in other parts of the international polity with the same internal security quandaries.

All legitimate national interests of Afghanistan appeared to have been grossly muddled in the Taliban's belligerent stand against the West and all that embodies Western values. This situation stood further worsened thanks to the lack of strategic foresight of the Afghan crown prince and his entourage, Zahir Shah. This international intrusive nature of the internal set up of Afghanistan definitely sets up a theme of sub- national and internal strife in the nation state of Afghanistan.

The issue of internal security in Afghanistan stands worsened by the fact that soon after the Taliban having been toppled, the international community failed to grasp the centrality of the comprehensive reform of the police and justice sectors to the rebuilding of the state.[2] The Afghan hoi-polloi has been largely susceptible to the practice of external intervention and the other international instrumentalities of the order of NATO and ISAF which have now become a common element in the internal security situation of the state of Afghanistan. The ISAF or the International Security Assistance Force has been involved in the upkeep and maintenance of peace and a tranquil state of affairs in the country in the light of terror attacks in Kabul and other places in Afghanistan.

The pattern of terrorist attacks is seasonal, generally peaking from June through September each year which definitely poses as a majorly significant anti-national threat to the already strategically bedeviled Afghanistan. Reconstruction projects have been soured by the gloomy spate of security conditionalities disruptions, and for this the Report states how the special representatives for Afghanistan and Pakistan have professed the need for greater security cover for civilian personnel and contractors to carry out their work.[3] The Mission document of ISAF contends that, "In accordance with all the relevant Security Council Resolutions, the main role of ISAF is to assist the Afghan government in the establishment of a secure and stable environment and to develop the Afghan National Security Forces."[4] Thus, the theme of reconstruction and the staffing and training of the forces of Afghani origin emerge as the twin percepts and the cornerstones of the security operations of the International Security Assistance Force in Afghanistan. The ISAF also undertakes reconstruction work in the turmoiled and charred remains of Afghanistan through its Provincial Reconstruction Teams in coordination with the GIROA and the UNAMA representatives which have area available on the ground.

Adding on to the plight and penury of the Afghani population as an aftermath of the stand-off between the Karzai Government (supported by the West) and the Taliban, the displacement of specific population groups has marred the internal security paradigm in the nation. However, in mid-2011, the United States and several other troop-contributing nations announced they would begin a drawdown of ISAF, with a view to complete withdrawal by 2014. The prevailing ISAF assessment is that current security conditions are conducive to Afghan forces assuming primacy in some areas and not in all the strife torn regions in the country.

The United Nations Office for the Coordination of the Humanitarian Affairs reports in one of its releases that, "As of August 2011, an estimated 500,000 people had been displaced from their homes. A further 4 million Afghan refugees continue to reside in Iran and Pakistan. An estimated 4.5 million refugees have returned, many of whom require assistance to re-establish their lives and livelihoods."[5] Thus, akin to other displaced populations in the regions in Sri Lanka, Bhutan and Bangladesh, the scenario calls for immediate attention. Since the law and order and the rule of law conditionalities have been somehow tackled in some of the won back regions in the state of Afghanistan, so there has been also 'a witnessed return' of the refugees from the border regions across the dreaded Af-Pak or the bordering regions

The Brookings Institution's reports on the internal displacement of population in the nation also is a deft reminder of the state of affairs. Outreach efforts by the Government-supported High Peace Council have been undermined by the threat of or reality of violence in many parts of the country. This culminated in the September 2011 assassination of former President Rabbani, Chairman of the High Peace Council, effectively halting the peace process. The Report contends "The presence of a growth of unmitigated stress on refugees in Pakistan and Iran to come homewards to Afghanistan. Around two million Afghan refugees in Pakistan and about 900,000 in Iran are the bone of contention.[6]" Another prominent area of concern is the theme of largely felt persecution by the Pashtuns in the north which have led the populations to flee to the Southern and the Eastern segments of the nation, thus rendering the cause of security mobilisation much more intricate and tough in the region and the territory of the nation.

The Ethnic cleavages in Afghanistan: A threat to the national rubric of the state of Afghanistan

An ethnic imbalance between the various communities in the country of the order of the Uzbeks, Turkics, Pakhtuns was aggravated by the two successive wars which had gripped the country and had torn it apart, leading to an absolute form of chaos and disharmony in the landlocked nation.

The Question of Identity for Afghanistan

And as Emile Durkheim has commented on the raging issue of identity which serves as the choking point for every nation state to delineate itself from the rest of the milieu, and this is one aspect where the Afghan identity has wobbled amidst much angst and despair. These cultural posers pinpoint to the word 'Afghan'[7] which is depicted as the common national identity all across the global polity. There have been a lot of discussions and debates over this word which according to us is quite a natural corollary of being an Afghan national. If one analyses the origins of the word, 'Afghan', one can hark into one mention of it in Ahmed Shah Abdali's epistle to Sultan Mustafa III, his parallel Ottoman emperor.[8]

Those who use the word 'Afghanistani' in place of "Afghani" are neither making a mistake nor committing a crime. It is a mere thaw in the national ethos of Afghanistan that such a spat about nomenclature has emerged in the South Asian nation. It is all about stoking the fires of unpatriotic and sub-national sentiments in the body politique of Afghanistan.

Drug trade in Afghanistan: A Major destabilising influence on the national ethos, internal security

Drug Trade is also another spanner in the works of the Afghani internal security situation which has to be delved into with some incisive detail. Since the US led invasion of Afghanistan in October 2001, the Golden Crescent opium trade has soared. According to the US media, this lucrative contraband is protected by Osama, the Taliban, not to mention, of course, the regional warlords, in defiance of the 'international community'. The heroin business is said to be 'filling the coffers of the Taliban'. One can conveniently refer to Taliban as an older and much internally pervasive genre of sub-national threat to the body politique of Afghanistan which is tearing apart the nation and sucking dry its the resources along with the honest efforts of the international community. In the words of the US State Department:

"Opium is a source of literally billions of dollars to extremist and criminal groups... cutting down the opium supply is central to establishing a secure and stable democracy, as well as winning the global war on terrorism."[9]

Thus, the culture of Opium running in the confines of the tribal belts of Afghanistan also leads to the creation of an Opium lethargy and Opium syndication with the younger section of a nation's population which debilitates the socio- economic construct of that country in particular. The nation too seems to be running through a similar morass which has been further bedevilled and scarred by the greedy ministrations of the external agents along with the suicidal friction betwixt the myriad tribal belts and sub-nationalities in the nation. These can be easily accounted for as the 'Unbounded-Risks' in the internal security framework of the Afghani nation state which goes well with the neo- international relations scenario of Afghanistan being a Risk Society akin to other contested territories in the South Asian region and other territorial expanses in the international realm.

It all seems very clear that a peaceful path towards democracy is overshadowed by the menacing cry of drugs and warlords, and be that as it may, soon after the overthrow of the Taliban dispensation, poppy production saw an increase on an extensive basis. Poppy Cultivation is an eminent threat to the younger and a nearly spoilt generation in the South Asian nation of Afghanistan. Poppy Cultivation has to be controlled and well regulated if not completely curbed in the country if the economics of the nation has to be balanced in the longer run and in the contemporary context as it definitely runs as a significant threat to the body politique of Afghanistan.

The menace of drug trade in Afghanistan has had a telling and a deleterious impact upon the economics and the general stability and solidity of the beleaguered nation. Though an agreement has been reached between the nation's political interests and the NATO commanders serving as the international interlocutors, still the conditionality of ensuring a smooth and subtle right of the NATO and soldiers belonging to the International Security Assistance Force (ISAF), will ensure the smooth and efficient working of the NATO instrumentality in Afghanistan. Also, the coupling of the general security and reconstruction work of the Western interests and the attendant NATO forces with the impinging upon the narcotics trade in Afghanistan can also be reviewed, as the Westerners are able to reach a great deal of success in this dual responsibility of ensuring security and a drug free Afghanistan.

Thom Shankar reports in the American national daily, New York Times that, "American policy makers and military officers say it is critical to choke off the drug money that sustains the insurgency, much as they are working with Pakistan to halt the use of its tribal areas as a haven by the Taliban."[10] Thus, the origins of insurgency and internal security strife in the nation has been aptly related to the context of the drug money in the nation, as it definitely serves as a source of money and finances for the Talibasnists, too.

The question which can be definitively posed is that, is Afghanistan a narco state in the making or is already one. The theme to be underscored is that both the Taliban forces and the supporting forces led by President Hamid Karzai are drawing their succor and support from the drug money which is present as the cultivated poppy fields in the rural and interior hinterland of the nation which has a more than debilitating impact upon the notion of peace blenees and tranquility in the nation. It was reported in the New York Times that, "We had just learned that in the two previous months Afghan farmers had planted almost 60 percent more poppy than the year before, for a total of 165,000 hectares (637 square miles). The 2006 harvest would be the biggest narco-crop in history[11]". Thus, it is an open secret of sorts in Afghanistan that poppy cultivation and the attendant trade will lead to a strengthening of the final resources of both the Talibanists and the forces led by President Hamid Karzai. Eradication was an essential component of successful anti-poppy efforts in Guatemala, South East Asia and Pakistan. It was proposed in various international for a that aerial eradication of the poppy cultivated crops could take place like it had been attempted in the infested nation states of Guatemala, South-East Asia and Pakistan, but the process was initially opposed by Hamid Karzai in the year 2006 where an effort was afoot to hide before the international community that the year 2006 witnessed the highesy poppy yield in the territory of Afghanistan.

The Americans were part of the drug related internal security strife in Colombia in cahoots with the Colombian authorities but the same problems of replication in the Afghani firmament have occurred in South Asia, too. One of the reports of an American national daily contends that, "The Drug Enforcement Administration worked the heroin trafficking and interdiction effort with the Afghans. They targeted kingpins and disrupted drug-smuggling networks[12]". The Americans too talked about the introduction of a court based penalising of the drug traders and the peddlers in Afghanistan, but the culprits after having been incriminated often utilised the escape routes by paying a bribe and winning their freedom after an adversarial court indictment of their culpability in the crime of drug over lordship and trade.

One open truth that further endorses US foreign policy's moral degradation is the notorious Golden Crescent drug trade which was the manifestation of US dependence on Pakistan for a regional geo-political influence in the aftermath of the Soviet-Afghan war.[13] The CIA-backed drugs trade stands conservatively estimated by the UN to be at $ 400-500 billion, the third biggest global commodity in cash terms after oil and arms trade.[14] The beneficiary of the drug trade is never the farmer who grows the opium but it is the forces along with the Western conduits and instrumentalities which go ahead with the theme of vitiating the economic and the moral fabric of Afghanistan which is already truncated into a twilight existence due to the volatility of internal strife and the ethnic sectarianism prevalent in the whole Afghani tale of attrition and vitiation.

The Global Scenario of the Afghanistan's drug Scene

The global proceeds of the drug trade stands at $ 51.4 billion dollars where Afghan contribution accounts for 3600,000 kg as of 2003. This is estimated by computing the final heroin retail price and factoring in the retail margins.[15] One can delve inside the theme of opium trade and cultivation as viewed and perceived through an international standard.

Afghanistan stands eighth in the itinerary of most volatile nations.[18] Notwithstanding all this, the neophytic nation state needs to forget the past and pursue a dual paradigm for meeting the menace of drug proliferation. As an initiatory exercise in Afghanistan, the poppy fields need to be decimated and their

Table 1
Opium Poppy Cultivation in Afghanistan[16]

Year	*Cultivation in Hectares*	*Production (tons)*
1994	71,470	3,400
1995	53,759	2,300
1996	56,824	2,200
1997	58,416	2,800
1998	63,674	2,700
1999	90,983	4,600
2000	82,172	3,300
2001	7,606	185
2002	74 000	3400
2003	80 000	3600[17]

destruction ought to be a continuing process. Organised and targeted efforts, all drug shipments originating in Afghanistan are stopped before initiation. Thus, the nation state of Afghanistan cannot be returned to a state of normalcy if the illicit drug trade and the international networks attendant to the practice and exercise of drug trade are not officially and formally discouraged and brought to the national rule book, which emerges as a waxing and waning and faint possibility that notwithstanding the state of anarchy and pandemonium in some regions in Afghanistan. The nation of Kazhakistan placed in the Central Asian region too survives in the same context, where-in drug trade hampers the institutional and civil societal stability and stolidity of the nation state.

Kenneth Katzman contends in one of his reports for the Congressional Research Service in United States that, "The limited capacity and widespread corruption of all levels of Afghan governance are growing factors in debate over the effectiveness of U.S. strategy in Afghanistan, as expressed in an Administration assessment of policy released December 16, 2010[19]". Thus, though the realisation can be recorded that normalcy has still not returned since the ouster of Taliban from the stead of power in Kabul, still the performance of President Hamid Karzai's Regime in delving inside what ails the nation and devising administrative solutions and law and order solutions has not been very feasible and satisfactory both in the eyes of the local populace and the international observers who have more than a simple stake in the internal security situation in Afghanistan.

Another debilitating development has been the tokenish pandering to the official American policies aimed at welfare in Afghanistan and along with that practice, Hamid Karzai has maintained and spawned new clandestine and open linkages and relationships with such elements in Afghanistan's political and economic firmament which goes against the comprehension of an alliance between the Western interlocutors and the Domestic Regime of the day.

Katzman contends in the same piece that, "Then-head of the U.N. Assistance Mission Afghanistan (UNAMA), Kai Eide reflected in a news event in the year 2010, that improving governance and political processes are 'indispensable' for resolving the conflict in Afghanistan[20]". Thus, the internal maladies of the nation need a humane and a soft security approach for a long lasting solution so that peace and stability become so much a part and parcel of the internal fabric of the political culture in Afghanistan that even after the outward drift of the NATO instrumentalities from the besieged battlefields peace and area domination in the rescued regions of Afghanistan can be made a reality and maintained in the longer run.

The "Bonn Agreement," signed in the year 2001 serves as a *tabula rasa* for the ferment and the stabilisation efforts which have been undertaken till date in the Afghani turmoil and strife which no Loya Jirga[21] has been able to solve till date. It also included the passage of the U.N. Security Council Resolution 1385. The Bonn charter, if we may call it so, involved a great iota of Iranian official help because Iran had supported the military efforts of the Northern Alliance faction. The further text of the Bonn agreement legitimatised the spawning and a creation and an establishment of the international peace keeping force to maintain security in Kabul, and Northern Alliance forces were directed to withdraw from the capital[22]. Thus, internal strife has been, as can be conveniently observed, a kind of a common occurrence along with the notion of cabals of clans, tribes and kith and kin ties subverting at times the emergence of a national, conjoined and cosmopolitan fabric of Afghanistan.

Afghanistan has definitively improved since the days of the Bonn Agreement as novae and practicable ventures in tandem with both the tribal chiefs and the professionals close to Hamid Karzai have been undertaken by the Kabul denomination. The presence of a solitary football stadium in Kabul and its deft utilisation by the Afghan cricketing team in order to win laurels for the nation and ultimately win a place for itself in the Cricket World Cup can serve as an encouraging instance of mobilisation of normalcy in the besieged political-social and economic tumult. This can serve as a silver lining within the confines of a grey and darkening cloud cover over the socio-political skies.

Also, to deface the notion that Afghanistan is a nation divided by the tribesmen, a mission civiltraice has to be accomplished by the nations before real dividends of development can accrue the way of the denizens of the nation state of Afghanistan. Nadeer Naderi and Hasb Humaoon contend that, "Around 11 million turned up for casting their votes in the first elections held in the year, 2004.[23] Professor William Anthony Hay of Mississipipi State University contends that, "A long view suggests that few nations will create sustainable liberal democratic regimes. Some nations like Singapore sustain a relative liberal order without complete democracy. Thus there is not a rather grave disparity between democracy and despotism and it is a give and take measure[24]". Still a larger than life game of Buzkhazi goes on for the Afghans as the different tribes muster together for the notion of political one upmanship as a consequence destabilising the general societal and the political applecart in nation state. Also, all in all the northern territory of the nation has been dominated by the Tajiks which have been traditionally supported by the Indians, Russians and the Iranians. The southern Pashtun belt is the one region where the Taliban belt hails from and has been historically supported by the people from the nationalities of Saudi Arabia, Pakistan and the United Sates. Thus, the international fulcrum since the cold war days has always been playing a prominent role in the niceties and the roughage of politics in the nation.

There is a dual crisis in Afghanistan. There is a Western and the general international fear that the tribes and the groups formed during the Jihadi groups in the days of complete strife and turmoil need to be taken note of as such Jihadi forces can mobilise the political process in a very different manner in the nascent democratic process.[25] One of the lacunae's of the Afghani system remains the notion that the national economy is premised upon the linkages of personal illicit linkages and guarantees with the activities of opium trade, quarrying and the want of sanitation and a dearth of clean drinking water along with a macabrely scanty social infrastructure remain the perennial sore points in a divided and straengegloved Afghani polity. The international aid programme also intends to largely solve the poverty hunger trap for a war ravaged nation state wherein the ailments such as Malaria under the Malaria Roll Back programme along with the initiative to get rid of Actual Flaccid Paralysis (AFP) are existing as menaces to the health of the nation. Still, if the Bonn consensus is followed verbatim with making changes for the transforming international fulcrum along with the regional tribes dynamics then the road towards a stable democracy can be attained very willfully and wholesomely in a nation state presently faced by infratructural, health, internal security and challenges of economics with a parallel national economy fraught with all national ills ruling the roost in the nation state of Afghanistan.

References

1. News Report aired on 10th of May, 2010 in Headlines Today in a Special Report on Afghanistan, Swat and the North-West Frontier Provinces.
2. Afghanistan's Security Environment (Online: Web), Accessed on May 11th, 2010, URL: http://www.gao.gov/products/GAO-10-178R.
3. "Peace Operation in Fcatsheet Series", "Views on Security in Afghanistan: Selected Quotes and Statements by US and International Leaders" (Online: Web), Accessed on May 11th, 2010, URL: http://www.stimson.org/pub.cfm?ID=119
4. "The Mission of ISAF," www.isaf.nato.int (Online: Web), Accessed on January 11, 2012.
5. United Nations Office for Humanitarian Affairs in the year, 2012.
6. "Internal Displacement in Afghanistan," URL: http://www.brookings.edu/speeches/2007/1 (Online : Web), Accessed on January 12th, 2012.
7. According to history and language books, 'Afghan' is a Persian word which means "to shout" or "to whine" and it has been referred to one of the original ethnic groups of our country.
8. *Ibid.*

9. Statement of Assistant Secretary of State, Robert Charles. Congressional Hearing, 1 April, 2004.
10. Thom Shankar, "Obstacle in Bid to Curb Trade in Narcotics," (*The New York Times*, 22 December, 2008).
11. Thomas Schiech, "Is Afghanistan a Narco State," (*The New York Times*, 22 July, 2008).
12. *Ibid.*
13. The Golden Crescent is the name given to one of Asia's two principal areas of illicit opium production, located at the crossroads of Central, South, and Western Asia. This space overlaps three nations, Afghanistan, Iran, and Pakistan, whose mountainous peripheries define the crescent, though only Afghanistan and Pakistan produce opium, with Iran being a consumer and trans-shipment route for the smuggled opiates. The United Nations Office on Drugs and Crime (UNODC) heroin production estimates for the past 10 years show significant changes in the primary source areas. Heroin production in South-East Asia declined dramatically, while heroin production in South-West Asia expanded.
14. United Nations Drug Control Program, Report of the International Narcotics Control Board for 1999, E/INCB/1999/1, United Nations, Vienna, 1999, pp. 49-51, and Richard Lapper, UN Fears Growth of Heroin Trade, *Financial Times*, 24 February, 2000.
15. "The State of Afghanistan" (Online :Web), Accessed on May 11th, 2010, URL:http://www.unodc.org/pdf/publications/afg_opium_ economy_www.pdf.
16. UNDCP, Afghanistan, Opium Poppy Survey, 2001, UNOCD, Opium Poppy Survey, 2002, http://www.unodc.org/pdf/afg/afg_opium_ survey_2002.pdf.
17. "Press Release United Nations" (Online: Web), Accessed on May 11th, 2010, URL: http://www.unodc.org/unodc/press_release_2004-03-31_1.html, and 2003 Survey: (Online: Web), Accessed on May 11th, 2010, URL:http://www.unodc.org/pdf/afg/afghanistan_opium_ survey_2003.pdf.
18. *Ibid.*
19. Congressional Research Service, "Afghanistan: Politics, Elections and Government Performance," (CRS Report for Congress, Prepared for Members and Committees of Congress, 2011).

20. *Ibid.*
21. The last pre-Karzai *loya jirga* that was widely recognised as legitimate was held in 1964 to ratify a constitution. Najibullah convened a *loya jirga* in 1987 to approve pro-Moscow policies,
22. Text of Bonn agreement at http://www.ag-afghanistan.de/files/petersberg.htm.
23. Nader Nadery, Hasseb Humayoon, "Afghani Women March and America Turns Way," (New York, *New York Times*, 19 April, 2009).
24. William Anthony Hay, "Democratisation, order and American Foreign Policy (Online: Web), Accessed on May 21st, 2011, URL: www.fpri.org/ e-notes.
25. Afghanistan: From Presidential to Parliamentary Elections, *ICG Asia Report, N'88*, November, 2004.

8

The Rise and Upsurge of Islamic Fundamentalism, Illicit Migration and its Regional Ramifications in Bangladesh

The state of Bangladesh was restored to its national and ethnic status with the advent of the Indira Gandhi regime in the Indian union. Bangladesh was freed from the exploitative and discriminative rule of Western Pakistan in the year, 1971. Mohammed Ali Jinnah led to the conflict betwixt the Hindus and the minority Moslems in the Indian subcontinent. The Punjabi defense Generals and the intelligentsia premised in Western Punjab, incremented the disgruntlement amongst the denizens of 'Eastern Pakistan' which later on was freed through the deft utilisation of the *"Mukti Bahini"* under the directions of Prime Minister Indira Gandhi under the rubric of the Indo-Pakistani war of the year 1971, when Indian sovereignty was transgressed upon by the Pakistani Military establishment in the subsequent incursions of the order of 1948, 1965 and the year 1971, which was the birth of a new nation state (in the momentous year of 1971) under the leadership of Sheikh Mujibur Rahman, who played a pivotal role in the spawning of regional cooperation in the form of the spawning of the South

Asian Association of Regional Cooperation, SAARC[1] with subsequent bottlenecks being created by the Indo-Pakistani rivalry in the South Asian political firmament.

Still, with the advent of the Jatiya Party in the form of the rule by Mohammed Ishaq, the fundamentalist and the extremist forces in the nation state of Bangladesh were given a predominance in the domestic domain of Bangladesh. Zia-ur-Rahman also established the popular Islamic University[2]. Subsequently, the JEI party supported the BNP in establishing the government in the year 1991 and Mujib decided to remove the citizenship for the Golam Azam, and the BNP-JEI coalition castigated the Babri Masjid demolition in India. Internal political limitations and the succor of the Gulf nations, Saudi Arabia in particular, reorganised the Islamic factions in the micro nation state of Bangladesh[3].

Political pragmatism and compulsions of religion patched the old thaws in the relationship between the nation states of Bangladesh and Pakistan[4]. Though, the nation state of Pakistan was largely responsible for a genre of genocide of the intellectual class in Bangladesh, still the ways of the twin nation states of Pakistan and Bangladesh have not parted ways. General Zia-ul Haq 'islamised' Pakistan completely. In the news release by John Mark Ministries, it was reported that, "On 1 October, 2001, as U.S. and coalition forces were assembling in Pakistan in preparation for the bombing campaign in Afghanistan, Bangladeshis were heading off to vote in their national elections[5]". Thus, it can be safely commented and discussed that the lore of the fundamentalism does run itself anew all the way in Bangladesh and the religious and the old connections with the State of Pakistan have always run true in the South Asian context, too.

Thus, there is definitely a connotation of a connexion betwixt the fundamentalist umbrella which ensconces both the nationalities of Pakistan and Bangladesh, and it is this lately found conjointedness which creates confoundness and an attendant sense of instability in the internal security scenario in the Indian North-East and other strife affected regions of the Indian Union militating against what all Declarations as adduced in Addu in Maldives have to present before the international community in general. There is nothing ill placed within the confines of a religion and a specific faith which is believed in by the people but when a reinterpretation of the scriptures takes place to ascertain certain political objectives with no care being taken for the intertwined lives of the innocent in shopping malls, cinema halls, airports, bus stands, railway stations and other places of public congregation, then the accountability-sufi-finger has to point towards the transgressors of public morality both in the regional and a much larger international context.

Later on in the Bangladeshi political firmament, riding to victory on an enormous wave of religious fervour was the pro-Pakistan, Bangladesh Nationalist Party (BNP). It was also supported by the pro-Shari'a Islamist Jama'at-e-Islami and Islami Oika Jote parties and the election was an alternate protests anti-the coalition forces in what was being touted by Islamists as a "crusade against Islam[6]". A secular Islam is what Bangladesh can aim for on the lines of what is being practised in the twilight zone nation state of Turkey which makes a tight rope walk betwixt the traditional tenets of religion and the attendant Western and secular "best practices" of the Occident in the contemporary context.

The theme of extremism as an eminent internal security threat has been elaborated with great zest and brio by South Asian and international observers. Sudha Ramchandran contends in a piece, "The World Bank's Director premised in the micro nation state of Bangladesh, was threatened and she was the first foreigner in the country to be warned in such a manner[7]." She further asserts that, "Apart from India, the international media has reported extremism, including Al-Qaeda activity, in the nation state of Bangladesh. New Delhi tends to call it as the 'talibanisation', of Bangladesh[8]". Thus, this intended talibanization of Bangladesh is not a positive development for the micro nation state as it is still in the nascent developing state of a LDC and then domestic bottlenecks only add up to the internal security obfuscations in the national firmament, as the nation needs all the positive visage internationally and regionally which can make it go ahead with the rest of the region and the global polity. The rue of political instability to be germinated amongst the masses and the myriad sub-nationalities is the norm of talibanisation and the word Taliban, might be a regional phenomenon but the ambit of fundamentalism of all genres has a much larger global impact zone which ruins the societal and political fabric of very many nationalities at large, including nascent nation states of the order of the micro state like Bangladesh.

The country has a proud history of linguistic nationalism triumphing over religious nationalism with a dominant Bengali culture, which is an undercurrent in the State of Bangladesh. In the words of Sultan Shahin, "New Delhi and Washington realise the phenomenon occurring in India's troubled North-East. The United Liberation Front of Asom (ULFA) has conjoined with the Pakistan-based Muttahida (United) Jihad Council (MJC)[9]". Assam Chief Minister, Tarun Gogoi has referred to the Bhutanese angle, too, which is embroiled in the state of instability in the Indian North-East as the entire region of the Indian North-East along with the nations of neighbouring China, Burma and of course out state of Bangladesh are part and parcel of a contiguous zone which have spilled over effects in each other's territories, as the transgression and trespassing in the entire region is not both a difficult task and an ask in the context of the porous nature of the borders and the inability of the national border establishments to ascertain the impermeability of the adjacent borders which further brings the threat of secessionism, separatism and illegal migration into the foreground as a preeminent threat to the internal security fabric of the states of Bangladesh, India and Burma. An official report further contends that, "New Delhi has provided lists of rebel camps inside Bangladesh[10]". Thus, the notion of internal turmoil and the much desired internal stolidity in Bangladesh is much intertwined with the larger neighbourhood in South Asia. Despite the developments since the September 11 catastrophy, the practical realities include the gravest danger from clergies.

Alok Kumar Gupta of Jawaharlal Nehru University contends that, "The militant ranks have expanded because of the influx of alumni from the estimated 64,000 *madrassas* of Bangladesh that have grown significantly in the past decade. *Madrassas* disseminate primary education and establishment does not commander these seminaries[11]". Without any need arising out of the internal turmoil and the state of indecision residing in the Indian Union, the people in the Bangladesh are definitively faced with the scourge of a rising tide of fundamentalism which tends to destabilise relations with the neighbouring India as part of the functioning of the fundamentalist apparatus in the micro nation state of Bangladesh.

Enclaves remain a big disputed issue in normalising the relations between India and Bangladesh which has a direct reflection in the conditionality of internal security and the demographic relief in Bangladesh. In the words of Alok Kumar Gupta, "The border between Bangladesh and India is defined along fixed lines. In some cases, they pass through the middle of common rivers. It is a misconception that if the river shifts, then the line separating the two countries will also move[12]". Thus, border problems further accentuated by the internal political vexations in Bangladesh sour the regional playing ground for Bangladesh in connexion with an equally anxious India. A scholar Shariar Kabir contends that, "The Islamic rebellion has been generated in Bangladesh out from the Middle Eastern nation state of Saudi Arabia. Communalism and religious extremism has existed in Bangladesh in one form or another[13]". Sufis have been a historic force in Bangladesh but they have not been politically much significant as they lay more of a stress on the notion of spiritualism and mendacity of the individual and the society in the general sense of the term. It is the powerfully inclined zealots who are politically aligned to self interested forces in the power corridors in Bangladesh.

The Attendant Indian Concerns

Praveen Kumar, an analyst working on the theme of Bangladesh narrates that, "Inter-regional linkages of the separatist groups further worsen the internal security situation in India. For instance, beyond its intra-regional linkages, ULFA sustains intertwining with the Maoists in Nepal and the LTTE. The latter have links with various Naxalite groups."[14] Thus, apart from the internal security framework of Bangladesh the neighbourhood too takes the shape of a strategic malfeasance in the larger context of the region.

Bangladesh might transform itself into a kind of "Neo-Afghanistan," according to one observation. In a report by IPCS, Praveen Kumar contends that, "*Amra Sobai Hobo Taliban, Bangla Hobe Afghanistan* has become a rallying cry and the same slogan of the Bangladesh's main Islamist extremist group, Harkat-ul-Jehad-ul-Islami (HuJ-uI) has to be taken seriously by India[15]". The stark realities that are associated with a failed nation state are there to be witnessed in Afghanistan but no one can portend that kind of a bleak and a dystopian future for the factionalism and trite political legerdemain which form an interesting and a challenging attribute of the internal security paradigm in Bangladesh, as Bangladesh has performed remarkably in the context of the human development indicators and in the sphere of soft security after being once ensconced in the South Asian region as an American surrogate state in the cultural sense of the term.

Women Capacity Building is also a major human developmental concern in the nation state of Bangladesh. Bangladesh ranks 108th out of 109 countries in the GEM, with a value of 0.264[16]. Migration too is a significant notion to be encountered in the theme of human and comprehensive security in the nation along with the gender concerns in the South Asian region.

In the realm of literacy in the subcutaneous context of the nation the standards and the figures have improved reasonably. Rated in the year, 2000, the literacy bar stands as follows:

Literacy Rate	*Illiterate Population*
40.0 %	50.6 million

Source : 2000 figures estimated by UNESCO Institute for Statistics, July 2002.

The Bangladeshi Government tackling the handicap of literacy in the nation has very high goals according to some official releases. The following table reflects the prime concern trained by the government on the idiom of universal literacy which is even more ambitious than the Indian literacy goals, since the time illiteracy was identified as a force majore in the undeveloped state of affairs in the Indian nation state. One can have a look at the undersaid national literacy goals of the nation state of Bangladesh:

National Literacy Goals

National Literacy Goals

Year	*2005*	*2010*	*2015*
Total adult literacy rate (%)	100	100	100
Female adult literacy rate (%)	100	100	100
Male adult literacy rate (%)	100	100	100

Source : http://www.accu.or.jp/

Thus, these above mentioned figures of attaining cent per cent literacy can be a bit too much of an ask but with the new resolve it might not be too far in the offing in the Bangladeshi firmament. Apart from the notion of literacy in the nation, another soft power aspect of the order of gender empowerment has been well ascertained by the Bangladeshi strivings at providing micro finance to the Bangladeshi women to initiate their entrepreneurship skills.

In a report it has been contended that, "Women have been more politically stable in the last two decades. A quota has ensured women's presence in the local government and national parliament. Among women politicians, the older group entered politics through social work[17]". Thus, the era of freedom and liberty and one upmanship coming the way of the Bangladeshi women had been taken up through the twin prongs of institutional uplift and the civil societal betterment of the conditionality of the women in Bangladesh.

Mohd. Joynal Abidin remarks in one of his papers that, "Most of the violence towards women in Bangladesh takes place within the households. The increased awareness of violence against women has facilitated uncovering occurrence of violence. Rural women are faced with the ideology of patriarchy, too[18]". Thus, the quintessential pretext and the context of domestic and familial violence remains the same in the Bangladeshi context akin to the trails and tribulations of the women brethren too, in the context of the South Asian condition of women, with India being another instance of the malady in the sub continent in certain selected quarters.

Added to all these conditionalies, the nation of Bangladesh has a very well defined and well intentioned poverty reduction strategy and a whole plethora of such related plans to surmount the debilititating factor of poverty reduction. Though there is a well defined institutional framework for the solution of endemic poverty in the nation, still a great deal of loopholes remain embedded in the planning and the implementation mechanism. What has been tokenism for the Bangladeshi strategy to eradicate poverty has been the multifaceted approach towards poverty alleviation. Dr. Salahuddin Aminuzzaman writes that, "Different agencies of Government of Bangladesh (GOB), international donors and the Non-Government Organisations (NGOs) have experimented with different models and approaches of institution building for rural and local level development[19]". A singular panacea for the abolishment of Poverty is not a tailor-made and a suitable solution for a developing nation state such as Bangladesh. The same author further contends that, "What causes poverty in a typical third world country like Bangladesh? In fact there is no single cause of poverty, the plight of some poor could be due to several factors[20]". The size of the land holding by a peasant family can be earmarked as one of the root causes of poverty in the nation along with a want of novae technology which is employed by the peasant in the field, thus adding on to the established causes of poverty in any developing context of which the nation of Bangladesh is an apt example. Still, one factor can be emphatically underscored in the realm of strengthening the security of a nation state that, with the appendage of extreme and harsh and biting travails of poverty in the Bangladesh along with the stark and stand out dependence of Bangladesh on the foreign aid metamorphosed the nation into a routinised model for rural development and poverty alleviation model building, which further hindered the indigenous and a self sufficient trend of policy making for effective poverty reduction.

In a related security development, premised on the lines of the 2010 'graves scoop' in Bangladesh, one news report by Radio Free Europe and Radio liberty went on to contend that, "Bangladeshi troops uncovered a mass grave believed to hold the bodies of some 20 officers killed by mutineers. Reports say scores of officers from the Bangladesh Rifles Guards remain missing after the mutiny by their men[21]". The report further went on to add that, "Nazrul Islam, a senior correspondent for the English-language "New Age" newspaper in Dhaka, tells RFE/RL that the mutiny was not linked to Islamist extremist violence and it was a demand for better remuneration[22]". Thus, despite the buttressing of democracy being established in the micro but fast emerging state of Bangladesh, the schisms and the pangs of a developing but politically divided nation mar its general visage, too, akin to any Latin American or an African upstart nationality.

Akin to Pakistan to a certain extent, the role played by the military in Bangladesh has not been appreciable in ascertaining the attainment of a stable and democratic buttressing in Bangladesh and the trails and tribulations of the liberation struggle of 1971, notwithstanding. According to a Media report, "In January 2007, the Bangladeshi High Court suspended general elections due to allegations of a lack of transparency and fairness within the voting system.

Concurrently, the country is under a national state of emergency with 35,000 Bangladeshis arrested[23]".

The Freedom house too reported about the state of instability and internal turmoil in the interior dynamics of Bangladesh. The 2007 boycott of general elections by Awami League and other political outfits raised a great deal of international clamour and an equally unsuitable pattern of scare mongering relating to the internal stability in Bangladesh. In a BBC report it was contended that, "While Henry Kissinger was wrong to describe Bangladesh as a "basket case" in the mid-1970s - it has for the most part been more than capable of feeding itself since independence[24]". Thus, it is due to the bipolar nature of politicking in the political firmament in the nation along with the immaturity of the political class to a certain extent that sometimes the socio-political turf resembles a shamble, otherwise for a nation doing pretty well in its human development indicators and other international concerns keeping in view its well inscribed limitations and constraints.

There is also a xenophobic schemata to the whole socio-political scenario in Bangladesh. According to a British Broadcasting Corporation issued report, "Some 150,000 Urdu-speaking Muslim refugees have the right to be Bangladeshi citizens, a court has ruled. The Dhaka High Court decision refers to the Biharis, who migrated from the Indian Union and were caught in the Bengali-speaking Bangladesh[25]". Thus, internally displaced populations in the country too need to be envisaged a proper place in the national narrative with tangibles flowing their way, as has been the ministrations of the Indian nation state, where in the minorities and the so-called marginalised classes have been provided a centrally situated socio-political space through government policy making and under the constitutional fabric through the ambit of fundamental rights in the socio-politico-economic context of the Indian nation state. Thus, as can be cannily perceived, the notion of migration, that too of the *illegal and accounted for* variant, has been a debilitating thorn in the flesh of the internal security fabric of Bangladesh. The same theme in its extension in the regional realm westwards, has scarred the turf of bilaterals betwixt the Indian Union and the micro nation state of Bangladesh, which in many ways has a reflection in the internal security dynamics of both the nation states.

As and when one refers to the notion of internal security how a nation maintains its welfarist and internal scenario is largely reflected in the externalities associated with that nation state in the immediate regional zone and the larger international firmament. As an instance, India has been able to bell the cat of liberalisation, privatisation and globalisation to a certain imaginable extent, which renders it accouteted enough to gerrymander and negotiate with the super and multilateral actors and players with much ease and convenience, as it is evident in the Indian role in climate change, non proliferation and security/ economic parleys of the highest order, and the associated great power status along with the People's Republic of China, Brazil, Eurozone, etc., is conveniently tagged with the benign Indian presence.

Illegal Migration: A Cause of Concern for Bangladesh

Demography plays a great and subtle role in deciding the regional and international future of a nation. Thus, if the internal stolidity and stability of a nation has to be attacked, then the notion of the majoriatarian population residing in a nation has to be impacted upon with transfer of people of a different ideology and a generally different way of life into the already established substratum of the previously settled population, which is not very much a diasporic *sine quo non*. Such an engineered exodus into an established enclave of well settled population since the ages has to be dovetailed with a strategic change in the foreign policy of the sending state, which might not be true in the case of Bangladesh. but tone of the Indian meta-narratives run thus. Illegal migrants scatter throughout the confines of the Indian nation and work as household helps and construction workers in the country, which ought to be cause of concern for the establishment of the Indian Union with the advent of cross border terrorism in the South Asian firmament. Frequent news of illegal immigrants getting caught in India are widely reported in the Indian media. In one of the reports in the national daily. The Hindu, contended that, "Twenty two Bangladeshis, who illegally migrated to Hyderabad and even secured ration and voter identity cards, were arrested by the city police here on Monday. Some of them had been living here for years[26]". The national daily, The Hindu further reported, that, "The Bangladeshi denizens confessed to the police that they managed to sneak into India by bribing brokers at the bordering towns like Raj Sahi and Murshidabad[27]".

Prostitution too is a notion of concern, wherein the nation of Bangladesh contributes a significant section of skin trade in the Indian nation *in the South Asian neighbourhood.* The chief mode of transit centers around the axis of Dhaka-Mumbai-Karachi-Dubai, all leading up to the shady destination of the Middle East. The Penal Code of 1860 Bangladesh contains provisions for kidnapping, which in general covers trafficking also. Inspite of there being provisions in the Penal Code, these were not being effective in stopping trafficking because of various implementation problems.[28] In a news report by Roland Buerk in British Broadcasting Corporation, it was reported that, "Don't stray off this road, that is where India starts," said Lt Col Rahman, pointing with his silver-tipped swagger stick at the ground a yard from our feet. "They may shoot, they are so brutal[29]". Thus, internal scaremongering has become part of political rhetoric in the subcontinent when it comes to the regional grappling with border issues and the contextual themes of illicit migration of people and labour across the Indo-Bangladesh border.

The fencing on the border has spawned conflict and occasionally there have been gun sinstances between the soldiers. Roland further narrates that, "It was made of wire, 12 feet (3.6 m) high, and stretched out in a straight line across the fields to the horizon. Bicycle rickshaws drifted along a raised road behind it, and every so often the silhouette of an Indian border guard stood out[30]". Fencing on the porous borders can be an effective modicum of separation of territory if it is further amalgamated with a separate practice of policing the borders with adequate personnel and equipment aiding the transport and communication patterns in the system in the border terrains with the specificity being the Indo- Bangladesh border over here in the present context.

Illegal immigrants from Bangladesh are a cause of concern for the South Asian region in the sphere of internal security. In a piece by Anand Kumar, he posits the illegal migration as a concern for the whole of the internal security dynamics of South Asia. He goes on to contend that, "The illegal immigration from Bangladesh has become a serious problem for India. In order to tackle it the regime had transported three thousand migrants from Bangladesh[31]". The fence which has been constructed by India is built on its territory and not on Bangladesh's territory, while the Bangladeshi denomination clamours that the Indian fencing has a great deal of symbolism attached to it in tandem with the Indian expansionist and hegemonic credentials attached to the whole fencing exercise. Despite the barricade several people cross over inside Indian terrirotory. This position might be completely uncalled for and might be politically unfeasible and non-terminus with regional security concerns. Thus, the theme of fencing remains a major bone of contention to this day which accounts for illegal immigrants in India varying from an exaggerated 20 million to about 2 million in the context of the immigration problem betwixt the twin neighbours.[32] The voices by Bangladesh have been raised as early as in the late seventies during the tenure of General Ershad in the nation state of Bangladesh.

Political parties in India of the order of Bhartiya Janta Party have raised their voice over the notion of orchestrated demographic changes and transformations in the Indian north eastern underbelly in the context of the perceived extra-sensitiveness of the North-Eastern region, courtesy, the all over-arching and an all-pervading presence of a neighbouring People's Republic of China and the subversive presence of the Inter Services Intelligence in the same region of the country which also has proverbial *tentacles* in the micro state of Bangladesh. Though the populations in the North-Eastern are

are very much endowed by God with the same linguistic, ethnic and regional attributes and characteristics, still the preponderance of anti-national and anti-country elements in the neighbourhood sour the turf for the upkeep of a stable internal security scenario and platform. This is not a standard nationalistic rhetoric but the appraisal of a very realistic nihilistic project which can tar and mar the internal security rubric of any sovereign nation which intends to keep intact its power and territorial integrity in the commonest sense of the term, with India and Bangladesh, being no exception to the universal rule of national well being and national upkeep. The treacherous terrain of such demographic profiling can run the immediate errands for the antagonists of the Indian nation and a largely peace loving South Asia.

The national daily, The Hindu, reported, in the context from illegal border cross-overs from Bangladesh that, "The Bangladeshi denizens confessed to the police that they managed to sneak into India by bribing brokers at the bordering towns like Raj Sahi and Murshidabad."[33] The internal instability seems to have spilled over into the neighbouring India from Bangladesh as is manifested in a court decision to express concern over the steady influx of immigrants from Bangladesh into the Indian soil.

Article 364A of the nation's constitution provides that, "Whoever, kidnaps or abducts any person under the age of ten, in order that such a person may be or subjected to slavery or to the lust of any person shall be punished[34]". Still as a neighbouring land of milk and honey in the form and size of India pulsates in the neighbourhood, so the agent provocateurs from Nepal and Bangladesh indulge in such nefarious acts and ministrations as to tide up their coffers, and thus human trafficking with an attendant want of protection by the Statal apparatus remains a genre of internal security threat to the entire South Asian region.

Laws countering human trafficking abound in the Bangladesh polity but the execution of the same remains tardy and insufficient in the micro and nascent nation. In the related Human Development prism, according to a Bangladesh CEDAW report, actions and cognizance have been taken of the crimes against women but still it only a noble and small beginning in rendering succor to the women and the general populace. The beleaguered state needs to firm up its women empowerment record and other social welfarist norms with an appropriate normalisation and interpretation of the notion of constitution and rule of law in Dhaka, if the spillover impact in other South Asian neighbours have to be prevented. Still, in the realm of human development Bangladesh has improved beyond a degree and can move along the lines of a reformed Sri Lanka, the South Asian Emerald Isle which too boasts of impressive human development indicators, though hailing from the LDC belt of the Oriental global society which is what the standard Western narrative contends.

Akin to the nation state of Pakistan, the novae nationality of Bangladesh has been exposed to and marred by the similar legerdemain of political and dictatorial hiccups in the country. The state forming personage of Sheikh Mujibur Rehman was promptly followed by the rule of Zia-Ur-Rehman and Generals and commander-in-chiefs like General Ershad in the seventies and the eighties, and it was only during the rule of General Ershad before the advent of the political outfits of the order of BNP and Awami League that both Bangladesh and the Indian Union entered into a treaty to share the Teen Bigha Corridor and to sort out other border disputes in the vicinity of the commonly shared frontier. Bangladesh was under military and quasi-military rule between the year 1975 and 1990 and was ruled by General Rehman and later General Ershad. During this scenario, India's political situation also fluctuated very fervently with Indira Gandhi losing the stead of power in the year, 1979. The intervening years witnessed the Janata Regime enjoying and firming up good and cordial relations with other neighbouring South Asian nations of the order of Bangladesh.[35]

Thus, as the Indian Union was turmoiled by the notion of coalition governments along with the internal security destabilisations of the order of terrorism, insurgency, cross-border illegal immigration, human trafficking, etc. in the same vein the Bangladesh was bedeviled by the notion of frequent military interventions in the power structure at Dhaka along with the oscillations in Regimes between a pro-India Awami League and an anti-India, BNP, thus souring the pitch for the spawning of a stable and stolid governmental denomination at the center in Dhaka which could be regionally, internationally and nationally respected and venerated in the Indian nation state. This inter-connection between the international visages of both India and Bangladesh is significant pathfinder, as the internal security scenario in both the nations, specially in the context of the Indian North-East, is part and parcel of a combined strategic and locally political matrix. The Pakistani Inter Services Intelligence, which intervenes in the internal security scenario in the domestic polity in the nation state of Bangladesh, too, is responsible for destabilising the turf in the Bangladesh nation state and the intertwined zone of North-Eastern India which pips to the post, *all the talk as palaver* about the peaceful co-existence amongst the nation states in South Asia.

There is always a tenor of growing uncertainties akin to the failed nation state mantle which Pakistan has acquired. Sreeradha Dutta contends in one of her comments that, "Akin to the rise of the Hindu right in form of the upsurge of Bhartiya Janata Party in the Indian Union, the rise of HUJI in the micro state of Bangladesh has too soured the internal security pitch of both the nation states."[36] This argument might not hold much water as the national rubric of India is permeated since time immemorial by a majority populace of the Hindus which makes them a vocal, dominant and fervent majority without being subversive to the cause of the minorities. Thus, the Indian scenario is far better, far more advanced and a front ranger in the international firmament which cannot be compared so blatantly with neophytic micro states of the order of Bangladesh, though some of the North-East in India along with states like West Bengal and Assam bear close resemblance to the culture, lore and myth of the neighbouring Bangladesh.

The internal stability scenario in the North-Eastern segment of the South Asian region is also threatened by espionage and subversion carried out by the Inter Services Intelligence of neighbouring Pakistan as mentioned above. In a book penned by Dhar, who is an ex-Intelligence Bureau chief, he contends and relates a real time tale of subversion pertaining to both the Indian and the Bangladeshi internal security contexts. He contends that, "In the military cantonment in Malda in West Bengal, there lived a Dhobi (washerman) who was very friendly with the defense personnel in the locality of Malda and went to the cantonment to have a good time with the defense people." The author further contends that the person was of a Bangladeshi origin who would repeatedly visit his native place in Bangladesh. The personage was then, one day found dead in an accident as he traveled in a bus from Dhaka. When the unknowing police personnel were checking the casualties, they found strategic and sensitive maps in his luggage which was found to have a kind of letter which used a strange language. The letter was aimed for some Pakistani ISI operatives and used the following language in a clandestine and symbolic fashion. The letter went on like that, "The Dulhan, (Missile) is yet not prepared for the marriage procession and still intends to stay in the house in Malda. It is now being decked up with all ornaments and accouterments and the paraphernalia which one associates with a marriage occasion. Soon it will leave for its in-law place."[37]

Herein, the missile stored in the Malda cantonment and the airbase somewhere in Southern India is being talked about as a kind of in-laws, place.[38] Thus, this incident as enumerated in the book pinpoints at the notion of ISI sponsored and linked personages roaming scot free and doing incalculable damage to the internal security and security of the nations of the order of India and Bangladesh both, as their international boundaries are intertwined with each other in a strange matrix of demography and geography in the region in the North-Eastern fringe of the South Asian Association of Regional Cooperation (SAARC). The strategic situation is such in the North-Eastern segment of South Asia that the internal, religious, linguistic and ethnic predilections in the region have an impact on the respective foreign policy handlings and negotiations of the nation states of Nepal, Bhutan, India, Bangladesh and Burma forming one sub-set of interactions in the region so undemarcated by reigning territorial delineations. Akin to Pakistan, there is a discernible tendency amongst the political mandarins of Bangladesh which tends to pinpoint towards India as a perennial spoiler of the internal security and as a regional arm twister, which is nothing more than a strategic and political device to divert away the attention of the people from the internal failings of the regimes so as to spawn a perennial bugbear in order to keep on stirring the pot of regional animosity through the menace of terrorism and separatism. This is a brew which is very much foreign to the Indian comprehension of stability, stolidity and international cohesion of all variants including the economic perspective being attached to the theme of regional security.

References

1. Kamruddin,Ahmad, A Social History of Bengal, Dhaka: Progoti Publishers, 1978, pp. 91-92.
2. *Ibid.*
3. Rahul Bedi, "Cross-Border Links Strengthen India's Insurgent Groups," Jane's Intelligence Review, November 1, 2004.
4. US Department of State, "Country Reports on Terrorism," 2008, available at www.state.gov/s/ct/rls/crt.
5. "Bangladesh-Sytematic Persecution of Religious Minorities," (Online: Web), Accessed on May 6th, 2010, URL: http://jmm.aaa.net.au/articles/11127.htm.
6. *Ibid.*
7. Sudha Ramchandran (2010), "Bangladesh Treads Fine Terror Line," (Online :Web), Accessed on May 6th, 2010, URL: http://www.atimes. com/atimes.
8. *Ibid.*
9. Sultan Shahin, (2010), "A New Dimension in India's North-East Woes," (Online: Web), Accessed on May 6th, 2010, URL: http://www.atimes.com/atimes/South_Asia/FJ23Df02.html.
10. *Ibid.*

11. Alok Kumar Gupta (2002), "Islamic Fundamentalism in Bangladesh and Pakistan: Role of Madarssas," (Online: Web), Accessed on May 6th, 2010, URL: http://www.ipcs.org/article/terrorism/islamic-fundamentalism-in-bangladesh-and-pakistan-role-of-madrassas-753.html.
12. Alok Kumar Gupta, "India and Bangladesh : Enclaves Disputes," (Online: Web), Accessed on May 6th, 2010, URL: http://www.ipcs.org/article/india-the-world/india-and-bangladesh-enclaves-dispute-493.html.
13. Shariar Kabir (2006), "Jamat-E-Islami and Islamic Militancy in Bangladesh," (Online: Web), Accessed on May 6th, 2010,URL: http://www.secularvoiceofbangladesh.org/Islamic.
14. Praveen Kumar (2003), "Bangladesh as India's Internal Security Concern," (Online: Web), Accessed on May 6th, 2010, URL: http://www.ipcs.org/article/terrorism-in-northeast.
15. Praveen Kumar, "Bangladesh: Turning Into Another Afghanistan," (Online: Web), Accessed on May 6th, 2010, URL: http://www.ipcs.org/article/terrorism/bangladesh.
16. "Human Development Report: Bangladesh 2009" (Online: Web), Accessed on May 6th, 2010, URL: http://hdrstats.undp.org/en/countries/country_fact_sheets/cty_fs_BGD.html.
17. "Women's Rights in Bangladesh," (Online Women in Politics. Org.).
18. Mohd. Joynal Abidin, "Women Empowerment in Bangladesh," (Papers, Social Science Research Network, May 8, 2008).
19. Dr Salahuddin Aminuzzaman, "Institutional framework of Poverty Alleviation: An Overview of Bangladesh Experiences," url: http://unpan1.un.org/, (Onl;ione: Web), Accessed on 1st January, 2012.
20. *Ibid.*
21. Abubakar Siddique (2009), "Fears of Instability Haunt Bangladesh After Army Mutiny," (Online: Web), Accessed on May 11th, 2010, URL: http://www.rferl.org/content/Fears_Of_Instability_Haunt_ Bangladesh_ After_Army_ Mutiny/1500592.html.
22. *Ibid.*
23. Bangladesh Halts Elections, Arrest 2500," *CBS News.com-News-World*, 13 January, 2007, http://www.cbsnews.com/stories /2007/01/13/world/main2358638.shtml; "BD Crisis

Deepens After Election Suspension," *The News-International*, 28 February 2007. http://www.thenews.com.pk/daily_detail.asp?id=40931.

24. Waliur Rehman, "Is Bangladesh heading towards disaster?" URL: http://news.bbc.co.uk/2/hi/, (Online: Web), Accessed on January 11th, 2012.
25. "Citizenship For Bihari Refugees," (Online: Web), Accessed on May 11th, 2010, URL: http://news.bbc.co.uk/2/hi/south_asia/7407757.stm.
26. Hindu Staff Reporter (2007), "22 Illegal Immigrants from Bangladesh Held," (Chennai: The Hindu, October 9, 2007).
27. *Ibid.*
28. Bangladesh CEDAW Report, 1 April, 1997.
29. British Broadcasting Corporation, "Roland Buerk" "Villagers Left in Limbo By Border Fence," (Online: Web), Accessed on May 11th, 2010,URL: http://news.bbc.co.uk/2/hi/programmes/from_our_own_ correspondent/4653810.stm.
30. *Ibid.*
31. Anand Kumar, "Illegal Bangladeshi Migration :People Take the Mantle When the Government Gives up," (Online: Web), Accessed on May 11th, 2010, URL: http://www. south asiaanalysis.org.
32. Praful Bidwai, "Beggaring the Neighbour," New Delhi: Frontline, 20 (4), 15-18.
33. *Ibid.*
34. The Constitution of Bangladesh.
35. Sumit Ganguly Ed., "India's Foreign Policy: Retrospect and Prospect," (New Delhi: Oxford University Press, 2010), p. 65.
36. Sreeradha Data, "Bangladesh's Political evolution: Growing Uncertainties," (Strategic Analysis, 27)2), pp. 23-49.
37. K.N. Dhar, "The Fulcrum of Evil: The triumvarite of Pakistan, China and United States".
38. *Ibid.*

9

Internal Security Threats to Maldives: Turmoil in the Indian Ocean

Maldives happens to be ensconced in the southern bed of the Indian Ocean and it is a blissful, little and peaceable Republic. It happens to be a vastly and often sought retreat for the denizens of South Asia, especially the Indian denizens who need to embark on a long and restful furlough of a holiday in the confines of a sleepy little Maldives which boasts of fishery, a little bit of shipping and a great deal of the azure beauty of the high seas.

In the words emanating from a Maldives introductory portal, "Scattered across the equator in the middle of the Indian Ocean, the gem like islands of the Maldives depict the rare vision of a tropical paradise. Maldives is configured by Palm suffused islands with enciting pristine beaches, breadth takingly beautiful lagoons."[1] Thus, lesser said the better about the scenic beauty of the nation state of Maldives which will be sufficient to make a nature agnostic swoon in anticipation of something better. But, such a largely sequestered scenic island nation faces the twin threats of Climate change in the form of the impact of the recent Tsunami and the newly bridled threat of terrorism which seems to rearing its ugly head in the South

Asian region and also in the micro and idyllic nation state of Maldives which can categorised as a Banana Republic in more senses than one. It is one of these impediments of the nation states such as Maldives, Monaco and Vatican and Luxembourg that they need to be gauged as the new dependencies which do not want to remain a slave and in a subservient status owing to their small territorial extent and the resultant paucity of resources in these realms in the South Asian subcontinent.

The Indo-Maldives Bilaterals: A Delving inside the Theme of co-existence

India and Maldives share a long and rich history of bilateral relations with the Maldives being regarded as a co-partner with India in several of its national and international endeavours. In the aftermath of Military instigation an attempted Regime change was contrived in Maldives by the Piratical attackers and the Indian governmental denomination supported by the Indian navy saved the day for the beleaguered Government of Maldives and extricated it out of the 'political quagmire' by subverting the coup. This rescue operation by the Indian Union further cemented the bonds of friendship and the notion of '*Pacta Sunta Servanda*'[2] meaning the notion of mutual Faith and good faith between two bilaterally disposed nations who happen to be in political and strategic contiguity with each other.

The Indian-Maldives bilaterals have enjoyed the characteristics of mutual cooperation. Disparate spheres such as economic and technical cooperation, defence, education and public health tend to be the spheres in which the two South Asian nation states are engaged in. The warmth of the Indian-Maldives bilaterals has been kept alive through pristine and well felt for diplomatic exchanges. President Gayoom of Maldives has visited India twice since January 2007 to participate in the International Seminar organised by the Indian National Congress in January 2007. As part of the diplomatic deliberations, Mr. K.D. Ahmed Maniku, the personage in-charge of the nation state of Maldives arrived in Delhi in the month of March 2007 to confabulate with the Chief

Election Commission of India, wherein he dwelt upon the practice of the initiation of the Electronic Voting Machines in the nation state of Maldives.[3]

The Process of Development in the Nation State of Maldives and the Role of Indian Friendship

India has been in the forefront in providing economic and technical aid to the nation state of Maldives in its developmental efforts especially in the areas of human resource development and general health. A Military of External Affairs source premised in India reported that, "The cooperation in the area of defense and security forms an important component of our bilateral relations. The Indian Navy has gifted INS Tillanchang to the nation state of Maldives in April, 2006."[4] Thus, in the environment which reeks of a Chinese intrusion and a Han expansive exercise in the Indian Ocean and the South Asian subcontinent in general, the Indian defense partnership with Maldives becomes more than a strategic necessity which has been very ably initiated by the Indian lending of a frigate to the Maldives Navy.

The Nature of Indian Settlers in Maldives

In the age of Globalisation and other attendant dynamics of the network, denizens and the myriad diasporas of the world, Indians are found to be the largest expatriate community in the Maldives with a total strength exceeding 19,430 followed by Bangladesh and Sri Lanka. The Indian expatriate community consists of doctors, nurses, technicians, teacher, labourers, tailors, etc.[5] The Indian settlers are affluently ensconced in the micro nation state of Maldives lying perilously close to the Indian Ocean rim nations and the various maritime pathways which criss cross the region in and around the micro island state of Maldives which too has now acquired a new denomination in the strategic architecture of the region and is not a volatile or an unstable nationality on the lines of nation states such as Sri Lanka, Pakistan and a strife torn India in some quarters of its confines as the stakes are much lower in the context of the international polity and the attendant dynamics of separatism and popular disaffection. It has been observed in South Asia and internationally, too, that the smaller nationalities in the context of a smaller territoriality and the paucity of natural minerals and resources to support an fervent and effective industrialisation in the nation, such nations in the micro mould are generally elitist oriented at least in the context of who rules the power corridors and the much often instability can only be in the form of a natural catastrophe. The establishment of a super power or a great power base along with a power change in the political system of the state under consideration can be another cause of concern in Maldives. Much of it runs true to the nation state of Maldives, which has been unfortunately effected by the menace of Wahabi mould of terrorism along with being impacted upon by the scourge of Tsunami and the attendant natural disasters and the perils in the Indian Ocean.

The foundations of India's foreign policy were laid during the freedom movement when the founding fathers were intertwined with the greater and pressing themes of the time. The principles of the country's foreign policy include the norms of conflict resolution by non violent and diplomatic means, the sovereign equality of all states, sovereign inclinations as reflected in the dictum of Non-alignment, and equity in the conduct of international politics. The upgradation of 'bilaterals' with the neighbourhood is one of the cornerstones of Indian foreign policy. Apart from successfully evacuating the coup in Maldives, India played an historic and unique role in the liberation of Bangladesh which attained independence in the year, 1971.

In an Indian Embassy release, the following facts have been highlighted, "Through the implementation of the 1964 and 1974 Agreements, the issues of the stateless people of Indian origin in Sri Lanka were resolved."[6] The South Asian Preferential Trade Arrangement (SAPTA) became operational in December 1995. Maldives, too, has been able to deal with the theme of regional security and bonhomie with the aid and support of the Indian Union though in a secondary but not in a gullible capacity.

At the 9th SAARC Summit in Male in May 1997, a historical decision was undertaken in order to objectify a South Asian Free Trade Area (SAFTA). There has been an establishment of the Indian Ocean Rim Association for Regional Co-operation (IOR-ARC) in March 1997, which again has the Indian support and diplomatic succor. A threesome set of threats have been encountered by the nation state of Maldives. There has been a history of military coups and resettlements in the political denomination in the nation state of Maldives since its short national history which brought in one of the famed Indian interventions in order to maintain the peace and tranquility in the micro nation state with all its dependencies along with a well witnessed want of an independent and powerful Defense force and the presence of a strong network of bilateral, multilateral and global ties with significant players in the international polity. There are prescriptions inscribed in the myth and legendary lore of the people of Kautilya and Sun Zu which pinpoint towards the stratagem for a small and a weak nation state to survive when there are stronger and more rampant actors evidentially operating in the neighbourhood and the immediate playing field in the strategic region. Then, the options become rather paltry and few for such a hard pressed micro nation state.

Hideyuki Takahashi contends in one of his research papers, "The theme of the protection of micro nation states needs to be reasserted and such states fall in the Third World where external threats constitute the omnipresent mercenaries. Maldives has been through periods of insecurity itself during the failed coup."[7] The nation states of the order of Monaco and nationalities and principalities of the order of Vatican and various free trade zones in and around the international polity, tend to be in a precarious state and strategic and political position, where in they require the help and succor of the prominent and powerful nationalities in the region and in the much larger international firmament after getting over and tidying up the much larger and nearer home threats in the realm of internal security in the region and the individual nations.

Internal Conflict and Insecurity as Perceived in the General South Asian Narrative

Maldives is a classic case of a micro state in which it is generally difficult to apply a framework of South Asian conflict with the a redefinition of the theme of Internal security threats to the region as a whole and to the nation state of Maldives in a singularity. A United Nations, report provides us with a framework which can be appended with the situation in Maldives. The UN report contends that, "A Country Peace Commission (CPC) could be established through a legally binding Charter with a statutory body, but enjoy a higher level of independence from the executive than is the case in democratic dispensations for judiciary or election commissions"[8]. Thus, international professional encouragement and assistance is very much the need of the hour for the denizens of Maldives and some such programmatic ministrations and exchanges have been observed with the aid and the succor from United Nations and various international agencies.

Non-Traditional Threats to Maldives and South Asia

The Ford Foundation project on Democracy and Terrorism as part of RCSS, zeroes in, on the following themes:[9]

The South Asian region is significantly prone to both natural and man-made catastrophes. Over the last 25 years, disasters have killed nearly half a million people in South Asia besides inflicting colossal financial damages worth US$ 59,000 million. Over 60,000 people were killed by Tsunami in India, Sri Lanka and Maldives.[10] Thus, Tsunami had a significant factoring impact on the general frailties of the socio-political system in the micro nation state of Maldives and a great deal of Indian and international aid went inside the rubric of the general betterment of the coastal and affected populations in Maldives and in the other contiguous areas in the maritime context. In such micro nation states such as the states of the order of Maldives and Pakistan (the earthquake a few years back), the nationalities have to face the ferment of the Climate change and Global warming which in the context of the nationalities makes them open to the futuristic menace of the inundation by the melting sea caps in the Artic zones leading to the overflowing of low lying coastal regions and islets in the case of a severe metamorphosis in the context of coastal, maritime sea side belts which the micro nation state of Maldives is an instance of.

The scourge of glacial and Artic melting has had a major impact upon the existential dynamics of Maldives with a great deal of attendant political and leadership overtures on the part of the Government of the day. In the year, 2009, along with the marine creatures, in a symbolic exercise undertaken by the Maldives power mandarins, the President of Maldives and his Cabinet wore scuba gear and used hand signals at an underwater meeting to highlight the threat climate change poses to the archipelago nation in order to send a message to the international community and the myriad stake holders involved. At the meeting, the Cabinet signed a declaration calling for global cuts in carbon emissions.[11] *The Telegraph* has reported that it is not internal political violence but Climate change which militates against the fate of Maldives as a territorial expanse. [12]Also, the smaller and micro nation states of the order of Maldives have raised a voice about an international concern to be raised about the swamping of the Islet nations in the gargoyle of rising sea levels as a result of global warming. All this amounts to a general sense of insecurity and uncertainty in an already hard pressed micro nation of the order and categorisation of Maldives.

Environmental Paradigm: The Internal Security in Maldives

As an extension of the Maldives' Government going for a scuba dive, Environmental security moves beyond the environmental segment of the order of interrelated realms such as, Water scarcity, Air Pollution, Energy security, Environment sustainability for the idiom of the age. The Millennium Development Goals too include the themes such as Environmental degradation and resources going dry in the womb of mother nature. The idiom of environmental damage can threaten to security in the region on the whole. This rings true in the context of Maldives.[13]

The Anti-National and Internal Strife in Maldives

The constitutional and the internal establishment in Maldives are spawned like other ordinary nationalities as the internal bureaucratic and administrative structure in this micro nation state of South Asia. Recently, the Maldives Association of Judges communicated a letter to the Chief Judge, which contained the information that the political outfits accused the Judiciary since the separation of powers under the new constitution. The epistle was encouraged by President Mohamed Nasheed's recent criticism of the judiciary. The fundamental freedom of expression in Maldives media was tainted in a recent incident when four men mishandled DhiTV studios and later a Haveeru employee was stabbed in the back, in a related accident.[14] Thus, such a morass which the Maldivian politics can enter into is a kind of political tide which needs to be supplanted by a healthy and mature political culture. It is the plight of smaller islet nation states such as Maldives that the definitiveness of a genuine political culture is not recognised in the norm of a genial political development and as a consequence the repetition of political coups, a want of general accountability of the political class and a circulation of the elites in the firmament of the political system tend to stymie the healthy, transparent and effective rendering of governance in the nation states which are internationally politically and industrially challenged due to the pygmiesation of their national and political character.

The Scourge of Fundamentalism in the Micro Nation State

There is also an internal threat of rising Islamic Fundamentalism in Maldives which is such a sought after hospitable, peaceable Archipelago in the South Asian sub continent.[15] In a related incident, two Maldivian citizens were taken into custody in the context of a violent incident, wherein they carried on their day to day ventures disguised as 'Jewellery repairmen'. The veil controversy which has been till now a concern of the French political scene has erupted anew in the Maldivian firmament. Jennifer Latheef, a Maldivian human rights activist, has contended that, "The number of women wearing the veil has risen dramatically."[16]

In a related incident, Christian Donelan and Jennifer, were injured in a terrorist attack in Male, the capital of the Maldives, but, they were kept unattended as bystanders sparred over as to who would undertake of the expenses for the treatment of the injured protagonists in the terror incident, who[17] were spending their time on a honeymoon. The authorities in the micro nation state of Maldives have contended that such acts of subversion and terrorism tend to vitiate the international visage of Maldives as a kind of much sought after tourist destination along with letting open the Pandora's box over the question of internal security in the State of Maldives which plagues its much larger neighbours of the order of India much so in the besieged State of Jammu and Kashmir which used to be a much sought after tourist destination in the Indian Union. It was in the aftermath of the spread of terrorism in the state, the national tourist destination since ages dwindled into a troubled spot and a security concern for India.

Maldives is facing an eminent terror threat from the anvil of the international terror mongers. Maldives has not suffered a major terrorist attack since 2007, when a bomb exploded at Male's Sultan Park on September 29, injuring 12 tourists of different nationalities.[18] This network is starting to rear its head again in security briefings for the region. Investigations showed that the terror threat from radicalised youths in Maldives had reached high levels with indoctrination being received from Wahabbist schools of thought. The Federal Bureau of Investigation in the year, 2002, arrested Ibrahim Fauzee in Pakistan and he remains under surveillance by Maldives security apparatus.[19]

One author related in one of his statements that, "The fact that Al-Qaeda operatives and Afghan and Pakistan Taliban elements are known to operate in that region further realised the fears that the training had reached a superior level."[20] The role of the Lashkar's patronage to the Maldivian youths is further mentioned that Jamia Salafia Islamia, was the school for Mohamed Halim, Vice-Chief of administration for the Laam atoll.[21] The Islamic Studies Institute in Male has been established in Maldives, wherein students are taught in

Arabic.[22] Thus, fundamentalism seems to be rearing up its ugly head in the nation state of Maldives, where in the scenic beauty and the pastoral quality of lifestyle which is very much tranquil, is being hampered in a considerably significant manner. The international and the universal veneer of the threat of political violence might be in an incipient stage in Maldives but the dangers are there to be seen, perceived and executed upon by all and sundry as observers of the security situation in Maldives.

Tourism happens to be the mainstay of the Maldivian economy and the rise of fundamentalism was not commensurate with a corresponding increase of attacks on foreign tourists in Maldives. The Domestic people visualised the consequences of the foreign clerics in Maldives and in the words of Jennifer Latheef, a local human rights activist "the number of women wearing the veil has risen dramatically[23]". Furthermore, the radicalisation of the state also had an impact on the linguistic culture of the state. The domestic population is being changed not to refer to God 'Maaiyraskalaange' and move on to the nomenclature of 'Allah[24]'.

India has played an active role to counter terror in the nation state of Maldives. The Indian Space Research Organisation facility in southern India was too mired in an espionage incident when a Maldivian national backed was involved in a stratagem to mar the organisation. Lashkar agents perceive Maldivian national's superior knowledge of the sea as a major asset in spreading their terror tentacles.[25]

There has been an advent of the Maldivian and Indian governments to open up floodgates to counter the new brand of 'Sea Terrorism. Maldives is being misused as a principality islet in the larger framework of fundamentalism, which is very much in a neophytic stage in the micro mould in Maldives. Still, as early as in the year, 2003, some activity in the form of political violence has existed in Maldives. One instance has been pointed out by Dr. S. Chandrasekharan, "On September 20, 2003, a large number of people in Male went on a rampage to protest over the killing of a prisoner Naseem in jail. This sparked off riots in the prison and many prisoners were shot."[26] As the Maldivian population is young in age and the impact of economic dissensions have fallen upon them, so the floodgates of infestation by terror modules, has become a grave reality in the nation state of Maldives. Thus, the theme of human rights resuscitation has already emerged in the young and naive political narrative of the nation state of Maldives with all the quintessential trials and tribulations being perceived to exist and having a political impact in Maldives in the accurate realm of internal security in the small and beatific nation.

The Jamestown Foundation of United States of America further highlights the linkage between the nation state of Maldives and the Wahabi influence.

Terrorist organisations such as the dreaded, LeT have attempted to set up bases in uninhabited islands in the Indian Ocean. The Pakistani national daily, *The Dawn*, reported that, "The island paradise has seen attempts by India to take it over and it has rested all attempts at absorption into its larger neighbour. In November 1988, a group of Maldivians headed by Mr. Lutfee, took over the island."[27] Thus, such isolated and scenic locales lying ensconced in the blues of the Indian Ocean are too being tethered to the dust bags of terror mongers by the clandestine and anti-humanity exigencies of the region, now owing their origins and connections to the larger universalistic dictates of the fundamentalist genre which very much infests the expanses in nations such as India and maldives through its variously vicious denominations in the region. Terrorism is a genuine threat to the tourist prospects of Maldives. In one of the UNISCI Discussion papers, Ahmed Niyaz contends that, "Incidents such as the Malé Sultan Park bomb blast and Himandhoo island mosque confrontation in the Maldives suggest that the society is losing its tolerant and moderate nature towards other cultures and ideas."[28] It might be too early to call the micro nation state of Maldives as a terror hub but the portents point in the similar direction if the on-ward march of the terror modules and espionage related centers are not curbed within the territory of Maldives.

Maldives itself has raised a voice internationally through the platform of the hallowed portals of the United Nations in order to circumvent the nebulous cataclysm of terrorism in the South Asian region and particularly in the body politique of the micro nation state of Maldives. The statement of Mohammed Lateef, permanent representative to the United Nations from the Republic of Maldives, contended in one his exhortations to the knighted world body that, "To us in the Maldives, any terrorist attack anywhere brings back memories of the carnage caused by terrorists in our country nearly two decades ago. We have strengthened our national legal framework to counter terrorism."[29]

He further went on to contend that, "However, with the limited human and financial resources at our disposal, for small states like the Maldives, combating the increased activities of international terrorism has always been an uphill battle."[30] Thus, the scourge of international terrorism is not an entity which was unknown and undeciphered about five years back in the micro nation state of Maldives, but it has been the national bone of contention much before the Bali and Philippines terror incidents began to shake the world out of its strategic and pre-ordained slumber.

The internal security scenario and the exercise of maintaining the house in order gets a significant beating in a small nation state with a dearth of national means and natural resources to counter both externally and internally generated threats. This grave conditionality brings about a demand for the bigger and resource rich bigger players in the regional and international firmament to play a role in a 'no-winner takes all' game with an intent to better the internal condition of the next door neighbour which is not as well equipped and gifted to tackle the national challenges of both traditional and non-traditional variants. A philanthropic spirit can do no ill for a better resourced country such as India.

It has been contended that, "These events imply a need to develop policy measures to counter the extremism in the country. For a determined extremist group the Maldives tourism industry is an easy target."[31] Linguistic conflicts, too, exist in Maldives which very much makes this South Asian nation state suffering from a genuinely regional malady on the lines of the language conflicts in India, Bangladesh and Sri Lanka and the race question in South Asia. The lesser said the better about ethnic strife in the region. Chandrasekharan in his paper highlighted that "many critics are quick to blame President Gayoom for past mistakes like the introduction of Arabic in schools in the late 70s and 80s, revision of text books, creation of Arabic medium schools, or letting in all dubious characters[32]".

Some observers contend that there are news reports that India is constructing a premise in the nation state of Maldives which might endanger Pakistan and China and these propagandists further contend that India too has bases in Tajikistan and Afghanistan. This Indian nation state does objectify to circumvent the string of pearls as appended by the Chinese strategists. Thus, the Chinese design of a futuristic stratagem of the encirclement of the Indian Union by extending hands of friendship to the various islets and island nations and regional conclaves including the IOC-ARC rim and the SAARC nation states will amount to a lot if the Indian think tanks do not counter the Chinese move in the Indian Ocean and the threat is further exacerbated by the development of a Blue water navy by the Chinese mandarins in Beijing. If the Indian Union requires a stationing place for it's newly acquired Arihant and the other nuclear submarine, then Maldives can very much serve as a kind of appropriate station which will render good the Han Challenge in the Indian Ocean strategic belt.

In the context of a turbulent world polity which witnessed the notion of convergence and transnational, the American recession along with the attendant developments in Italy and Greece and the consequential crisis in the Euro Zone, the Maldivian applecart too has been unsteadied in the aftermath of the resignation of the President in Male in February, 2012 which comes as a blow to democracy in the Island nation as

Democraty in the real sense of the term took roots in the nation state of Maldives in the year, 2008. Also, the nation was steadied with Indian hands during the tenure of Abdul Gayoom, in the coup year in 1988 by a noble Indian intervention. The Indians still need to replicate the older *avatar* of being a democratic interventionist in the unsteadied political system of Maldives. The person of the order of Abdul Gayoom has been allegedly involved in a conclave with a Judge in Male who was fired by President Mohammed Nasheed.[33] The political crisis leaves the Maldivian nation state in the lurch with more of political instability to follow.

In an interview with the Indian Press, Mohammed Nasheed, contended that, "There is no contradiction between Islam and democracy with a cent percent Muslim population. Maldives now has room for political activism, a Constitution, political parties, free and fair presidential, parliamentary and local elections".[34]

Thus, the outgoing President has been a relentless votary for the terms and conditionalities of a democratic ethos along with a supporter and activist political leader for environmental dangers and the human rights concerns facing Maldives. The underground ministrations of fundamentalism were effectively combated by him during his tenure. His departure from the political firmament can serve as a blow to the idiom of democracy, rule of law and participative governance in the micro nation of Maldives. He contended that Theocracy is a mere front shop for dictatorship, which was never present in Maldives.[35] Also, the nationality of Maldives, cannot be compared with the general activism which has been witnessed in the Middle East principalities along with the notion of Twitter activism which was tailored by the youth in the effected region which later on received the support of their parenthood also once the larger than life and the life changing contour of the movement was realised across all quarters. The micro nation state ought not to become a classic and a test case of observers drawing correlations and differentials between religion and democracy, as even Prophet Mohammed had established the community of

Medina which was one of the earliest hallmarks of religion ordained democracy in historical precedents.

Every nation has its own cultural experience which spawns a political and social system and it is the deft art work of a chosen leader who happens to be in the helm of affairs to amalgamate and sublimely draw blood with the democratic and liberal tenets of the day. The traditionality and the indegeniety of the nation state of Maldives serves as a substratum for a liberal and open society and a deftly practised political system which can severe the civilisation ethos of the nation from the tentacles of illeberalism. Saddam Hussein too was brushed aside in order to usher in an era of reconstruction and rehabilitation. But, Maldives is a different test case in South Asia, altogether which has not been severely tested by the vagaries of fundamentalism. Religion itself is not erroneous but its mutilated interpretations are, a cause of concern internationally. Thus, internal stability in Maldives erupts in a boil which engenders the much feared anarchy but the existence of a well enshrined constitution and rule of law is enough to restore internal order in Maldives.

To Conclude

Thus, Maldives is faced with a great deal of the vitiating impact of international and across- the-sea-terrorism, which has to be taken cognizance of Maldives' happens to be a sea bound nation state and thus it relies upon the support of its power throwing neighbouring states in the South Asian firmament. Thus, the dependency of Maldives and the infliction of fundamentalism cannot be denied which places Maldives in a precarious strategic and political position which needs all the international cooperation and transactions in multilateral, bilateral and regional groupings, all across the North and South divide in the international polity. The nation can emerge as a classic tourist destination as it is imbued with scenic and beatific value in great abundance which need not be marred by the scourge of political instability and terrorism. The Indian role in the year 2012 Regime change in Male also left a lot to be desired as political support for Nasheed would have given an impression to the extended neighbourhood beyond South Asia, as taking political sides but the stringency of a singular stance would have showcased India in a better light with definitely repercussions for the internal polity of Maldives.

References

1. "Maldives: The Largest Group of Islands in the World" (Online: Web), Accessed on 16th July, 2010, URL: http://www.maldives.com
2. In its most common sense, the principle refers to private contracts, stressing that contained clauses are law between the parties, and implies that non-fulfillment of respective obligations is a breach of the pact. The general principle of correct behaviour in commercial practice — including the assumption of *good faith* — is a requirement for the efficacy of the whole system, so the eventual disorder is sometimes punished by the law of some systems even without any direct penalty incurred by any of the parties.
3. Government of India Documents, Ministry of External Affairs, BSM Division, "India Maldives Relations".
4. *Ibid.*
5. "Indo-Maldives Relations,"Accessed on 16th July, 2010 (Online: Web), URL: http://meaindia.nic.in/foreignrelation/maldives.pdf
6. "India's Foreign Policy: Fifty Years of Achievements",(Online: Web), Accessed on 16th July, 2010,URL: http://www.indian embassy.org/policy/Foreign_Policy/fp(intro).ht
7. Hideyuki Takahashi, "Maldivian National Security: The Threats of Mercenaries" (*The Roundtable*, Volume 88, July 1999).
8. Shiva Hari Dahal, Haris Gazdhar, Padmaja Murthy, "Internal Conflict and Regional Security in South Asia: Approaches, Perspectives and Policies" (Online: Web), Accessed on 17th July, 2010,URL: http://www.unidir.org/pdf/ouvrages/pdf-1-92-9045-148-3-en.pdf
9. Dr. Sayyid Riffat Hussein, "Non-Traditional Security Challenges in South Asia" (Online: Web), Accessed on 17th July, 2010, URL: http://webcache.googleusercontent. com/search?

q=cache: 2gx3xuBmU VoJ:www.rsis-ntsasia.org/resources/publications/policy-briefs/

10. *Ibid.*
11. "From Underwater, Maldives sends warning on Climate Change", URL: http://articles.cnn.com/2009-10-17/world (Online: Web), Accessed on 19th December, 2011.
12. "Island States Criticise the slow progress on Climate Change" URL;:http://www.telegraph.co.uk/earth/environment/climate change/8868655 (Online: Web), Accessed on 19th December, 2011.
13. *Ibid.*
14. "Maldives in Brief: Judges Association Vs Chief Judge" (Online: Web), Accessed on 17th July, 2010, URL: http://www. asian tribune.com/news/2010/03/17/maldives-brief-judges-association -vs-chief-judge
15. "Maldives were warned of Islamic Danger" (Online: Web), URL: http://www.telegraph.co.uk/news/uknews/1564729/Maldives-were-warned-of-Islamic-danger.html
16. *Ibid.*
17. Peter Foster, "Maldives Bomb Couple With Air Ambulance Fight" (Online: Web), Accessed on 17th July, 2007, URL: http:/ /www.telegraph. co.uk/news/uknews/1564728/Maldives-bomb-couple-win-air-ambulance-fight.html
18. "Two British tourists injured in bomb attack on Maldives" (*The Independent, 30 September, 2007*).
19. B. Raman, "Al Qaeda in Maldives - International Terrorism Monitor"-Paper No. 308", South Asia Analysis Group, 19 November, 2007 (Online: Web), Accessed on 20th July, 2010, URL:www.southasiaanalysis.org/%5Cpapers25 %5Cpaper 2466.html
20. *Ibid.*
21. Swami, Praveen, "Maldives: militant Islamists on the rise" (Chennai: *The Hindu*, 24 November, 2008).
22. Upadhyay, R., "Islamic Radicalisation of Maldives", *South Asia Analysis Group,* paper 2610, 7 March, 2008 (Online: Web), Accessed on 20th July, 2010,URL:http://www.south asia analysis. org/%5Cpapers27%5 Cpaper 2610.html
23. Maldives were 'warned of Islamic danger', (*The Telegraph,* 1 October, 2007).

24. Upadhyay, *op. cit.* (Online: Web), Accessed on 17th July, 2010,URL: http://www.southasiaanalysis.org/%5Cpapers27%5Cpaper2610.html
25. Swami, Praveen, "INDIA: Mumbai: The Road to Maximum Terror" (*South Asia Intelligence Review,* volume 7 number 23, 15 December, 2008).
26. "Misuse of Terrorism Laws Should Cease", URL: http://www.southasiaanalysis.org (Online: Web), Accessed on 18th December, 2011.
27. "Pakistan and China Should Save Maldives From Indian Clutches" (Online: Web), Accessed on 20th July, 2010, URL: http://thedawn.com.pk/2009/08/20/pakistan-and-china-should-save-maldives-from-indian-clutches.
28. Ahmed Niyaz, "Terrorism and Extremism: A Threat to Maldives Tourism Industry" URL: http://www.ucm.es/BUCM/revistas (Online: Web), Accessed on 19th December, 2011.
29. Statement of the Representative of the Republic of Maldives to the United Nations, 10th October, 2005.
30. *Ibid.*
31. *Ibid* http://www.rediff.com/news/slide-show/slide-show-1-how-maldives-is-fast-becoming-lets-terror-hub/20111121.htm
32. Chandrasekharan, S. (2007), "Maldives: Sultan Park Explosion-Dealing with Religious Extremism" *South Asia Analysis Group*, no. 2476, at http://www.southasiaanalysis.org/%5Cpapers25%5Cpaper2476.html
33. See *Indian Express*, 7th February, 2012.
34. See *Indian Express*, 8th February, 2012.
35. *Ibid.*

10

The Indigenous War Against Terror Mongers: The Prime Anti-National Threat

Threat to the Beleaguered Indian Nation State

"Acquiring weapons for the defense of Muslims is a religious duty. If I have indeed acquired these weapons [of mass destruction], then I thank God for enabling me to do so."

Osama bin Laden as interviewed in Time Magazine in December, 1998.

Notwithstanding the question as to whether or not Osama bin Laden has acquired nuclear weapons, the world must respond as though he has, and that too without fail. Stability and peace, if is to be restored, governments all across the political and economic divide need to acknowledge its brute reality. A comprehensive assessment of current threats and a coherent strategy for combating the same in a wholesome manner is the need of the hour. Public opinion never came around to concede its inception with the unprovoked attacks in India and Israel, but only when a real threat seemed portent after 9/11, did the US set in stone its policy of a global war against terrorism, relegating public opinion to the backburner[1]. The exhausting exigencies of the current crisis could all be traced back to damage to American naval property in the form of assailing of the USS Cole and the horror of September 11 that made the international community sit up and take notice of a potent threat to the "international peace and security" as embalmed in the United Nations founding Charter.

India faced its initial brunt of the menace of terrorism through the demand of a separate nation state in the form of Khalistan which was spawned as a result of Operation Blue Star and the names of Tarantaran and the sacred Golden temple lie embalmed in the memories of the people all for the wrong reasons and rationales of separatism, though, the State of Punjab is known to serve along with Rajasthan as the traditional bulwark against foreign aggression of the physical genre so the State of Punjab going the way of terror path did add to the misery of a beleaguered Indian nation state. Who can but forget the daily news bytes from the news channels accounting for the staid statistics of the killed Punjabi youth and the assertions from Canada and Britain about a need for the liberation of the Sikhs in those dark days of the Indian Republic. The North-East definitively remained a threat from much earlier time period, but only as a hoary non-mainstream threat which could not at anytime climb down from the remote heights in the North-East much to the glee of New Delhi. Still India is no stranger to terrorism and the attendant parabola of destruction attached to life and property all translating into playing havoc with the law and order entitlements of the state.

For functional purposes, the terror apparatus in the international polity can be divided into the twin categorisations of the suppressor and the suppressed nation states. The countries which are supporting both directly and indirectly the menace of terrorism and insurgency and low intensity warfare in other nation states are termed as suppressor nation states'. The nation states of the order of Sudan, Islamic Republic of Pakistan, Cuba and the nation states of the order of Saudi Arabia, Iran and Iraq can be clubbed under this categorisation of the 'rogue nation states', which are able to spawn 'terror modules' and 'sleeper cells' in the neighbouring nation states or plainly in the name of an 'international armageddon' conspiratorially perched against the United States of America and the so-called 'neo-imperialistic agencies' of the international polity. This is a western nomenclature as perceived by the 'rest'.

Then, there are those nation state actors such as India, Israel, the US and the UK which fall prey to the diabolic designs of the terror modules and sleeper cells funded and patronised by the suppressor states and are to be termed as suppressed states. The modules have an obsessive and omnipresent focus on these states among their leaders and strategists and this ubiquitous threat has permeated the entire body *politik* and now only when it looms as a 'clear and present danger' to the US that it has lumbered along supporting India as the receptacle of terrorism in the region. Thus, only when the moments of revelation came thick and fast since the 9/11 did the US acknowledge that India has been subjected to the same malady which is the much festooned and demonic and diabolic visage of international terrorism, since the last two tumultuous decades.

The actions in India which have elicited sharp denunciations of Pakistan for its sustenance of the groups responsible were in the nature of super-terrorism, a doctrine which involves a deft utilisation of the resources and infrastructure of the state that is to be attacked. The Aum Shinrikyo cult's using sarin nerve gas has raised the eyes and radars of the international experts who are tackling the scourge of terrorism of which India as a nation state is a sad victim despite its assertion of the principles of non-alignment and peaceful co-existence with the neighbours of the South Asian region.[2] Super terrorism happens to be a phenomenon, wherein the personages of the terror groups deliberately choose a node, which is a hub of habitation such as a shopping mall, cinema hall, railway station, airport terminals, market places and temples in the latest edition of terror strategies. Apart from these, the internodes, too, can be attacked which are the interconnectivities between, let's say, two internodes which comprise of railway tracks, highways, roads between city centers, telegraph and internet superhighways and other such connectivity ordained paraphernalia. Thus, the terror mongers intend to deftly and cannily utilise the infrastructure of the targeted nation state in order to rely less on the weaponisation of their operation, but pit the state against the state. Also, as an instance, the highways in uninhabited regions in the country scape in states like United States of America tend to be attacked in a strategic fashion. Also, the power distribution network in the form of an sequestered electricity transformer can be attacked by letting loose an avalanche of iron fillings through a gas balloon mounted on a high truck which will gradually incapacitate the power distributing transformer which will eventually curtail and deaden the wires supplying electricity to the nearest 'Node' in the region's habitation.

Thus, such innovative but deleterious schemes intended to destabilise the state will lead to the subversion of the state supplies leading to a dark age thus eliciting looting and arson and community violence in the darkened region or the city which only a psychedelic *Batman and robin* with a gymnast, "*Alicia Silverstone* can only tackle, when the security apparatus of the community" has given way to a complete situation of anarchy and pandemonium hurtling the state in the existentiality of neophytic organicity. The strange case of such a scare scenario can be easily replicated in an Indian and South Asian setting too, with much more of an ease and devastating impact as the internodes remain unchecked and no patrolling takes place in the interior regions and the inner countryside for months together. This happens to be not a mere harking back to the days of a 'Mad Maxian' futuristic dystopia, where in the tenets of dusty rebellion along with a withered human visage looms large over the country-scape, as Mel Gibson, the blue eyed male protagonist/highway cop lets loose his guns and bikes over the murderous gangs of the vast and inundated ravines of South Australia much in the tradition of the American wild west.

Alexander and Hoening define terrorism as the calculated employment or threat of violence by individuals, sub-national and state actors to attain political, social and economic objectives in violation of law, intended to create an overwhelming fear in a target area larger than the victims attacked or threatened.[3] Nation states such as US, India and Israel are at a heightened risk today than ever before. The psychological damage which is caused to a person wilting under the notion of 'relative deprivation,' can thus be an origin and a root cause of the existence and the functioning of such terror modules in India with young people's psychology being mutilated and scarred by the diatribes, repetition and an amplification of the ills and sins committed by the state apparatus in a mad cap drive to attain superlatives of the order of 'good governance' and 'best practices' in the context of the region, individual, national and the international scenario.

The History of Terrorism

The history of terror mongers in the nation state can be conveniently related to the international ramifications of the terror threat in the global polity. The days of anarchism in the European and the French society and polity all the way to the IRA and the Basques in the European scenario have been replicated in the Indian scenario too, where in a strong and well resourced nation state actor is pitted against a weak but phoenix like non-state actors which are perennially on the look out for a 'spectacular effect' of gargantuan proportions in the larger rubric of things. The history of terrorism at least dates back to 1500 years wherein the people in Jewish lands were made the victims. Zealots killed Roman soldiers and destroyed Roman property. The term assassin comes from a Shi'ite Muslim sect (Nizari Isma'ilis also known as hashashins 'hashish-eaters') fighting Sunni Muslims (1090-1275) and during Medieval Christendom resisting occupation during the Crusades (1095-1291).[4] But, ancient Greek historian Xenophon contends that, "The effectiveness of psychological warfare against enemy populations is of paramount significance amongst the observers, commentators and the victims of terrorism."[5]

In the Indian context, the days of Sikh militancy, the Lal Denga days along with the mayhem and the blood bath in the state of Jammu and Kashmir has led to the hiking of security imperatives directed towards scathing the menace of terrorism in the nation. A report in the Week contends that, "A recent haul of weaponry has been ceased in the Chittagong jetty, in the nation state of Bangladesh, where in the weapons originated from Qindiang in China, all the way across the nationalities of Thailand, Vietnam, Myanmar and finally setting foot upon the Bangladeshi soil."[6] The report further contends that the top most functionaries of the Bangladeshi intelligence agencies too have been made inroads in by the Pakistan's ISI with direct assistance to ULFA and other organisations in the north eastern section of the nation.[7]

Sikh militancy has more or less disappeared from the State of Punjab but reports about the Canadian and European connections reflect towards the fact that the pot is still boiling somewhere and another heady brew might be in the offing. It was contended by the Intelligence Bureau Chief, Mr. Mathur, that, "There have been clear attempts by inimical agencies abroad to reactivate Sikh terrorist elements, forge nexus between LeT and terrorist groups like Babbar Khalsa International and the Khalistan Zindabad Force."[8] The attitude of the government along with the sense of alienation being felt by the Sikh youth fuelled the fire of militancy in the northern State of Punjab which had always acted as the frontal frontier of the nation at large along with the role played by the Royals of the Rajputana. In the words of Birender Pal Singh, Punjab University, Patiala, the Indian government categorised the militants as separatists and fundamentalists, while on the contrary the militants were seen to be fighting for a 'just cause' which meant their rights against socio-economic and political discrimination along with a clear self perception, a distinct goal and a professed logic of violence in their struggle against the state.[9] He further goes on to contend that the agricultural, economic, the rural and the religious idiom of the State of Punjab can be factored in as the dissatisfaction of the hoi-polloi in the Punjab state. The juxtaposition of all these factors led to the tumult in Punjab with a specific and characteristic security dilemma.

The Indian Context of Terrorism

The Indian scenario is replete with its characteristic hues and chromaticities. Right from the dreadfully flawed equations, between Jarnail Singh Bhindranwale and Prime Minister Indira Gandhi that led to the latter's demise, down to her son's assassination at the hands of the LTTE, challenge to the state power has swept the entire countryside today from beleaguered Jammu and Kashmir to the besieged North-East and the ravaged estuaries of Sri Lanka. Ever since the Instrument of Accession was signed by the then Hindu Maharaja Hari Singh, trouble started brewing as Pakistan launched its *Kabaili* invasion while India came to its aid, demanding its legitimate suzerainty in return[10].

The gory incident of partition created two antagonistic nations of the order of the Indian Union and the Islamic Republic of Pakistan and the Kashmir schism along with the lore of the Pakistani interventionism in the internal matters of India along with the flawed decision of Prime Minister Jawaharlal Nehru to internationalise the *Kabaili* incursion by taking recourse to the portals of United Nations Security Council. This has been the norm of legend and the lore of the incessant and perennial contest between India and Pakistan. Horace Alexander relates how on 22nd October, Pathan tribesman recruited by the Poonch dissenters rode into Kashmir, looting and killing whatever came their way, as a revenge for the killing of their Muslim brethren.[11] The matter was sealed and the much vitriol which has been spawned between the twin estranged neighbours has been a figment of political legerdemain with the political mandarins playing the game of one-upmanship, which also is the origin of the Pakistan sponsored tenet of 'bleeding india white' by the stratagem of fomenting internal dissensions in India through the creation of Inter Services Intelligence sponsored terror modules, midwived by Pakistani origin terror groups of the order of Lashkar-I-Toiyaba, Hurkat-Ul-Ansar, Hijb-I-Mujahideen along with the latest edition of the terror dragnet in the form of the Indian Mujahideen. A state's intentions are not being questioned over here but the drift of the neighbour which might be on an irreversible trajectory, makes for a primal cause of concern.

Thus, the Pakistani terror spawning in India is also part of a grand vendetta as India supported the nascent rebellion in the nation state of Bangladesh through the year, 1971's war and the complete Pakistani apparatus since then has been geared towards the garnering of dissensions and spiteful propaganda against a much more powerful, stable, democratic and an internationally valued India after the initiation of the liberalisation, privatisation and globalisation policies since the momentous year of the year, 1991. Differences in interpretation of the procedure for demilitarisation on both sides failed to give out a concrete message as it was still unclear whether the Azad Kashmiri army was to be disbanded at the truce stage or during the plebiscite stage.[12] Communal violence has been the bane of the peace scenario in the State of Jammu and Kashmir. Pandits become the latest victims of communal retaliation, a motivation which JKLF denies and any future reconciliation efforts between the two communities are actively discouraged by Jagmohan leading to the exodus of estimated 162,500 Hindus from the Valley by the end of March.[13]

Other stories apart from the dehumanisation and the alienation of the Kashmiris from the Indian mainstream too need to be heard to arrive at a completely wholesome and a fulsome picturisation of the terror situation in the State of Jammu and Kashmir. Praveen Swami draws a searing picture in which the Hindu partisan-led Village Defence Committee backed by the Army and the Muslim militia in their supposed defense of the Muslim community have fed each other, leading to the killing of 307 Hindus and 377 Muslims in Doda and Rajauri districts in 1998.[14]

The troubled North-East has always been traditionally out of bounds ever since access was restricted, and entry was granted only upon the furnishing of special permits from the Centre in five of the seven sisters barring Meghalaya and Assam. Being plagued with inter-ethnic clashes, unceasing separatist demands and dreadful insurgencies, it has earned the unenviable and proverbial epithet of 'sick man' of India.[15] The North-East has now become India's neglected child.[16] Renaud Egretaeu laments that the North-East has become a strategic area adequate enough to acquire proportions of a 'dangerous cross-roads of instability' with the advent of globalisation as with the setting up of external linkages, the strife by the insurgent groups have spilled over to neighbouring countries and the regional underground networks.[17]

Wajahat Habibullah, a renowned bureaucrat who served as the Information Commissioner of the State of Jammu and Kashmir, has suggested a novel way of containing the situation in Kashmir by festooning the flank of governance in the frontline.

The author advocating for the hapless disposition of women, who though are not the primary instigators of war and conflict figure adequately among their victims and yet the activities they engage in during times of conflict, are, the ones which prepare ground for peace to return. Any modicum for relief after this is snatched away by violence at home.[18] The Marxist notion of 'Estranguffen' i.e., alienation in German, bears resonance here. The notion encapsulates a four-fold alienation felt by the people with the advent of industrialisation in the Occidental developmental pattern which leads to the disaffection of the citizen-cum-worker from the human race itself. Thus, the seeds of rebellion are sown here where the government of the day is increasingly seen as an instrumentality of violence and exploitation.[19] In the Cuban context, Che Guevara apart from being a rebellious personage pitted against the menace and the all arching tentacles of neo-imperialism as reflected by the legerdermian of nation states such as United States and other colonial conquistadors of the European ilk, instituted agrarian reforms. He also served as a national bank president, donned the cap of instructional director of the armed forces and traversed the globe as a Cuban diplomat.[20] His work, Motor cycle diaries has grave consequences for the instigators and the rebels alike. His works and life are blazing a trail of glory with the cornucopia of Che t-shirts and his attendant memorabilia which inspire generations of youth since his demise in an uncharted and untrajectoried conflict in Latin America and much of the 'beyond'.

The North-Eastern concerns further on in India, too, pinpoint towards the notion that social conflict is a significant pointer in the direction of the troubles in India. The people of Mizoram for instance were faced with the rise of Mizo National Front (MNF) which put to demise the political and the statal fortunes of the political outfits such as the Mizo Union (MU) and the UMFO (United Mizo Freedom Organisation) which were sharing the power and political pelf in the confines of the Lushai Hills which was the nomenclature given to the Autonomous District Council near the State of Assam which happens to be the receptacle and the symbolic force of exploitation and regional and developmental prejudices against the people and the authentic concept of the 'Mizo-ness,' of the people and the tribal denizens residing in the state of Mizoram while it was emerging out of the colonial rule and the attendant divisive policies in the larger and the general realm of the North-Eastern region of the Indian state. Thus, akin to the threat of the ULFA and the MNF, the Lal Denga's (the ideologue and the person chaperoning the MNF) philosophy surmises the tribal discontent and asymmetry with the Indian nation state.

Lal Denga goes on to contend in an excerpt that, "The Mizos from time immemorial lived in complete independence... the Mizo people are inseparably linked through bonds of tradition, custom, language and religion, whereever they are. The Mizo people feel that they have never felt one with India and have never been able to share the joys and sorrows with the Indian nation."[21] Thus, the North-Eastern imbroglio happens to be that of a permeating nature which has engulfed the national security super structure in the 'Far East' of the Indian nation state. Insurgencies[22] have recurrent patterns in various places and stations and if a cookkie cutter approach of 'shock and awe' does not suit the need of the strife torn area then an ink blot approach might as well work. Still, the conflict of insurgencies and terror acts in the North-East remains that of insurgents and counter insurgents which inevitably remains a conflict between the human forces within an improved and an enhanced high technology and high communication, 'small wars'. Internationally, too, the cult of rebellion has been much posited as an act of freedom from tyranny and oppression.

In the international hall of fame, after de-boarding from the old, creaky cabin cruiser, the Granma that served as their primary transport, 82 of their comrades fell prey to bullets fired from the guns of Batista's military, and only 22 survived and it was here when Che picked up a box of ammunition dropped by a fleeing comrade and figuratively speaking, underwent transformation from physician to combatant. The life and times of Guevara continues to serve as an unceasing source of inspiration for many youngsters in India, where in in the face of exploitative and lopsided development patterns, they hold a candle not to legends of the likes of Maharana Pratap or Netaji Bose but rather lean towards equating the crass pandemonium and anarchy as an upshot of the Western imperialistic policies, in effect fostering mass upsurge against the Indian state apparatus. Such centripetal tendencies are in the long haul deleterious for the survival of the Indian nation-state or for that matter any normalcy loving nation state in the South Asian

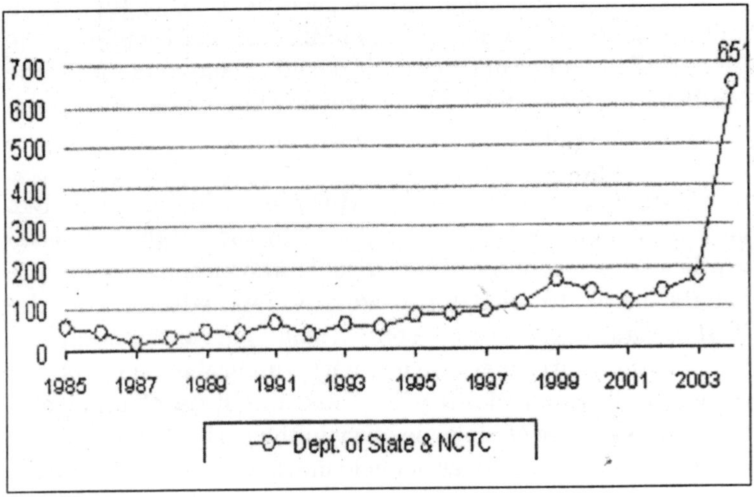

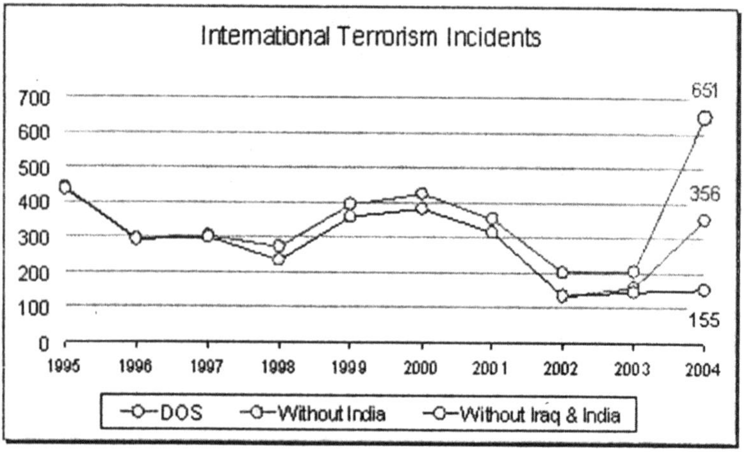

subcontinent to utilise an older terminology. This notional dream for anything anti-establishment and self-determination runs riot in the imagination of the young minds of some of the younglings and this foments neophytic revolutionaries that challenge state authority, a temperament capitalised upon by our neighbours to the west and north through arms and propaganda supply.

The cult of rebellion can be further surmised with the aid of the psycho-socio set up of the separatists and the avowed terrorist running asunder the democratic ethos of the nation and the South Asian region in general. Van Der Dennen in the context of the ethos of the cult of rebellion contends that, "The conflict is basically the one of contrasting human nature, where-in it is an amalgam of highly complex and elaborate constructs of reality. Man also creates psychologically distancing devices, to dehumanise, diabolise, to exterminate his enemies like vermin in fantasy."[23] The sociologist in the context of social conflict further contends that, "People who metamorphose into rebels tend to cultivate worldviews which are the *Weltanchauunegen* in which only a small part of the humanity fits. Furthermore, men have a very vulnerable sense of self esteem and group identity"[24]. Thus, the state of mind of a terrorist is a state of art gone awry in the early romanticism of the days of yore which does not hold much water in an utilitarian and instant *nirvana* world of the contemporary times. The state shuns all but not an insurgent.

Some Interesting Statistics about Terror in India

Terrorism has been there right from the start. Cain committed the first murder known in human history. Al Qaeda has been in many ways an exception to the generally held notions of terrorism as they have no reason or logic and are never open to any dialogue, and till now no attempt has been made to at least talk with them.[25] The ugly contours of terrorism took shape with the gruesome Munich massacre in 1972 followed by recurring events of plane hijackings and this has now developed into a more ghastly and macabre mode of 'human shields' and 'suicide bombers'[26]. The year, 2011, was very acceptable as a year when the casualties were of lesser nature in number and the year 2012 reflects a trend which pinpoints towards the fact that by July, 2012, around 93 casualties have been already recorded in the year.

The argument here should run as that, to begin with poverty creates fertile ground that provide succor and sustenance to terrorists who in turn find a support base and safe haven amongst the general populace who are alienated from the world order which the terrorists are ostensibly attacking and militating against. It is not just poverty but a sense of exclusion and marginalisation that people are driven to support and orchestrate terrorism as the only hope for outwitting the political dispensation that alienates them, but can symbolic violence earn the earth and the world for the same runs the poignant question. The thematic reality of class finds a pervasive resonance in the notion of a terror war 4,108 terrorist incidents occurred in India between the years 1970 and 2004. During this period, India ranked sixth among all countries in terms of terrorist incidents (behind Peru, Colombia, El Salvador, the United Kingdom and Northern Ireland and Spain).[27]

The National Counter Terrorism Center report, its questionable methodology notwithstanding, claims that there were 651 significant international terrorist incidents in 2004, from 175 in 2003 out of which 295 could be attributed to militant action in Kashmir.

The Rand Corporation does not mention any incident for India in 2004 while the State Department pegs it at 53. This is probably a result of Rand having historically applied a narrower definition of terrorism.[28] Thus, there happens to be an inherent discrepancy in the estimates concerning the terror victims in India and the South Asian region as a whole. The United States as a responsible nation and the international super cop in the visage of Uncle Sam turned a transient blind eye to the notion of Indian claims in the early nineties that India had been a victim of Pakistani transformed terror module perpetrated as a vendetta regimen against the nation state of India to tide over the national loss and humiliation of the year, 1971. Thus, even the Under Secretary of United States's State Department, Robin Raphael, contended that India ought not to blame the State of Pakistan at accentuating an imagined proxy war against the nation state of India. This infuriated the public opinion against the Americans in India but the Indian diplomatic and marketing vigil did not have much of an impact upon the foreign policy mandarins of United States in a world which had not witnessed the *'Boomrang phenomenon"* in the form of the Black Tuesday and the September 11 catastrophe in the context of the World Trade Tower bombing and gutting. Thus, when United States was awakened to the threat of international and cross border terrorism in the case of India, that India was able to fight forth with its case as a regional victim of terrorism in the South Asia. It was only that the spectacle of terror mongering came of its own age in the regional and the international context that the universality of the locally violent concerns came to be realised by the great powers of the international polity.

Margaret Atwood, contended in the Oxford Book of War Poetry, in the year 1988 that, "Even my passive eyes transmute everything I look at to the pocked black and white of a war photo, how can I stop myself, it is dangerous to read newspapers, each time I hit a key on my electric typewriter speaking of peaceful trees, another village explodes."[29] The condition of peace is a much wanted conditionality in a strife torn region or a nation state which the poet yearns for in the thematic sense of the term. The idiom of persistent reportage of the terror spectacles in the State of Jammu and Kashmir and the region of North-Eastern states in the Indian Union is sought to be strived for by the national government. No critical discourse[30] on political violence can be complete in the absence of consideration of the means by which humanity could transcend the conditions of war and internal strife which India and South Asia have witnessed in the context of the scourge of terrorism and separatism. Under the rubric of the Christian edicts of Saint Augustine and Saint Thomas Aquinas, the war and the struggle for justice had to be fought in the context of a 'Just cause'. This leads to the notion that the struggle being waged by terror groups in India also attribute their causes to the notion of a 'Just and an avowed cause,'[31] which replicated itself in the shape and form of an 'international' edifice of ideology which permeates the nook and cranny of the terror ideologues in the global firmament. Also, the norm setting of the international law, which some contend is no law at all, also finds it difficult to tackle the international and converging phenomenon of global and cross border terrorism.

Thus, the genre and the *avatar* of cross border terrorism which India and the South Asian firmament in South Asia faces is definitely ensued by the neighbours which has *belied* all expectations of a staunch and stable understanding in the context of multiple and myriad mechanisms of confidence building measures between the twin antagonists of the order of India and Pakistan in the South Asian firmament. 'The discourse ethics', of conflict indicates an enunciation of communicative action through the folds of iterative games betwixt the various nation states especially in the context of the South Asian region. The theme of terror imports to India very much falls in tandem with the International relations theory doctrine of prisoner's dilemma and chicken hunt, wherein the notion of uncertainty and the want of mutual trust, faith and reciprocity leads to the notion of an uncomfortable and suspicious existence between the adversarial nations in the immediate context of bilateral and internal conflict.[32] The terror imports to India are not random in nature and they tend to transfix the comprehension of the political mandarins and the national security mandarins of the country as a long pronged and a futuristic strategy of tackling terrorism needs to be coalesced out of the multiplicity of incidents which mar the internal security fabric of the Indian nation state.

References

1. Kumar, Rajiv and Menon, Admiral Raja, "The Long View from Delhi: To Define the Indian Grand Strategy for Foreign Policy," 2010, Academic Foundation, New Delhi, pp. 236, 258.
2. Adam Dolnik (2002), "Thirteen Years Since Tokyo: Revisiting the Super-Terrorism Debate" (Perspectives on Terrorism, Volume 2, Issue 2, 2002).
3. Yonah Alexander, Milton Hoening (2001), "Super Terrorism: Biological, Chemical and Nuclear", (New York: Transnational Publishers, 2001).
4. "The History of Terrorism-More than 200 Years of Development" (Online: Web), URL: http://cjc.delaware.gov/terrorism/history.shtml, Accessed on 19th December, 2011.
5. "The History of Terrorism" URL: http://www.terrorismfiles.org/encyclopaedia/history_of_ terrorism.html, (Online: Web), Accessed on 19th December, 2011).
6. See *The Week*, 15th December, 2011.
7. *Ibid.*
8. "Sikh Militants, LET Trying to Revive Terrorism in Punjab", *The Economic Times*, New Delhi, 25th August, 2010.
9. Birender Pal Singh, "Rise of Sikh Militancy and Militant Discourses: An Appeiasal of the Economic factor" Paper presented at the Summer Conference of the Association of Punjab Studies held at the Oxford on 25th June, 2005.
10. Vohra, Kiran, Enemies at Rest: The Simla Agreement, New India Publishing House, 1995.
11. Horace Alexander (1952), "Kashmir" (London: 1952, p. 8).

12. UNCIP Resolution, 5 JANUARY, 1949; UNCIP Resolution, 13 August, 1948; UNCIP Resolution, 30 March, 1951; *Official Records of the United Nations Security Council*, Meeting No. 534, 6 March, 1951, pp.13-20.
13. Pankaj Mishra (2002), "Kashmir: The Unending War," (2002)
14. Praveen Swami, *The Kargil War*, New Delhi, 1999, pp.71-2.
15. S. K. Sinha (2002), " Violence and Hope in India's North East ," (New Delhi: *Faultlines*, Volume 10, 2002). S. K. Sinha, a former Governor of Assam, was also Vice- Chief of Army Staff in India.
16. Rammohan, E.N., Insurgent Frontiers: Essays from the Troubled North-East, 2005, pp. 45-51, 54.
17. Renaud Egretaeu (2006), "Instability At The Gate: India's Troubled North-East and Its External Connections" (Online : Web), Accessed on 1st of March, 2010, URL: http://www.csh-delhi.com/publications/downloads/ops/OP16.pdf
18. "Missing Links in Sustainable Development: South Asian Perspectives" (Online: Web), Accessed on March 28th, 2010, URL: http://www .sdpi.org/9thsdc/sd_conferences.htm
19. Karl Marx, (2001), "The German Ideology" (New York: International Publishers, 2001).
20. Rodriguez, Felix & John Weisman, Shadow Warrior: The CIA's Hero of a Hundred Unknown Battles, 1989, pp. 21-22.
21. Eds. N. Jayaram, Satish Saberwal, "Social Conflict," (New Delhi: Oxford University Press, 1996). pp. 165-167.
22. *Ibid*
23. Eds. N. Jayaram, Satish Saberwal, "Social Conflict," (New Delhi: Oxford University Press, 1996) pp.15-17.
24. *Ibid.*
25. Kennedy, Baroness Helena, Legal Conundrums in our Brave New World, Sweet and Maxwell Ltd, London, 2004, pp. 234-35.
26. *Ibid.*
27. "India Terrorism By Numbers : Statistics From University of Maryland Global Terrorism Database" (Online: Web), Accessed on March 28th, 2010, URL: http://www.newsdesk.umd.edu/sociss/release.cfm? ArticleID=1797.
28. *Ibid.*
29. Margaret Atwood, 'The Oxford Book of War Poetry (United Kingdom:1988).

30. Vivienne Jabri, "Discourses on Violence: Conflict Analysis Reconsidered, (Manchester: Manchester University Press, 1996), p. 145.
31. E.D. Vattel, "The Law of Nations," (AMS Press, New York, 1987).
32. See Bayllis and Smith "Globalisation of World Politics".

11

The Myth of Benign Neighbourhood: Neighbourly Contributions to India's Internal Security

A country's ability to pursue interests for its own sake is contingent on its management of relations with neighbours. India being the proverbial benign, non-interfering neighbour has extended its hands too often in the neighbourhood, though this act of brotherly disposition has not been wholesomely reciprocated by nation states of the ilk of Pakistan, Sri Lanka, Bangladesh and Nepal. Themes in academic debates have gone from India being a benign superpower to a neighbourhood bully, the country has been for long tolerant towards its neighbours, especially in the case of China, the most significant determinant of Indian foreign policy. With an aim of collective good in mind[1], the discourse on democracy has been put paid while it does business pragmatically with Pakistan's military regimes, all this while one knows that a truly democratic system in Pakistan would limit the influence of both the armed forces and extremist groups. Also, India hankers and longs for a trail of benignness in the South-Eastern nation states[2]. AK Verma, a prime observer on South Asian security, expresses cautions at the steady rise of China in terms of its military and economic might as it readies itself to be the main counteract to the US. India is the unlikeliest of nations to have earned the uncalled for sobriquet of a 'benign hegemon', a country known for its glorious Nehruvian past. Be it the Mahakali Treaty with surrogate Nepal or the exchange of blasé pleasantries with Begum Khaleda Zia on border segregation and insurgency in the North-East. India has had always clamoured for collective co-operation and growth of the sub-continent and it goes without saying that a lot needs to be done on the part of its neighbours in acknowledging its benign and generous ministrations despite it being scathed with unceremonious and illegitimate ingresses[3] of insurgent and separatist forces. India's benign face and regional policy needs to be studied and narrated upon as the nation is truly emblematic of the South Asian sub-continent in the truest sense of the term and though the world is realistically ordained, the notion of India getting its rightful place in the friendly nations pantheon is the need of the hour in the South Asian context and structurally all so significant, thus emerges the need to discourse upon the 'Benign' nature of Indian foreign policy and its meandering but well meaning attitude towards its neighbours with whom it shares contiguous borders and others too not so far off in the regional realm.

Aiding in and abetting of terrorism activities by the hydra-headed juggernaut of the Army-ISI combine is consistent with the 'scarring India with a thousand wounds' policy as was espoused by a renowned Pakistani head of state. When such a gross and scathing violation of the diplomatic norms are committed by a head of state and when the Indian Union merely asserted itself in the norm of the commonly available foras, then, the palaver and the general understanding of the people and their leaders in the South Asian sub-continent cannot be of a negativist genre if the overall and comprehensive picture of the camaraderie in South Asian comity has to be comprehended and an organisational and systemic understanding in the norms of an European Union in the days of 'Erstraz Capitalism' has to be comprehended. Thus, the military and the defense aspects of a new South Asia need not dominate the discourse and the narrative in the realm of the sub-continent but a soft security idiom ought to be the guising light of the day.

India has never played the role of a history sheeter with a 'Big brotherly' attitude with the notion of a regional hegemon being attached to the Indian standpoints in the multivariate issues in the South Asia region. India cannot be construed as a benign hegemon in any sense of the term in the light of the ministrations of the United States of America and the People's Republic of China in the context of the Asia Pacific region and the larger Asian *millue*. Great Britain can be considered as the Benign hegemon in the pre-independence days of the Indian Union but not an independent and democratic India as we as a nation state were the champions of the right of self-determination and freedom the Asian *minnows* of the order of Burma, Sri Lanka and Indonesia and much before the hey day of the Hindi-Chini Bhai-Bhai days, the Indians were supporting the claim of PRC to become a full fledged member of the international institutions. History showcases it all.

Realistically speaking, the Chinese interest in the South Indian region needs to be countered by the Indian action and pro-activeness as the various nations of the order of Nepal, Bhutan and Bangladesh are being wooed by the expansionist designs of the People Republic of China. It would be naïve to compare the Indian position in South Asia with that of Russia in the Central Asian region. Professor Stephen Blank has written that, "Russian specialists also have developed a plan to re-establish a common CIS energy space including and threatening the Baltic states, and of late, the three South Caucasian Republics"[4]. India's parallel inclination in the pantheon of development activities meant for the development of the South Asian states, will definitively accrue with some gains for the country as part of a bargaining or a non-bargaining scenario along with a strategic and political pedestal. The term benignity can be conveniently associated with the Indian state but not the notion of hurtling hegemony as it leads to a negativist positioning of the nation state of India which merely earns good breathing space for stiffer challenges ahead by fostering a tradition of good trend of friendly ties with the South Asian neighbours.

Paul H. Godwin contends that, "Few doubt that China is now a great power. China's population and land area are huge, and its geopolitical location means that no part of Asia is without a Chinese presence or interest"[5]. Thus, the theme of a hegemonic Chinese Monroe Doctrine is very much true but the notion of India having its own South Asian version of the doctrine does not hold much water as competing from energy resources in the nations of Syria, Ecuador and Angola and in the Vietnamese oil fields with other nations does not amount to being bequeathed the sobriquet of a Hegemon, whether it be benign or malefactory. Nations such as Pakistan harp repeatedly about the notion of an Indian regional hegemony. The question can be that the Indian hegemony tends to harm the regional applecart or is it its foreign policy.

According to the United States National Intelligence Council Report titled as 'Mapping the Global Future,' by 2020, the international community will have to confront the military, political and economic dimensions of the rise of China and India. This report likened the emergence of China and India in the early 21st century to the rise of Germany in the 19th and America in the 20th, with impacts potentially as dramatic[6]. Thus, in actuality, it is the mere fact of India and China becoming the great powers that they have become and their ascendance cannot be construed as a dismal strategising on their part which is intentional and not too much of a malefaction can be read inside the narrative of two steadily developing and expanding economies and societies which is a natural outcome of the universal percept of the shifting of the internal power zones from the all powerful West to the upstart Eastern sector of the international polity.

The Gujaral doctrine has been emblematic of the notions of continuity and change which have been the hallmark of the foreign policy approach of Gujaral. During the times of I.K.

Gujaral, the American pressure was rampant on the Indian Establishment to sign the Comprehensive Test Ban Treaty and to *kow-tow* along with the Non-proliferation regime of the day which was much largely and still is ordained by the nuclear haves of the international system.

The militarisation of South Asia witnessed in the present times which is very much associated with the notion of American and Western led intervention in Pakistan and Afghanistan has led to the theme of an around hardening of positions in South Asia which have a direct impact on the 'internal security' scenario in the sub-continent. Ravi Sundaralingam contends in the context of the way India is perceived by stating that, "India might be big and strong but the neighbours don't care a wee bit." The same author goes on to contend that, "Nepal is another small nation-state, in the Ganges-plains, on the northern border of India in a more strategic location than Ceylon. It is going through a process that gives similar, more serious worry to India."[7] Even nations historically close to India, such as the Nepalese Hilly Billy Kingdom chose to stay away from the Indian quarters. The Foreign minister of Nepal has gone on to remark, even gave a stark warning to India saying that if anyone is foolhardy enough to attack Nepal, they would have to confront China beside. Thus, the instability and the anarchy which persists in the domestic realms of some of the South Asian counterparts surrounding India, has led to the vision and the missions of their respective statal establishments being coloured by the twin themes of sectarianism and fundamentalism which culminates in the general concomitant sense of the term in a distrust and suspicion of the Indian intentions which are definitely influenced by the Pakistani and the Chinese factors, as in the recent past the People's Republic of China too has initiated its *tentacalising* of the South Asian firmament. The Bangladeshi scenario vis-vis too deserves a *dekko* in the context of what all has transpired between the Indians and the Bangladeshis.

A divided thinking and a sheer lack of consensus among policy makers is apparent in India's dealings with Bangladesh.

Ever since emerging as the liberator when it played a critical role in ousting the outmoded, exploitative West Pakistan imposed administration, it has gone on to provide patronage and support in opening up borders, infrastructure building and sharing of Brahamaputra waters, all the while being benign and conveniently oblivious to the insidious designs of General Irshad[8].

The themes of the Ganga Water Sharing Treaty, Joint Rivers Commission, the Tipaimukh Dam and the Asian Highway have caused much consternation in the bilateral ties between India and the micro nation state of Bangladesh.[9] The 2010 jaunt undertaken by the Bangladeshi Prime Minister has resulted in three agreements which have been reached in the much besmirched bilateral narrative between the twin nation states:

1. Agreement to provide mutual legal assistance in criminal matters;
2. Transfer of persons, who are sentenced by each other;
3. Agreement to fight against terrorist activities, organised crimes and illegal drug-trafficking.[10]

The Indian establishment is aware and sensitised about the migration from the micro nation state of Bangladesh as the demographic profile in some of the regions of West Bengal has been changed drastically since the last few years as a consequence of the illegal hordes of migration from Bangladesh. It has been reported in the International Organisation for Migration reports that, "It is estimated that over five million Bangladeshis are currently working overseas, contributing greatly to their families, communities and the country's economy through remittances"[11]. Poverty, internal environment factors of the order of internal natural disasters, cyclones, etc., too are a cause of concern for the internal stability and stolidity of the micro nation state of Bangladesh.[12] Apart from the threat of Bangladeshi migrants to India, the problem of internal migration in the micro nation state is also a compounding one.

In a research paper by Laura Giani, as part of the Sussex Working Paper serried, in Bangladesh, the adult-child relationship is characterised by an extremely high degree of asymmetry and non-reciprocity, within and outside the household, giving adults the right to dispose of the children as they wish. This is reflected even in the national laws which, for example, confer a special status on the father concerning important matters related to children's life and future development[13]. She further comments that, "The education of children who autonomously moved to Dhaka city is much likely to be affected by time constraints due to their need for work, therefore, it is assumed that their labour migration affects negatively their education"[14]. Thus, the educational parameters of the younglings of the micro state suffer given the parental negligence especially amongst the rural class in Bangladesh which adds up to the ugly rise of Islamic fundamentalism and the general political instability in the body politiyue of the micro nation state of Bangladesh.

Even the High Court in Delhi has registered the general concern of the Indian strategists in the context of illegal migration from Bangladesh. One Delhi Court decision thus speaks, "If someone is able to obtain a passport, ration card, election identification card and nationality certificate by illegal means, it doesn't meant that one is an Indian national, until and unless one gets his nationality through legal means."[15] Thus, the notion of Bangladeshi immigrants defiling the national security concerns and national health of the country is not merely a notion which is hobnobbed in by political outfits in India, but is a matter of grave and cautious concern for the general wellbeing and health of the nation at large. This judgment came into being in the context of the petition of Razia Begum seeking the citizenship of India but on non-production of the necessary documents, she could not be accepted as the denizen of the Indian Union. Thus, the theme of illegal migration in the Indian North-Eastern frontier in the much larger rubric is not a new phenomenon, much has continued as a perennial sore point which disfigures the demographic profile of the region every now and then.

India: The Benign

There is a need to stress the benignity of the Indian Union as a cautious approach to one's own house need not be construed as an act of intransigence and avowed transgressions amidst the comity of nations in South Asia. There are enough instances of perceived cooperation between the nation state of Nepal and the Indian Union in order to buttress the Indian claim of being a harbinger rather than a limiter for the smaller nation states and neighbours in the South Asian firmament. Combined studies with the able patronage of His Majesty's Government and the Government of India are being conceived in the context of the Sapta Kosi High Dam Multipurpose Project and Sun Kosi Storage-cum-Diversion Scheme, wherein, the following themes can be made as achievables:

(i) Hydro Power Generation;
(ii) Irrigation Development;
(iii) Flood Control/ management; and
(iv) Navigation.[16]

Waterways navigation can be the order of the day as far as the internal movement in the co-terminus rivers is concerned. Also, the norm of waterway faring way of life as witnessed in the beatific waterscapes of Europe can be indigenously replicated in the South Asian firmament when the contiguity of the rivers and multifarious waterways are there. This might be an exercise in the erosion of sovereignty which is much a fallout of the advent of globalisation and the withering away of the traditional state boundaries in the context of the South Asian nation states.

Water sharing is a paramount concern in South Asia much on the lines of Europe, as in a fast shrinking world the exigencies of the situation require that the rivers of the order of Sutlej, Jhelum, Bhramaputra, etc., are not the cause of conflict in the region. The Sharda treaty (1927), the Kosi treaty (1954, amended in 1966), the Gandak treaty (1959, amended in 1964) and the Tanakpur (1991) are some of the instances of water sharing in the region which goes a long way into emerging out of the strategic and diplomatic debris of the wars and various internal conflicts in the region. Also, the myriad legendary and hallowed tales about Pakistan fearing that India would flood the border rivers which flow from the inside fence to the Pakistani terrain, ought not to amount to much or hearsay, as the twin nations have to subsist together with a water sharing mechanism in the near future. It was observed in a Lecture in CSE, that, "The treaties are shorn of participatory processes, lack vision and have shown poor maintenance and absence of transparency and accountability. Kosi disaster of Aug. 18, 2008 is the best illustration"[17]. Rivers in the Indus Basin of the order of Chenab, Ravi, Jhelum, Sutlej and Beas, happen to be the bone of contention between the nation states of India and Pakistan. The notion of cost benefiting and mutual sharing for the respective human populations need to be the order of the day for the myriad nations in South Asia.

The water conflicts happen to be endemic in South Asia. The Indus water treaty sets out a legal framework for the sharing of water between the twin nation states of India and Pakistan. Ramaswamy R. Aiyer writes in *The Hindu* that water is once again becoming a core issue between the twin nation states of India and Pakistan. Pakistan has a few misgivings in the context of water sharing :

(1) India is storing or diverting waters to the detriment of Pakistan;
(2) The water scarcity in Pakistan is caused (or partly caused) by Indian action;
(3) The flows in the western rivers have diminished over the years, and India, as the upper riparian, must bear the responsibility for this.[18]

One of the allegations that India being the upper riparian state has dwindled the water tonnage happens to be a very sketchy one which needs to be countered by the Indian negotiators. In the related context, it has been contended that the Indian filling of the Baglihar reservoir also led to a kind of doomsday scenario in terms of water flows for Pakistan, is also a misreading of the water management scenario in South Asia in terms of India and Pakistan. In the context of Bangladesh, Sheikh Hasina visited India and opined that, "Bangladesh had a problem with India on sharing of the Ganga waters, but the countries resolved the issue and signed a 30-year treaty."[19] Though no separate treaty could be signed on the management of the Teesta waters but it has been officially sounded that an interim plan for the sharing of Teesta river has already been worked out by the twin nation states of India and Bangladesh. Such bottlenecks continue in the case of the Nepalese Kingdom and India, too. India ought not to be equated as having played the role of a regional hegemon as the nation has midwived several hydro power projects in the neighbouring micro states in the region and power, and water cooperation happens to be a new and much experienced realm of cooperation between the twin nation states.

A Bangladeshi think tank contends that, "It is evident that Bangladesh receives lower amount of flow as per 1996 treaty than the 1977 agreement and quantum of decrease varies from 7117 to 144 cusec during critical period from 21-28 Feb. to 11-20 May"[20]. There is an inbuilt loss and added cost to the nation state of Bangladesh which has been brought out poignantly by the critics of the Indus Water Treaty. This benefit even if it goes the Indian way ought not to earn it the epithet of a regional hegemon which in no way intends to be as perceived from the myriad water management agreements which the Indian establishment has entered into. On a second coming, larger than nationalistic approach can be the order of the day in the South Asian region, wherein the collectivist approach can serve as the panacea for the whole gamut of obfuscations and confusions that pervade in the context of water management duels in the region.

Ventures such as these make it difficult not to acknowledge India's efforts at spawning, maintaining and sustaining friendly relations with a non-malefactory intent with its South Asian neighbours. All this and more demands a certain kind of reciprocity, a subtle approval on the fence of the receiving neighbours with assistance in the sphere of combating internal security threats to India. The South Asian nation states are in a desperate need for greater cooperation and collaboration in development initiatives to accrue gains as compared to regional groupings of the order of Mercosur, NAFTA, EU, Latin America and such regional organisations of the same ilk.

The notion of India does not only rest on the theme of buttressing its gains in the international firmament, but it also does away with the a traditional fear psychosis which the micro nation states of the order of Nepal, Bangladesh and Bhutan have vis-a vis India. India is already harping over its United Nations Security seat which it deservedly demands with the developing world comity of nation states such as Brazil and the economic power, the Nippo. Needless to say that India has never been the transgressor and the aggressor in any sense of internal, regional and international understanding. The wars fought with Pakistan and PRC have been retaliatory efforts in order to strive to maintain one's independence, sovereignty and territorial integrity. Thus, India cannot be equated with the hegemonic prognosis which is heaped on a belligerent and interventionist United States of America (Uncle Sam) but only negative hegemonic pretensions can be attached to the Indian Union which has never been the neighbourly bully or a regional arm-twister as some of the fearful neighbourly micro states perceive the Indian nation state to be.

Anti-National Threats to South Asia

There are some students and academics who oppose all variants of nationalism, including legitimate ethnic nationalism among oppressed minority groups, usually the ones of Trotskyist temperament who are hell-bent on the strengthening an existentialist and utopian proletarian internationalism, albeit painful and unpopular as they might be[21]. Eric Hobsbawm, Benedict Anderson and liberal academic Ernest Gellner,[22] by resorting to the nastiest weapons that could be imagined. One of the traditional threats to the rubric of nationalism has been the notion of terrorism.

International terrorism is not a new phenomenon to the world or to India in particular. It is a manifestation of the anti-national forces and their surreptitious mandarins active in the Indian Union and the much larger ethnic and coalition politics realm in the much larger South Asia. The 11th September incident pinpoints towards the sheer and all abiding overarch of the multi-faceted tentacles of an all pervading technology and along with them the rising menace of Cyber terrorism and the scepter of Precision-Guided Missiles are a boon for terrorists by having exploited the revolution in the realm of IT. India's cooperation is denigrated as being 'interventionist' and a want of it considered as a genre of 'indifference'. There was a never lack of international cooperation when it came to dealing with terrorists until September 11. The Security Council Resolution (SCR) 1373 is a realisation which is yet to be implemented and adopted by various nations[23]. India in the recent past in the early nineties was not be taken in sincerely by the Occident and the West in the sense that despite India's repeated lobbying and espousal of its concern in the Western diplomatic foras and individual diplomacy, the Americans and the prominent stakeholders in the West were averse to the idea of India being a victim of terrorism in the larger context of the things. The statement of Robin Raphael, one of the under secretaries of the US State Department had led to the enunciation that all Indian claims in order to book the Pakistani side and all the gamut of evidence pinpointed by the Indian Union were not enough and were not authentic in order to bell the Pakistani cat of terror mongering in the Indian sub-continent and in the besieged State of Jammu and Kashmir in particular. It comes back at the person or the entity which threw the boomerang at the antagonist.

In a way, India, in attempting to set its own house in order by fighting shy of the terror threat unleashed on it by the regional state actors was pre-empting the terror threat to the international regime of peace and stability with a particular emphasis on the South Asia in general and the border regions of Jammu and Kashmir, Punjab and Gujarat in particular. When India was crying hoarse about the import of political violence by Pakistan, then at that peculiar point of time, the West failed to take notice of the rising scourge in India's neighbourhood. The Indian failings in the hallowed portals of the United Nations go a long way into discerning out the apathy of the West at the victimisation of India which was initiated by Pakistan after suffering defeats at the hands of a more powerful and capacitious neighbour. Thus, the nation state of India ought not to be castigated as being hegemonic and pretentious of its power, pelf and prosperity, as what it does best is to maximise its national security in the context of hostile and interventionist neighbours. When, one attempts to defile the security of the sanctum sanctorum of the Indian Union then acting in mere self-defense ought not to be construed as a stratagem to militate against the body politic of the aggressor nation state. It is the neighbouring environment which entails a face off between the aggressors and the Indian Union.

With such attendant notions of being a peaceable and norm abiding nation state, the Indian Union is largely considered to be the epitome of peace and cooperative existence in the context of a South Asia which is always on a boil in the light of various exigencies of the order of internal ethnic strife, sectarian violence, linguistic colourings being imparted to regional and national political issues, terrorism and the theme of political violence in all its various hues which have been repeatedly spoiling the national security of the specific nation state whether be it the LTTE infested Sri Lanka, a Taliban and Haqqani infested Pakistan, a Naxalism and Jihadi purloined India and Bangladesh suffering from the rising tide of Islamic Fundamentalism. Thus, the myriad and peaceable tenets of India are being tainted by the domestic press of some nation states in South Asia, of the order of Nepal, Bangladesh and Pakistan which do nothing but strive on the sense of immense and a deeply seated insecurity amongst the regimental set ups of these nations at the rising clout of an emerging India which is a rather special word as prophetically coined by Stephen Cohen. Thus, India needs to follow a well defined trajectory of counter-terrorism measures in its domestic terrain and the near vicinity of South Asia as political violence being imposed upon the country needs to be militated against and even if the weaker micro players perceive the ministration of self-defense as the 'shock and awe' stratagem, then, the flaw lies in the eye of the beholder and the receptacle nation state only, and in no way can the anointed democratic knights of the Indian Union be de-knighted as marauders and arm-twisters of the ilk of the developed West.

The Strategy to be Followed

Every nation state including the United States of America has a grand strategy to fall back upon in the times of a national crisis and it is there that national pre-emption to hunt down sub-national threats are not looked down upon in the mainstream political narrative of these nations. Lt. General Chandra Shekhar contends that, "There is no conception of a grand strategy as such and this needs to evolve from our obligation to protect some of the core values which amount to the following conditionalties:

A psychops operation is underway to derange the operation ability of the Defense forces and morally undermining the force, while the Indian soldier is perceived as the representing figure of the heavenly qualities of courage, sacrifice, integrity, strength of character and commitment to the cause of the nation.[24] The commentator is very correct in positing that the psycops are in full frontal operation from the other side of the fence in order to destabilise the functioning and the operationability of the armed forces in order to denude the Indian fighting units from their higher pedestal and from the high altar of sacrifice since the times of Major Shaitan Singh, Adbul Hamid and the likes, when the Indian soldier climbed heights of popularity and public respect and honour by laying down his life in the line of duty. The circumcision of the Indian courage and patriotic pantheon is not a new theme but when fissiparous elements in the Indian neighbourhood tend to foment the slide then it becomes a matter of concern for the Indian political culture and the proud national narrative. Then, whether, one remains attached with the 'Gandhian other

Cheek,' syndrome or not becomes a matter of secondary importance and significance.

India's benign nature of politics need not be extricated out of the garb of Kautilya's *Arthashasthra* but it ought to be viewed in the contemporary context. The Gandhian way of circumventing the brutal visage of the colonial state and declaring the village republics and the thematic percept of non-violent army and a non-violent state as the epitome of governance can be read as the cornerstone of the benign and peaceably inclined foreign policy and the attendant bilaterals of the country whether it be an engagement with the United States in the sphere of food security in the sixties or nuclear non-proliferation in the nineties or the Indian clamour for suppressing the alien hand in terrorism in the South Asian neighbourhood. Indian one-upmanship is not a consequence of the general strictural comprehension of being a regional power but it has always upheld a higher moral ground in the sphere of decolonisation, freedom of expression, international egalitarianism, secularism and a clamour for the right of self-determination. It is due to the notion of an enhanced and seven decades long role in the issues and developments in the sphere of international politics since the Korean war, that India has naturally as a result of its responsible and actually genuine role has earmarked itself as the agent provider in international politics and more so with the theme of being the economic power in Asia which has till the early 2012, faced and confronted the global economic spiral with resilience and sturdiness. Thus, it is the unstinting democratic ethos of the nation along with a genuinely expressed intent for internationalism through the past decades which have brought the requisite laurels to India in a world which indulges in a mad cap race of international balance of power equations in a fleeting floastsam of international politics. Thus, leading to the significantly large idea of India which ought not be an indigestible and a bitter pill for its South Asian neighbour. As it is contended in the superhero renderings of the present day world that, "With great power comes great responsibility".

References

1. Kanwal Sibal, "India and its neighbours", *Indian Defence Review*, Vol. 25,1 Jan-March, 2010, Available at http://www.indiandefencereview.com/geopolitics/India-and-its-neighbours-.html (last accessed on 12th April, 2010).
2. *Nye, Jr.,Joseph S.,* The Paradox of American Power: Why the World's Only Superpower Can't Go It Alone, Oxford University Press, pp. 34-56, 78.
3. Wilson John, Coming Blowback: How Pakistan is Endangering the World, Rupa Publications, 2009, pp. 313-317.
4. Stephen Blank, " Benign Hegemony: Russia's Grand Delusion" (Perspective, Volume 14, No.1, October, November, 2003).
5. Paul H.B. Godwin, 'China as a Regional Hegemon," URL: http://www.southchinasea.org/docs/Godwin,%20China%20as%20a%20 Regional%20Hegemon.pdf (Online: Web), Accessed on 19th December, 2011).
6. "Mapping the Global Future", URL: http://www.dni.gov/nic/NIC_redirect.html (Online: Web), Accessed on December 19th, 2011.
7. Ravi Sundaralingam, "In the Pursuit of Gujaral Doctrine: Amidst the Militarized Unconstitutional Neighbourhood" (Online: Web), http://www.southasiaanalysis.org/%5 , Accessed on 1st November, 2011.
8. Andrew, William Patrick, India And Her Neighbours 2010, Nabu Press, pp. 345-347.
9. *Ibid.*
10. "India- Bangladesh Relations", Accessed on April 7th, 2010 (Online: Web), URL: http://www.gscurrentaffairs.com/india-bangladesh-relations.
11. "Bangladesh: Overview of Migration" (Online: Web), URL: http://www.iom.ch/jahia/Jahia/bangladesh, (Accessed on November 4, 2011).
12. *Ibid.*
13. Laura Giani, "Migration and Education: Child Migrants in Bangladesh" (Sussex Migration Working Paper No. 33, March, 2006).
14. *Ibid.*

15. "Illegal Bangladeshi Immigrants: Threat to India", URL: http:/ ibn live.in.com/news/illegal (Accessed on 4th November, 2011).
16. "Illegal Migration into Assam" (Online: Web), URL: Ibidhttp:/ /www.satp.org/satporgtp/countries/india (Accessed on November 4th, 2011).
17. "Water sharing in South Asia: Cooperation and Conflicts" (Online: Web), URL: http://cseindia.org/challenge_balance/, Accessed on November 1, 2011.
18. Ramaswamy R. Aiyer, "Pakistan: Water on the Boil again" (New Delhi: *The Hindu*, July 26, 2011).
19. "Hope India, Bangladesh will work out the Teesta Water Deal" (Online: Web), URL: http://www.firstpost.com/politics/hope-india-bdesh-will-work-out-teesta-water-deal-hasina-88631.html, Accessed on October 1, 2011.
20. "Ganges Water Sharing Treaty: A Critical Evaluation" (Online: Web), URL: http://www.cyberbangladesh.org/ganges.html, Accessed on October 1, 2011.
21. It has become almost an orthodoxy to say that the great divide in the world today is between nationalisms. The talk of 'a new world order' and 'the end of history' may not have lasted long. But what has replaced it does not seem to have been class politics, but rather the rivalry of reborn, or sometimes completely new nationalisms.

    Yet those who speak in these terms have great difficulty in defining what makes up a 'nation'. It cannot just be those people who inhabit a certain geographical entity – otherwise what sense are we to make of minorities declining to be part of the 'nation' of the majority among whom they live? It cannot just be language – or what are we to make of Serb, Croat and Bosnian speakers of a single language declaring themselves to be separate nationalities, or of the founders of India attempting to impose Hindi, their own recently sanitised version of a regional dialect, Hindustani, as the 'national language' of a whole subcontinent? It cannot be that fashionable catch-all 'culture', since everywhere differences in culture, or ways of living, are greater between the rich and the poor or the workers and peasants, within a national state than they are between neighbours from the same class on different sides of national borders.

22. E. Gellner, *Nations and Nationalism* (Oxford: 1983); N. Harris, *National Liberation* (London : 1990).
23. Dr. Paul Norman, "The United Nations and Counter-terrorism After September 11: towards an assessment of the impact and prospects of counter-terror 'spill-over' into international criminal justice cooperation", Conference Proceedings of the British Society of Criminology Conference, 6-9th July, 2004, University of Portsmouth, UK.
24. *Ibid.*

Conclusion

Why Men Rebel: The South Asian Tale of Attrition via Sub-Nationalism Inclinations and the Tenets of Nationalism Threatened

South Asia is a *mélange* of a sub-continental diversities and a flux of changes and transformations taking place inside the sub-continent which provides an assiduous researcher with an overwhelming opportunity of research and investigation. Also, research, as it stands, posits that apart from the stereotypical key players of the order of India, Pakistan and Sri Lanka, other micro nation states of the ilk of Bangladesh too are coming into their own owing to their potential of a vastly improved performance in the sphere of livelihood, sustainable and human security concerns.

When one refers to the internal security and the attendant anti-national threats to the South Asian sub-continent and its internecine nation states then one needs to delve inside the notion of why men rebel in all developing and resuscitating societies and polities with South Asia being no exception to the rule of the upswing of the 'dissenters' and the 'violent, ideological and militarist upsurge' of the marginalised and the minority castes, creeds and mini/micro cultures and regional and linguistic groups interpersed within the territories of the South Asian nation states and the whole regional territory.

Whether be it Naxalism in the Indian Union, terrorism in the Islamic Republic of Pakistan or be it the threat of LTTE in the emerald Isle of Sri Lanka or endemic poverty in Bangladesh (which has improved since the last decade) or be it the internal political instability in Nepal and Bhutan, all these developments are fissiparous tendencies for the theme of national and internal security of the South Asian nation states which still yearn to live an intertwined existence akin to the regional groupings of the order of European Union, MERCOSUR or the NAFTA. With the advent of trade liberalisation across all the regimes in the international polity, the need for a conjoined trade regime for South Asia too has been institutionalised though in a very primordial and existential manner with the advent of trade regimes of the order of SAPTA and SAFTA.

Still, economic and social disparities along with the siphoning off of the public funds before the goodies actually trickle down to the poverty stricken masses in the hinterland of nearly all South Asian states, needs to be a cause of concern for all the denizens and the think tanks of the region in a conjoined regional/ universalistic manner. It is these lacunae which make a nation state fall short of the concept of a welfarist and a true blue nation state and the Laskian Model[1] and conditions serve as an ideal recruiting mechanism and as an instrumentality for the anti-national and alternate narrative purveyors in the Indian Union and also in the South Asian context. Separatist movements and demands for secession need to be analysed and an iota of reasoning for this debilitating dissidence needs to be fathomed out in the longer run. All such inclinations and anti-national murmurings which reflect in the form of political, ethnic and insurgent violence have to be clubbed together by the South Asian strategic community as a genre of sub-nationalistic threats, which tends to subvert the regional polity and society through the modicum of asymmetric and unconventional warfare and instability debilitating the applecart of peaceful and a development oriented approach to national sustenance and nation building.

Aggression emanates from frustration at the regional and the localised levels of existence which gets defined as internal security threats to a nation state or a region as a whole. One needs to explore why people involve themselves in political violence and what is the modicum of regimental response. An academic work titled as "Why Men Rebel", authored by Ted Gurr and published by Princeton University Press in the year 1970, resuscitates the realm of rebellion and angst amongst the common people.

In this book, Gurr examines the psychological frustration-aggression theory which argues that the primary source of the human capacity for violence is the frustration modulation of the *hoi polloi* in the South Asian region and the international system as a whole. The angst is further exacerbated and its consequences include anger and political mayhem which dilapidates the general political system. Political violence is considered to be a viable remedy in South Asia which is a developing region which will seek a safe passage through its material development but the attendant changes, movements, protestations and agitations, are proving difficult to be tackled by the establishments of these regional regimes of the day as present day conflictual turmoils contend and make us sit up and observe.

Relative Deprivation: What Does the Notion Lead on to

The theme remains that "Men are quick to aspire beyond their social means and quick to anger when those means prove inadequate, but slow to accept their limitations." This does not conflict with cognitive dissonance, which Gurr revies as what I think I can achieve and what I receive differ, I need to justify that, and justificiation doesn't require changing my expectations, it can mean placing blame on somebody else. Thus frustration leads to aggression.[2]

Another categorisation happens to be 'Progressive deprivation,' wherein the expectations spawn and it leads to continued growth, but potentialities either don't sustain themselves or begin to disintegrate which is happening in myriad Middle eastern and North African narratives of the order of Egypt, Algeria, Syria, Tunisia and Libya and the soft and subtle advent of the Jasmine revolution in the People's Republic of China.

In the current context, apart from the human security paradigm of experts and observers, the notion of terrorism and low intensity warfare, leads to the notion that the terror mongers are considered to be ideologically or psychologically motivated as they have been persecuted and maimed by the regime or the establishment of the day. They tend to have a 'persecution complex', which needs to be tailored to a civilised and trained mental and physical mode of operation and practice without becoming the naxals and the terrorists who fade away as wronged martyrs in the pathway of secessionism and separatism all of those amount to the notion of anti-nationalism in the contemporary context.

South Asia: Perceived as a Greek Analogy with the Intertwined Concerns of Politics, Economy and Political Class

South Asia persists with faults and internal discrepancies within its internal rubric and the political turmoil which engulfs nation states of the order of India, Pakistan, Sri Lanka and other micro nation states of the sub-continent. Greeks had a fine culture of a conjoined co-existence with City States of the order of Athens, Sparta, Thebes, Corinth, etc., having their internal differences but also their agglomerated identity as a unified and coherent Greece which did militate in a unified manner against the Persians and the Macedonians. South Asia too exists as a kind of mélange which has its internal rivalries and discords and the futuristic need is being felt to ingrain a combined ethos of a region which is on the move.

Let's move over to some Greek philosophy as a concluding essay on South Asia as a whole. The Greeks and the Romans had a strong sense and comprehension of the notion of nationalism and they dealt very severely with the anti-national elements. The American colonies when they became independent in the year 1787, they too adopted the nationalistic and patriotic fervour of the entrepreneurial Greeks in line with the conquistading Romans. Thus, the Indian security establishment as it was mired in the security and international ramifications of adhering to the ideal of Non-Alignment and non–involvement in the Blocs led to the following of a culture of tolerance and gratification of the fissiparous trends in the Indian nationalistic narrative and discourse.

The defeat at the hands of the Chinese and the incessant military incursions and bravados of Pakistan did add up to Indian Military awareness and preparedness but it could not firm up the ethos of an enlightened internal and national security operational bliss. Thus, India internally and gradually adopted the mantle of being a 'Soft State' which could be coerced through the modicum of asymmetric warfare and internal insurgencies without fighting a full fledged war. Thus, an aided and abated war of attrition was objectified by the neighbours by fomenting fissures in the religious demographics of the Indian and the South Asian nation states. Thus, the threats were encouraged by encouraging the elements of impoverished masses and the disaffected political lots in the idea of India. This is a pointer towards the threats of Maoism, Naxalsim, Casteist fissures, regional satrapism, ethnic cleavages and other localised conflicts in the South Asian region. The American creed as related by Gunnar Myrdal in his work American Dilemma tends to be an American reminder east of Atlantic which firmed up the American experience. Such a lorish and collectivised entity and idios defeat the life blood in the arteries of a fussilaged and tarred rationale of a destabilised South Asia.

The Greek idiom of nationalism and the attendant notion of integrity can be a sufficient pointer towards the theme of nationalism and the patriotic ethos in the South Asian region as a whole. Plato, the great philosopher can be consulted over here. Plato was an aristocrat par excellence born in an Athenian family, and the Peloponnesian War served as the test case of Plato's intelligentsia. Disgusted by the belligerent and self-destructive policies of his original city state, he stayed out of politics and spent most of his time and energy pursuing philosophy. Akin to the systemic dynamics of the Oligarchs, Pakistan and Nepal are instances of an oligarchy wherein they face insurmountable internal security threats and anti-nationalistic threats and the offiacldom in whatever frameworks and formats, they exist in the developing contexts of these two nations, whether it be the rusciticity of the Royalty, the aggression and the popular mobilisation of the Maoists or the pantheon of the Army cavalcade since the last few momentous decades in the context of the Pakistani Polity. The Greek denizens were aware of their social base and did not shirk aside the community at large. An individual who retreated from politics and public life was called an 'idiotes'.

Plato compares the state to an elaborate and expensive ship. Many a nation states in South Asia are akin to sinking ships which need to be rescued with an internal overhaul of the political, social and economic systems. A ship, to accomplish a safe and successful journey, needs an expert navigator at the helm, a captain who knows the capacities of the vessel, geography, meteorology, water currents, navigational astronomy, supplies management, and other related matters. An incipient person would be unfit to coalesce together the nation as the Gellerian life blood and thus would not serve the purpose of the national integrity and unison and the nation akin to a ship or a vessel would be laid astray in the chaotic tides of an anarchic and selfish trails and tribulations of time and international politics. Imagine then a ship or a fleet in which there is a captain who is taller and stronger than any of the crew, but who is a little deaf and has a similar infirmity in sight, and whose knowledge of navigation is not much better. The sailors are quarreling with one another about the steering—everyone is of the opinion that he has a right to steer, though he has never learned the art of navigation. Do we face such a slight on the hands of the politicians and the overall political class which reigns over the sub-class in the South Asian firmament. Thus, anti-nationalistic threats of the order of asymmetric warfare, low intensity conflict hewn from external forces along with the theme of casteism, religious and ethnic strife in South Asia, are some of the bottlenecks in the rubric of the regional security and nationalistic ethos of the sub-continent. The stewards of these respective ships like nation states in South Asia need to be aware of these sub-national and ethnic cleavages, if the notions challenging the South Asian nation states need to be circumvented. Thus, the threats in South Asia are both external and internal in nature which destabilise the nation states and tend to engender a negative public opinion against them in the international system. Thus, these nation states have to first of all go ahead on a roadmap for incremental changes including more of an accountability, transparency and democratisation in their internal security establishments and frameworks. Only then can the themes of nationalism, unity, integrity and prosperous stolidity can be prepared and sustained as an efficient bedrock for the future peacability and stability of the South Asian security environment. One can definitively hark back to political and civil-societal civil struggle and activism of the people of the order of Anna Hazare who based in his proud precint of Ralegan Siddhi goes on to term the struggle for a Lokpal and Lokayukt, in the aftermath of the Indian Governmental fiascos of the order of the Commonwealth games and the 3G scandal, in the Indian polity. Thus, in the realm of international relations the lore of repetitiveness and recurrence is the order of the day, wherein, such popular angst and discontent firms up the foundational elements of the order of a rebellion. The steward needs to be the calling duty of the day with the necessary were-withal to withstand the myriad vagaries which accost a nation state during its large and extended odyssey to prosperity, stolidity and all subsuming well being. The way to avoid the serious shortcomings of democracy as well as oligarchy is the installation of the government of technocrats that will make all relevant and necessary decisions on the basis of objective analyses and unbiased deliberations. Since neither the demos nor ordinary politicians can be expected to acquire this sort of competence, it will have to be the committee of philosopher kings (and philosopher queens) that guarantees justice, public welfare and peace.

In the words of Baseer Naveed, "An authoritarianism of reason is not welcomed much in the context of nation states. Expert knowledge is deemed essential for the upkeep of a commonwealth, and the *hoi pclloi* do not comprehend the social, administrative, legal and other relevant *brasstacks*."[3] Thus, the solution as advanced by the activism of team Anna will not be long lasting if the fundamental edifice of the Indian Parliamentarian system is jettisoned or is being vehemently attacked and castigated in the mad cap race to mollify the dissent though directed in the right direction and with a specific and 'Just Cause'. Also, the internal shenanigans of the nations have to be kept in the order, the house needs to be kept in the order if nations such as India, Sri Lanka and Pakistan aim and objectify to target their external platforms and if they need to vociferously project their power and in found globalised verve in the international firmament.

The Fragilities of Rule of Law and Democracy in South Asia: An Internal Security Discrepancy

In the case study of South Asia, to a certain extent, spawn a kind of a Pantopticon which tends to keep their denizens in a sort of 'reverent awe' and a conjoined distrust and suspicion of their political class and the people who have been engendered as their political guiding lights. Also, the Military rule and the *Junta* rules out much of a role for the subservient Civil Societal class on the whole in the Islamic Republic of Pakistan. The internal strife in the region is more or less fructifying due to the notions of sub-nationalistic dictates running at large in the internal civil- societal make ups of these developing and micro nation states. The South Asian nation states are struggling against a deluge of such developments which can be subverted by improving the human development situations and scenarios in the region along with sticking truly to the mandate of regional cooperation in the realm of the South Asian Association of Regional Cooperation (SAARC), which was established in the year 1985 to subvert the same anti-national and subversive threats which seem to be raising their ugly heads now in the regional firmament.

As an instance of these anti- national and internal security threats, the question of good governance cannot be completely ruled out. The judicial crisis witnessed in the Islamic republic of Pakistan after the removal of Chief Justice, Iftikhar Muhammad Chaudhary, traps the regime in its paradigmatic plan. The crisis has engulfed all departments and functionaries of the government so profusely that everyone in the government seemed to have lost their senses. The bureaucracy, law enforcement agencies and politicos in the government were getting comfortable in the army patronage and never dreamt that they would face a challenge from the people at the next elections. The judicial stalemate helped by mammoth protestations from the attendant Bar Associations have changed the contours of democracy in Pakistan. The Pakistani judicial class has recognised that it was not being much revered amongst the *hoi-polloi*.[4]

In *Stephen Cohen's Idea of Pakistan*, it has been pithily surmised that Pakistan is a military-dominated state that has experienced uneven economic growth, political violence and strife with its Indian neighbour. Pakistan's future is uncertain. Jayshree Bijoria writes for the Council of Foreign Relations, that the Pakistani Judicial community are ideally the protectors of the constitution but they have succumbed to expediency and accommodated constitutional changes by domestic mandarins. Legal history expert Tayyab Mahmud mentions in the Journal, *Utah Law Review* that, "The doctrinally inconsistent, judicially inappropriate and politically timid responses fashioned by the courts ultimately undermined constitutional governance."[5]

Harking back to the historical pragmatique of Greek thought, the engagement of the hoi polloi, as sanctioned by the Athenian Assembly, is a similar case in point. What Plato witnessed as a young man was not a lack of understanding of the technicalities of governing on the part of the *demos*, but rather poor judgment in the choice of major goals.

Instability in Nepal and India: Internal Security Defied

"You must come to Kathmandu with shroud cloth wrapped around your heads and flour in your bags. It will be our last battle. If we succeed, we survive, else it will be the end of our party." — General Secretary Badal of the Unified Communist Party of Nepal (Maoist)

In the words of Jed Brandt, "There are moments when Kathmandu does not feel like a city on the edge of revolution.

Shopkeepers sell vegetables and nail-clippers cramp the crowded streets. School children rush out of schools with ties in the testing clime[6]". It is further contended that, "Strikes paralyse portions of the nation and the southern Terai is in pandemonium with several power centers competing and peace is found to be a wanting entity.[7] In the Indian context, Naxalsim cuts a swathe throughout the red Indian corridor from the heights of Kathmandu down to the terrain of Chhattisgarh and Andhra Pradesh in India. The Institute of Peace and Conflict Studies in India contends that, "To understand the genesis of the Naxal movement, one needs to locate it within the framework of the Communist movement in India. To be more specific, any study on the Naxal movement cannot overlook the importance of the rise and fall of the Telangana Movement (1946-51)."[8]

The tale of Telangana too breeds the head of the menace of politicised regionalism which is much different than the democratic realisation of the theme of federalism which was rather ignored by the New Delhi Governmental dispensation as was observed by some media observers that the framing of the Lokpal Bill lead to the notion of a step brotherly treatment by the Centre to the Lokpal orientation in a much wider ethos of democracy in the Indian nation state. What needs to be earnestly realised by the political pontiffs in South Asia is the earth shaking development that the tenet of rebellion runs in the bloodstream of humanity whether it be the steppes and the Urbania of a Czar tortured Soviet Union or the charred hinterlands of the Indian Union. Reasons abound for the antipathy to the state but still the sores are there to be seen all across the length and breadth of the national polity. The images provided by cinemascopes of the order of Hazar Chaurasi Ki Man, etc., can provide one with what transpired in the seventies in certain tracts in the country which is witnessing further but interconnected fulmination now in the contemporary context. Naxalism with its advent has made the people eschew their tribal innocence and if one goes by the 2010 Bollywood flick's ditty, one can concentrate upon the theme song, 'Sasura Gainda Phool' which refers to the peace and tranquility of the life in the hinterland of the State of Chhattisgarh, wherein the people are alive to the natural rhythms of sequestered life away and ensconced from the Urban cacophony. Enter Naxalism and the innocent verve along with the tranquil village republics go off for a six and the rigmarole of security forces involved in seizures and the naxals blowing up of public vehicles becomes the staple fare of life in the land of God and the heart of middle India.

To Conclude : Keeping the House in Order ought to be a First Priority

As a case study in India which is often sobriqueted as the South Asian hegemon with an Indian refrain of being benign in its all dispensations towards the regional neighbours, Naxalism in the contemporary context happens to be the theme of an anti-national resurgence, wherein the clarion call given by Prime Minister Manmohan Singh wherein he described 'Naxalism' as 'the single most significant national security threat to the country', happens to become the defining movement of the day and the attendant debate in the South Asian sub-continent. The notion of why men rebel expounded by Ted Gurr, taken up in a social-psychological perspective, needs to be taken in with a grain of salt as according to the Statist perspective, the notions of State sovereignty along with the dictum of "Establishment runs the final writ in the country" can be adhered to if peace, stability and stolidity of the country has to be maintained despite the various discrepancies in hinterland governance in the country. The mere romanticism of 'Rebellion' cannot be the defining and the implementable idiom for a secure and safe South Asia despite the contradictions and the afflictions of political, societal and economic disequilibrium.

An opinion can be advanced very ditheringly that violence caused by determined rebels can leave a lot of harm in the lives and the times of innocent denizens in the country, so apart from being a domestic planning and disbursal failure, the rebellion needs to be given a humanly imagined solution. This imagined and foreseen solution can serve as an ideal recipe for the conflict ravaged societies of some of the sections and the populations of South Asia which definite have the question of race intertwined with the complete conflictual narrative. The whole debate is also about the safety, security and well being of the South Asian nation states at large and the circumstances tend to be very similar in various states in South Asia where internal separatist anti-national and secessionist movements tend to dampen industrial and economic development thus acting as a bottleneck in the general development, upkeep and progress of the nation states taken individually and the region as a whole, that is, South Asia. Practical governance concerns ought to rule the roost as against the tenet of romantic and superflucus rebellion and untrained disgust marked at the state. Still, the region ought not to earn for itself the Status Quo Ante, of a' Soft Region' as the region is bedeviled by the threats to lopsided or nullish development, and the themes of disaffection and political violence in the name of rebellion against the state can only be construed as an anti-nationalistic threat. Apart from the straitjacketed definitions of strategic warfare, the notions of human development being inclusive of the education, health and literacy levels of the *hoi polloi* of the nation states in the region, too, need to be taken into consideration which is admittedly not a novae approach at harbouring peace in a region and a nation state. The Indian visage of being a non-commital nation state and the Pakistan's standpoint as a 'failed nation state' and being an exporter of strife and instability, ought not to be the parameters for a futuristic and outward looking South Asia. The internal cooperation in the realm of general law and order problems and the attendant themes of anti-nationalistic and ethnic violence need to be subverted by the individual apparatuses of the South Asian nation states acting as responsible international actors.

Also, the theme of economic cooperation needs to be made a paramount fixture of discussion and application, as the myriad nation states in the region which need to be more economically intertwined with each other in order to beget prosperity and regional pelf thus nullifying the penury and the disaffection amongst the masses in the South Asian region. The regional instrumentalities of a common currency, SAPTA, SAFTA and the other tourist and cultural cooperation mechanisms can serve as an efficient bedrock for the sustenance and maintenance of the regional prosperity. Still, a regional mechanism to curb cross border terrorism, illegal migration, water conflicts and the instrumentalities of destabilsing the individual economies through the modicums of the order of Fake Currency, need to be delved inside with some strategic and cooperative insight. The effort for regional security has to be a deft amalgamation of the notions of both the dynamics of 'Soft Security' and 'Hard Security' wherein a collective internal stabilisation efforts and an internal cleansing exercise has to follow if the dream of a workable regional security has to be realised in South Asia per se.

Also, in the context of the Indian nation state and the South Asian region, it becomes pertinent to note that the usage of the terms such as 'Indian nation state', 'Nepalese nation state' and, 'Pakistani nation state' might just seem laboured and unacademic but they serve a clandestine purpose. For instance, the people and the denizens form the life blood and blood ties exist between the participants in any national endeavour, then, in that context, the nationalism scholar, Gellner's notion serves to consummate the conjoined ethos of the 'Nation state'. As in the general comprehension of the term, a state comprises of the conditionality of an institutional set up, a well defined territory along with the tangibilities of a Parliament, an armoured personnel carrier, a tank and the holding aloft of a national flag with untwisting honesty and honest clairvoyance of heart and soul.

Once a denizen enters the thematic rubric of a flag and an *Ashoka Chakra*, or a white star in a green background, then, the intertwined boundaries of symbolism tend to extend the word 'State' to 'Nation State' which not only becomes the *de-rigueur* linguistic nightmare of a national discourse but even the proud parable of a conjoined narrative and an amalgamated existentiality which moves beyond the mundane and mediocre mendacity of academia which takes false and convivial pleasure out of a quaint boredom borne out of an extension of mediocrity.

Thus, lies the staid tale behind the spawning of the term 'Nation State' bedeviled by the anti-national and sub-national discourses of the South Asian region factually filling the gaps by the order of Taliban, LTTE, Lashkar-E-Toiyyaba, and other non-state actors, the myriad of other centripetal narratives driving through the staid but peaceful stream of events rampant in the third world of South Asia.

Thus, the internal security threats are seemingly woven inside the texts as the much talked about incision of self determination in the light of a hijacked notion of 'life blood ties' in the misnomer world of nationalism which places the state in a neo-twilight zone of sorts in the contemporary context. The state in South Asia akin to other regions of the ilk of the Middle East and Europe is slithering into a sub-culture of protestations against the state which is being further midwived by the instrumentalities of Twitter, Facebook and the new found *gargoyle* of Social Networking which serves up a palate too strong and unsavory for the instrumentality of the state in more senses than one with the nations of Egypt, Syria, Iran, etc., being the living instance of what might follow in the internal political and societal dynamics of South Asia too in the light of the 'democratic unrest and the springs' of the Middle East.

Who knows, an unsuspecting, South Asia might be the next in the offing? Still, the diffused populations across larger landscapes in nation states such as India, Pakistan and Bangladesh might prevent the congregation of the vast crowds of flocking protesters but still the net-revolutions are seldom prevented by the divides of geography and demography as has been witnessed by the Facebook twitter of Mr. Navalny in Russia which makes the days of the Moscow Regime numbered in yet another episode after the anti-Yeltsin protests in the early nineties. Thus, the novae social revolutions perched atop undeniably the soft power protrusions of the state can conveniently tear asunder the framework of democratic and regimental peace in the myriad nation states in South Asia as one threat reminder to the establishments in the South Asian region as a whole.

Being an Indian author, one can take up the whole issue as the crisis of the state and the crisis of social change, if we perceive the developments in the sphere of sociology and political sociology. Apart from the notion of a dissolving stately apparatus, the resilience of a nation is a significant idea which must be delved inside with some detail. As an instance, the new found might and vocal quality of the Middle class in India and in the Urbania in South Asia, can serve as a receptacle of protest along with the younger section of the South Asian populace. Also, attendant to these factoids, the people will change themselves in the context of the internal security quibbles of the order of communalism, casteism and regional bias and other related non-military threats to the internal security of the nations in the South Asian region, whereever the civil societal bedrock is very well established. Thus, the Indian resilience as being a democracy and transparency loving *hoi polloi* group and being pervious to real public reflections of the defects in the social and political systems, is a case in point which will successfully counter the threats aimed at dismembering and toiling the nation. The other nationalities of Pakistan, Bangladesh and Sri Lanka have a long way to go before the issues of political accountability, democratic ethos, middle class meddling and the thorns of public opinion strengths become the bone of contentions in these second world nation states of South much on the lines of the Indian nation state. The political dénouement still awaits these nations in South Asia and unless that happens and certain phases of painful political and strategic growth have been reached akin to India, the internal security destabilisers will continue to have a formidably negative influence amongst these nation states in South Asia.

Thus, the themes and actualities of political maturity coupled with modernisation of South Asian societies will play a strong and unequivocal role in the furtherance of a stable and peaceful political culture in these nations. The shameful developments such as the Memo gate of Haqqani in Pakistan can destabilise the government in Pakistan and create a rift betwixt the Executive and the Judiciary, are some of the pointers to the reality that commensurate with the military and insurgency related menaces to national peace and interest, the want of a well shaped and wisened political maturity of the leadership and the institutions serves to act as a bane of internal security stability in some of the strife torn nationalities of South Asia.

As it has been pointed out that the notion of a Platonic ship going astray is not going to be of much help to the national mission and the imperative, so a steadying up effort by the institutional mandarins needs to become the order of the day. So be it if a controlled dose of centralisation and augmentation of the state responsibility becomes a dovetailing aspect of how to render a policy of maintaining law and order in the nation and in a beleaguered South Asia in general. The beauty of democracy in South Asia ought to be that the viscerality of the debates are brought out in a fully fanned out fashion by the Fourth Estate. The NCTC debate being an opportune pointer in the direction of the pointedness of a true blue democratic existence with the Maldivian experience having to vouchsafe a great deal for the nascent *Demos* in the South Asian sub-continent. The NCTC debate showcases that how the 'politics of policy' stultifies and hobbles the narrative of a stolid and a secure national security culture in the nation and slackens the national security understanding no bounds. The Chief Ministerial meet on the 16th of April, 2012 as another edition of the same jamboree entails a great deal of rethinking and synergising of the various federalist and regional concerns if a cohesive and a synchronistic culture of internal security which is amply buttressed by the Institutional framework in the nation has to be achieved in the context of the internal security imbalances in the nation.

Various Governments of the State have opposed the vehement and the open powers of the state to confiscate and sieze in the whereabouts of the country. One of the *Indian Express reports* contends that, "The state governments have objected that current provisions in NCTC give officers power to search, seize and arrest anywhere in the country. Such powers weaken the position of the state governments."[9] Thus, the freedom clauses of the *hoi polloi* might be marred by one specific reading of the NCTC in the nation but a centralisation of the internal security apparatus in the nation needs to be carried out with aplomb and immediacy if the myriad threats to the stolidity and security of the nation needs to be emboldened in the national security narrative. The Prime Minister, true to the spirit of the consensus building and the political coalition spirit in the national political firmament, has emphasised the need for a compromise on this issue pertaining to the internal security debate in the nation.

PR Chari contends that, "The Home Ministry has countered that a NCTC is unavoidable because, at present, the Union Government cannot deploy its military and para-military forces suo motu to deal with internal security problems in the states; often the states are unwilling to accept these Central forces"[10]. Thus, in the current framework of the national political debate the whole issue has attained the nature of a Federalist plebiscite. Still harking back to the Criminal Procedure Code, the magistrate can call upon the Union Government's permission to deploy military in the region if the state denomination has dried up and already explored all the dynamics of restoring order and security in the region and the State. This is what the law contends. The original mandate of NCTC does not seem flawed as "The NCTC would function under the Intelligence Bureau (IB); it would analyse the intelligence pertaining to terrorism and associated criminality; maintain relevant databases; develop appropriate responses; and undertake threat assessments for dissemination to the Union and State governments."[11]

It is the draconian dictate spirit as it is being observed by some state denominations which needs to be assuaged in the longer term if a well woven political scheme has to be reached in the light of the political fracas which has broken over the notion of the creation of the National Counter Terrorism Centre. Thus the rights of the people and the freedom of the regional centers have been made out to be the primal problem pointers in the entire debate surrounding the spawning of NCTC in the national firmament as an effective bulwark against the centripetal tendencies of the nefarious non-state actors in tieup with external agent provocateurs in the context of internal security in the nation. Definitively, the American import of the centralisation of security agencies is evidently reflected in the entire exercise but they have avowedly a successful and near to foolproof mechanism in place to counter all genres of internal security threats.

Another significant notion which can serve as a buttressing to the theme of Race in South Asia has been beautifully brought out by John Javos in one of his pieces. He concentrates upon the countries of South Asia Bangladesh, Bhutan, India, Maldives, Nepal, Pakistan and Sri Lanka are internally diverse and part of global flows of people, goods and ideas where along with Peter Robb zeroes in upon the theme of Indians and Sri Lankans, Pakistanis and Afghanis all serving under the divisive brass-tacks of ethnic separatism and the issue of identity in the larger sense of the term. It is this turmoil only which serves as the buttressing upon which the entire counter substratum of internal security rests. Thus, the separateness of existence as emphasised by the identity of race question in South Asia leads to firming up of internal discord and internal armageddon in the sub-continent. Attendant to this abovementioned theme, the cornucopia of nationalism tends very correctly to spawn the decibel of *'eu-sociality'* which can be savored as a new age phenomenon, wherein through cosmo generated notion of nationalism, the people are entreated to become part of a competitive and a consumptive social-political and economic order in order to ingrain the national ethnicity in them.

Ernest Renan too can be fruitfully recollected over here to contend that race has been too narrowly connected with the notion of being singular nation and the comprehension of sovereignty has been too narrowly straightjacketed with the idiom of ethnographic definition and understanding, which stultifies and the gravely jeopardises a South Asian nation state.

Anyway, the zoological origin of the human being is much a priori to the culture, nation and civilisational origins of people which bind together all the denizens of the international system and also very much in the South Asian context, as one boundless and seamless web of universality, spawning a premise for regional stability and stolidity, very much in the context of South Asia, which is very much bedeviled by the scapegoats of race and narrow identity considerations.

The Indian Foreign policy too is inextricably linked with the notion of internal stability and stolidity in the nation state and the South Asian sub-continent as a whole. The Grand Indian Strategy too rests on the theme of internal security. One can mull over a regionally contextualised, strategic Grand Strategy for the upstart region of South Asia despite its myriad of internal quagmires in the realm of ethnicity, self-determination, Maoism, terrorism, insurgency and the stalemate of poverty and development in the larger regions of the South Asian sub-continent. The Region can partake of the Indian expertise in a trustful manner of transactions and the senior partners of the order of Pakistan, Sri Lanka and Bangladesh can be co-partners in the regional visagewise uplift of the region in the international firmament. Still the attainment of the conditionality of keeping one's own house in order and then maintaining a conducive relationship with the neighbour is of paramount significance which can strengthen the internal strength and the national resolve of the hard pressed individual nationalities in South Asia in the face of a great iota of sub-national gerrymandering. It needs both a human security and a developmental approach but the grasping of an India ordained bargaining power in the international vetoing of concerns and interests. Also, in the end the road to a firming up of South Asian internal security definitely runs through the road of trade and colourful hollywoodian trucks trudging their ways across the dust bowls of Wagah and the initial tinkering at the *Khokrapar* and *Munabao* linkage joints between the twin un lucky neighbours in the sub-continent. Will imported cement and exported pharmaceuticals do a world of good for the twin nationalities of India and Pakistan which is the only way towards an internally stolid and politically demystified South Asia.

References

1. Harold Laski, "A Grammar of Politics" (New Delhi: Anamika Publishers, 2004).
2. *Ibid.*
3. Baseer Naveed , "Pakistan: People's Movement Will Overcome Military Tyranny" (Online: Web), Accessed on May 23rd, 2010, URL: http://www.hrsolidarity.net/mainfile.php/2007vol17no03/2531.
4. Ayesha Siddiqa (2007) "Military Inc: Inside Pakistan's Military Economy" (New York: Pluto Press, 2007).
5. Jayshree Bijoria (2010), "Pakistan's Constitution" (Online: Web), Accessed on May 23rh, 2010, URL: http://www.cfr.org/publication/15657.
6. Jed Brandt (2010), "Political Instability in Nepal" (Online: Web), Accessed on May 24th, 2010, URL: http://www. global research.ca
7. *Ibid.*
8. Rajat Kujur (2008), "Naxal Movement in India: A Profile" (Institute of Peace and Conflict Studies, Research Papers, September, 2008).
9. *Express News Service*, "Welcome Federalism: NCTC Debate, Says PC" (*The Indian Express*, New Delhi, April 1, 2012).
10. PR Chari, "National Counter Terrorism Centre for India: Understanding the Debate", URL: http://www.ipcs.org/pdf_file/issue (Online: Web), Accessed on April 19th, 2012.
11. *Ibid.*

Index

G

H

I